Writing Against the Family
Gender in Lawrence and Joyce

Cynthia Lewiecki-Wilson

Southern Illinois University Press
Carbondale and Edwardsville

Copyright © 1994 by the Board of Trustees,
    Southern Illinois University
All rights reserved
Printed in the United States of America
Production supervised by Natalia Nadraga
97 96 95 94   4 3 2 1

Library of Congress Cataloging-in-Publication Data

Lewiecki-Wilson, Cynthia.
    Writing against the family : gender in Lawrence and Joyce /
Cynthia Lewiecki-Wilson.
        p. cm.
    Includes bibliographical references and index.
    1. Lawrence, D. H. (David Herbert), 1885–1930—Political and
social views.   2. Feminism and literature—Great Britain—
History—20th century.   3. Joyce, James, 1882–1941—Political and
social views.   4. Domestic fiction, English—History and criticism.
5. Psychoanalysis and literature.   6. Sex role in literature.
7. Family in literature.   I. Title.
    PR6023.A93Z6556   1994
    823'.912—dc20   93-7829
    ISBN 0-8093-1881-4   CIP

For my children, *Kathrine Lewiecki, Amy Lewiecki,*
and *Sam Wilson*
And for my husband and partner in our family adventure,
Jim Wilson

Contents

Acknowledgments

Many people have helped make this book possible. In the early stages of this project, I received invaluable support from Michael Fischer at the University of New Mexico. He set the finest example as teacher and scholar, and his criticisms and suggestions led me to discoveries I might not have made. Thanks also go to Mary Power and Paul Davis at UNM for their helpful readings and suggestions.

I would like to thank friend and former colleague at the University of Cincinnati, Alison Rieke, for reading chapter 4 and offering suggestions, for our many stimulating conversations on *Finnegans Wake*, and for her sharing of her own work with me. Norma Jenckes, also of the University of Cincinnati, has my heartfelt appreciation for her convivial friendship in showing me Dublin and environs during the Thirteenth International James Joyce Symposium.

At Miami University, Karen Powers-Stubbs deserves thanks for her careful reading of the final stages of chapter 1. I also owe special thanks to the librarians and staff at the Gardner-Harvey Library, Miami University, Middletown campus—to Joe Phillips, library director, Nani Ball, Belinda Martindell, and Diane Miller—for tracking down research materials.

I would like to thank my editor at Southern Illinois University Press, Curtis Clark, for his efficient and thoughtful handling of this manuscript, and the anonymous readers, whose generous and sympathetic reading and helpful suggestions improved this book. Any remaining flaws and infelicities are entirely my own.

This book was written "against" the scene of family, having taken shape over the course of many years, amid the confusions and pleasures of my own turbulent and unique blended family.

Their confidence in this project sustained me many a time, and it is to them I dedicate this book. To my daughters, Kathrine Lewiecki and Amy Lewiecki, to my son, Sam Wilson, and to my husband, Jim Wilson, I thank you for your hard work in the daily grind, the love and support you have given me, and most of all for all I have learned growing with you.

Introduction

Writing Against the Family compares family relations in the major works of Lawrence and Joyce. I am interested in how Lawrence and Joyce portray the psychological and cultural formation of the individual, and in particular, how each writer conceptualizes gender. Besides mapping how Lawrence and Joyce portray family relations and gender formation differently from one another, this project necessarily entails a critical discussion of how theories of psychoanalysis inscribe family and gender. I read literary texts and theories of psychoanalysis from a feminist point of view. If there is such a category as feminist psychoanalysis, I do not believe it is a single theory or neutral methodology but a flexible point of view that questions how systems construe the female.

Lawrence and Joyce both write "against" the background of family; that is, they use family plots and family settings. A question I pursue in this study is whether Lawrence and Joyce also write "against" the family in a contrary way. What interests do their texts serve? Do they work to mystify, endorse, or do away with the family?

Feminists are particularly interested in the family because women historically have been defined by the family sphere. Feminists may not agree on what form the family "should" take or whether the family should be abolished or retained. However, all feminists agree that the term *family* is not neutral but historically variable and ideologically charged by religion, culture, politics, economics. The family, whatever its form, is also the location for the formation of the individual and for the reproduction of psychologies of gender. Thus social-historical, feminist, literary, and psychoanalytic concerns meet in the concept of family.

1

Most studies of Lawrence and Joyce proceed from the assumption that familial relations are universal and then measure the Morels or the Blooms against these assumed norms. This study differs because while reading the family relations in Lawrence and Joyce texts, I also analyze and question assumptions about gender lurking inside systems of meaning. Too often, readings that hinge on family theories depend upon an unexamined culture of gender.

Chapter 1, "Writing and Reading the Scene of the Family," examines the boundaries drawn across the territory of the term *family* when psychoanalysis and literature come together. The term *family* is a multiple site of competing ideologies, and those boundary lines often serve the interests of conservative theories of literature, social relations, and psychoanalysis. Using the theme of "difference" to break up the seeming unity of psychoanalysis, I explore the differences among Freudianism, Lacanian theory, object-relations psychology, and Marxist and feminist criticisms. A feminist psychoanalytic approach, I argue, is not a set of beliefs or a single, new theory but one that recognizes and examines how systems of meaning construe and construct gender. I briefly situate my reading of Lawrence and Joyce within recent studies and end by considering how each writer fits into a discussion of representation and gender, arguing against a theory of representation based on gender. I believe Lawrence's and Joyce's texts, in different ways, "test" the idea of a "female aesthetic" or of a theory of representation based on a direct relation to a binary sex/gender system.

Chapter 2, "D. H. Lawrence: The Sexual Struggle Displaces the Class Struggle," examines the contradictions in *Sons and Lovers* between social and class analysis on the one hand and gender critique on the other. Through Paul's intense mother love, I argue, Lawrence gives a voice to the contradictory position of the woman under capitalism and patriarchy. My analysis focuses most on Lawrence's third novel because historically *Sons and Lovers* begins the practice of psychoanalytic literary criticism. More briefly I look at *The Rainbow* and *Women in Love,* analyzing how these novels continue to explore the construction of gender, the conflicts caused by gender systems, and the limits of exploring gender boundaries within patriarchy. Lawrence increasingly moves away from reproducing family relations, preserving only the marriage quest, as he focuses more tightly on individual relations. *Women in Love* ends by tragically asserting the conflict between individual desire and cultural proscriptions about gender.

Chapter 3, "James Joyce: Overdetermination Replaces Cause and Effect," examines *A Portrait of the Artist as a Young Man,* briefly discusses *Dubliners,* and looks in greater detail at *Ulysses.* I conclude that Joyce's autobiographical text does not embody resistances and conflicts with the gender system, as does Lawrence's, but expresses a male Family Romance. However, *A Portrait* explores, works through, and deconstructs other broad systems of meaning adjacent to, and implicated in, the gender system. Stephen masters, debunks, and overcomes the spell of nationalism, religion, and systems of thought like scholasticism. *Dubliners* begins a critique of gender, but the focus is still dominated by men. Both works take causal analysis to its extreme limit, refining mimesis to the point at which Joyce's analysis of cultural paralysis threatens to look like, and collapse into, the very paralysis it means to expose, initiating the deconstruction of causal thinking itself and suggesting the shadow world of repression beneath the surface.

In *Ulysses* Joyce increases his frenetic pace of deconstructing systems, leading ultimately to the deconstruction of stable narrative itself. A by-product of increasing textual instability is that *Ulysses* deconstructs the cultural construction of gender. *Ulysses,* I argue, portrays the gendered individual formed by an overdetermined web of relations. Because it validates no system, it portrays both typical and atypical family relations, the womanly man and the manly woman, as well as their opposites.

Chapter 4, "'Retourneys Postexilic': Overthrowing the Christian Holy Family and the Return to Egypt," surveys common interests of Lawrence, Joyce, and Freud in Egyptology. I look at a late short novel of Lawrence's, *The Man Who Died* (also titled *The Escaped Cock*), two essays by Freud, "Leonardo da Vinci and a Memory of Childhood" and "A Special Type of Object Choice Made By Men," and Joyce's *Finnegans Wake*. All three writers are interested in relating family material to non-Western, Egyptian myth, but each one's attitude to Egyptian myth is different. Lawrence's last novella portrays a male/female relationship in abstract terms, welding Egyptian myth onto a Western and Christian psychology of gender. *The Man Who Died*, I conclude, focuses on and reifies gender difference itself. The plot dramatizes the Oedipal moment when the construction and valuation of gender under patriarchy are psychologically internalized. Lawrence's narrowing interest in abstract male/female relations as well as his increasing misogyny make sense if examined at the moment they come together, the Oedipal moment. *The Man Who Died* expresses the ambivalent wish to reenact the moment of gender difference under patriarchy as well as to undo the devaluation of the female by searching for the ideal, phallic female mate represented by the doubled female figure.

Finnegans Wake, Joyce's last work, continues Joyce's drive, discussed in chapter 3, to destabilize systems of meaning. The *Wake*'s fragmenting of language, narrative, and logic requires that a reader construct meaning and relations, foregrounding the process itself of constructing systems of meaning. As in *Ulysses*, a by-product is that the *Wake* implicitly portrays gender constructed by culture from an anarchic, polymorphically perverse, sexual base.

I explore two ways to construct the meaning of family relations and gender in the *Wake*: by reference to Egyptian myth and by reference to psychoanalysis and the undoing of repression. Both references come together in Freud's 1910 essay "Leonardo da Vinci and a Memory of Childhood." Joyce owned this text, and I argue it should be considered much more seriously than it has been as a creative source for *Finnegans Wake*.

There is a remarkable consonance in the portrayal of human drives in both psychoanalysis and Egyptian myth, two systems of meaning I use to construct a reading of *Finnegans Wake*. One way of reading the *Wake* is to see the sleeping and dreaming hero experiencing the undoing of repression in unconsciousness. At the level of the unconscious, according to Freud, every person is androgynous, narcissistic, and multiply perverse. One use Joyce makes of the *Egyptian Book of the Dead,* I believe, is to substitute the Egyptian view of the family, sexuality, and creativity for the Christian. Multiplicity, fragmentation, and reproduction, formal properties of the text, also characterize the figures and stories in Egyptian myth. Thus the characteristics of the unconscious mind and Egyptian myth unite in the unusual form of the book. The *Wake* uses Egyptian myth in an altogether more radical way than Lawrence's novella does. *Finnegans Wake* portrays beneath the gendered individual a root androgyny and asserts an evolutionary view of family relations. The *Wake* celebrates the creativity flowing from the perverse sexuality of the unconscious human mind as it adapts to, as well as changes, a random, natural world.

In chapter 5, "'*Afterthoughtfully Colliberated*': Resituating Lawrence and Joyce within Modernism and the Postmodern," I reflect on Lawrence's and Joyce's positions within the modern canon. While Lawrence and Joyce are not feminists, they write about issues that concern modern women writers. I conclude that Lawrence and Joyce inscribe family and gender in their work, not in opposite ways, but differently along a continuum. Both write against the Judeo-Christian family and patriarchal gender relations. Lawrence builds his plots on exchange relationships and preserves his ambivalence to patriarchy. Joyce develops serial relations by continual displacement using parody and reversals, wherein oppositions/identities collide with themselves and exceed their limits producing heterogeneity. Joyce, I conclude, approaches the postmodern, celebrating liberation and proclaiming collaboration.

1

Writing and Reading the Scene of the Family

The country around was beset by a frightful monster, the Sphinx, a creature shaped like a winged lion, but with the breast and face of a woman. She lay in wait for the wayfarers along the roads to the city and whomever she seized she put a riddle to, telling him if he could answer it she would let him go.

—Edith Hamilton, *Mythology*

The story of Oedipus should stand as a warning against reading the family relations of a literary text in a naive, "goahead" (to borrow a term from Joyce) way—in short, simply from the position of the male tragic hero as subject. Indeed, too easily trusting in naive instrumentality and autonomy led Oedipus to his fateful mistakes. Most often, though, literary interpretations of family relations do proceed by a single, simplified model of the family. Even when that model is deepened to include the psychic family constellation, complications and problems in the way systems of meaning construe family relations are repressed in favor of a smooth psychoanalytic narrative. Usually excluded entirely are questions of whether the construction of family under psychoanalysis should itself be analyzed.

As a feminist, I am interested in reading the full weave of family relations in Lawrence and Joyce. That means reading with and against texts, unknotting the threads of gender ideology woven into systems of meaning implicated in literary interpretations of family relations: in psychoanalysis, in social/political/

economic relations, and in epistemic categories that culturally construct the subject.

REVISING OEDIPUS

This study begins with Oedipus and theories of psychoanalysis because we cannot, I think, escape the net of that founding myth without understanding how enmeshed in it are discourse and desire. Although sympathetic to the motives and goals of feminists who reject Freud, I have found Freudian theories to be essential to my understanding of woman's position under patriarchy. Rather than mythifying Freud as the original misogynist who forced the Oedipus plot on our psyches, I think we should understand Freud's attraction to the Oedipus story as the result of his immersion in the culture of patriarchy and particular attentiveness to its structure. That structure was already there, and because it is still with us, we need to understand how that dominating force shapes us from within and how we reproduce it, before we can hope to change the world. Like the colonized subject Stephen Dedalus, we must begin by toppling the hierarchy within. There is no fleeing patriarchy's ubiquitous web, though. Instead women must work to change history from all the multiple positions they inhabit.

As important as it is to understand the internal, psychical forces of patriarchy, there is another compelling reason for interest in Freudianism. Psychoanalysis offers a theory of relations—hidden, oblique, and overdetermined—which in turn enriches literary theories of representation and reading. Shoshana Felman emphasizes interpretive play when she says that the great discovery of psychoanalysis may be *"as a discovery of a new way of reading"* (118; italics in original), where multiplicity in an endless chain of substitutions generates constant movement and guarantees ambiguity in opposition to the old way to knowledge in which the "quest for mastery" is ironically "to occupy the very place of *blindness*" (168; italics in original).

I would also stress that psychoanalysis is important to literary theory and feminism because of its understanding that a representation (a symptom, a dream, a narrative text, or even a social custom) is a secondary, symbolic formation whose underlying forces and relations are multiple and indirect but, nevertheless, connected to the surface. Freud's dream theory and later his theory of the unconscious explain that those forces and relations cannot properly be said to preexist their representation, since they can be approached only in represented form. Consequently, psychoanalysis understands "meaning" as that which is produced by the circulating energy of indirect forces and relations and then interpreted, not as a self-identical concept mirrored from some preexisting knowledge or condition.[1] Hence, psychoanalysis gives us a theory of the production of meaning that is nonmimetic but that is connected to subjectivity and moreover to the body. I believe feminism needs a theory of representation that relates the material world of bodies, subjectivity, and symbolic formation, but in multiple ways avoiding sexual determinism.

Generated out of the conflict between multiplicity and mastery, the Oedipus myth reveals that subjectivities are multiple. Jocasta is mother/wife/grandmother-mother. The Sphinx is self-divided between woman and animal, and Oedipus is son/husband/brother-father. "What overwhelms Oedipus is the burden of plural identities incapable of coexisting within one person," Edward Said writes. "In such a case the image of a man conceals behind its facade multiple meanings and multiple determinations" (170).

The plot of Greek tragedy insists that multiple identity be punished and punished differently for men and women. For Oedipus, there is self-mutilation and transcendence, blindness and insight. The myth also warns of the woman's fate under patriarchy: silence and suicide. Of the two female figures necessary to the myth, one—the Sphinx—does not even appear in Sophocles' tragedy, and the other—Jocasta—suffers in silence. She rapidly intuits the revelation of her husband/son's confused identities and rushes offstage to kill herself. Sophocles gives her no speech.

Whatever purpose they serve, whether for psychoanalysis, anthropology, or literary theory, most retellings of the Oedipus story follow the theme and plot of Sophocles, focusing on the lone male protagonist. Freud begins with the hidden desire of the son to kill the father and sleep with the mother. Others, and Said is an example, generalize from the plight of Oedipus to the state of *man*kind.

While Said deems plural identities a "burden," feminists such as Gloria Anzaldúa, Norma Alarcón, and Sandra Harding argue that for women consciousness may be a "site of multiple voicings," not "necessarily originating with the subject, but as discourses that transverse consciousness and which the subject must struggle with constantly" (Alarcón 365). Whereas Freud explains the female's less unitary, more multiple identity as the result of her weaker superego and less dramatic rupture with "infantile genital organization,"[2] feminists argue that multiplicity of (un)consciousnesses may be an advantage.

The tragedy of Oedipus is about patriarchy itself; its lesson reaffirms the kinship laws of patriarchy. Embedded within its structure are silent, almost invisible women or ones, like the Sphinx, who are fearful and ambiguous monsters—part human, part animal. They tend to know things before the men do, but knowledge does not do them much good. Once Oedipus correctly answers the Sphinx's riddle, Edith Hamilton tells us, she "inexplicably, but most fortunately, killed herself" (257).

Oedipus encountered the Sphinx on the roadway. He goes on to another momentous encounter at a crossroads, where he unknowingly kills his father and sets in motion the mix-up in family relations that will end in tragedy.

Anthropology reads family relations as a roadway—away from home in the rules of exogamy—and a crossroad where the merely natural capability to reproduce crosses over into some system of meaning assigned by cultures (such as kinship systems).

Freud emphasizes that family relations are also hidden or concealed relations, a matter of fantasy and desire, as well as intention. The crossroads of family relations also include the intersection between "work and relationship," as Terry Eagleton points out in *Exiles and Emigrés*. The material conditions of a culture—its systems of production, division of labor, health and housing—the race relations in a culture, and a family's race and class positions, all influence family relations and the psychological formation of the individual.

The family is also the place where the sex/gender system is produced and reproduced. Gender is a social and psychological product, a system of significance that human societies construct from the anatomical and physiological differences between the sexes. People born with different sexual characteristics are assigned at birth to one of two groups. An infant born with hermaphroditism, Nancy Chodorow points out in *The Reproduction of Mothering*, "tests"—that is, proves—the rule that the sex/gender system is a construction rather than a natural category. An infant with hermaphroditism is assigned to one or the other sex, and then its sexual organs are reconstructed to conform to the assigned gender model.[3] The behaviors and roles we expect from the person labeled as a given sex are shaped by the society and era we live in, the work we do and systems of production we are enmeshed in, our race, religion, education, and class. However, the sex/gender system, including its social construction of gender characteristics and the inferior value placed on women, is ancient and nearly universal, feminist historian Gerda Lerner points out. The family is thus an overdetermined site. "The notion of patriarchy," Annette Kuhn argues in *Feminism and Materialism*, "does indeed unite property relations and psychic relations" (65). The family, she concludes, is "the privileged place of the operation of ideology" (66).

Feminist philosopher Sandra Harding argues that feminist thinkers need to posit both a distinctly gender specific universal perspective in feminism and to recognize the pluralities of subjectivities. She contends we should also value this apparent contradictory dilemma as a valuable resource for new thought ("The Instability of the Analytical Categories of Feminist Theory").

A feminist reading thus requires interweaving seemingly disparate plural and universal perspectives, complicating the weave of family narrative with multiple threads. The scene of the family is a multiple site (psychological, social, economic, with anthropological roots and cultural differences) and also a universal structure of patriarchy. I would contend that it is most fruitful to revise the Oedipus myth for feminism not by turning away from the structure of patriarchy but by reading through it, restoring the multiple identities and omissions and articulating the plural voices in this ancient plot.

PSYCHOANALYSIS AND LITERATURE— QUESTIONING BOUNDARIES

This study also entails a practice, applying psychoanalysis to literature, reconceived by a feminist approach. Since a feminist necessarily has a partly adversarial relation to psychoanalysis, in questioning and exposing its ideology of gender, she reads against as well as with psychoanalysis.

The history and conventions of psychoanalytic reading were once dominated by strict Freudian interpretations that tended to ignore the plight of women and to psychoanalyze authors more than texts. Psychoanalytic studies of family relations in literature assumed that all individuals were men, analyzing characters from a male model of psychological development. In particular, psychoanalytic discussions of Lawrence's work almost always proceed from the "universal" male viewpoint. Perhaps Daniel A. Weiss's *Oedipus in Nottingham* is the prototypical study, but there are many others. For a reader interested in how literary works help produce, reproduce, and change systems of meaning (especially the sex/gender system), classic Freudian studies necessarily disappoint, even though the fine ones (like Weiss's or Mark Schechner's study of *Ulysses*) provide many rich insights. Traditional Freudian studies ignore any dynamic and different woman's experience, and they invariably end up focusing on the latent or secret psychological life of the author, rather than on a work's possible challenge to received notions.

In chapter 2 I argue that Paul Morel in Lawrence's *Sons and Lovers* develops "like a woman." I do not mean that he (or Lawrence) is a failed man or latently homosexual, a claim often made. One purpose of a feminist study is to point out the difference between being "like a woman" and being "a failed man." The latter judgment allows "no place" for "women in the calculations," as Hélène Cixous puts it (*The Newly Born Woman* 64). Whereas earlier Freudian readings acknowledge no female position or development that is not failure to be a man, feminist psychoanalysts such as Juliet Mitchell stress the importance of understanding the distinct psychological dynamic of female formation (within patriarchy), a dynamic either men or women can more or less go through. "[T]here is *no* absolute dividing line," Mitchell explains; men "can go through the Oedipus complex, or come out of it, in a way more typically feminine and vice versa" (*Psychoanalysis and Feminism* 112).

Many, though not all, of Lawrence's texts often seem hostile to women, and hence it might seem that the traditional, male-dominated psychoanalytic approach accords with Lawrence's own leanings. Yet I think there are two reasons why Lawrence's work may be profitably investigated from an alternative, feminist point of view. First, Lawrence himself "quarreled" with Freud (to use Frederick Hoffmann's term). Lawrence saw himself as a corrector of Freudianism in his two treatises on human psychology. Second, all Lawrence's work, I would argue, is in one way or another, about the problem of gender.

Traditional psychoanalytic studies also often suppress the role of the cultural construction of the individual in favor of analyzing personal relations. This particularly affects the interpretation of gender issues. Again, I might turn to *Sons and Lovers* as an illustration. Psychoanalytic critics label Mrs. Morel "phallic" and criticize her without examining how her psychology is formed out of her social relations, class conflicts, and position as a woman, and how those social positions inhabit her personal relations. In Lawrence's later work, he does create "phallic" female doubled figures. I believe Mrs. Morel is castrated rather than "phallic." In chapter 4 I explore the close relation between the phallic woman and the castrated woman. However close their relation, in literature I believe their plot functions are different.

Judgments about "normal" or "deviant" behavior are also problematic when psychoanalysis is applied to literature. The purpose of clinical practice is to bring patients to health, and mental health is defined by a consensus about social norms. Literary texts are not patients, however. And Lawrence and Joyce, in particular, do not share the ethical assumptions of psychoanalysis.[4]

Lawrence and Joyce both make claims that literature is so important that it should challenge and revise our notions of conventional behavior, of right and wrong, of perception. "No esthetic theory," Stephen in *Stephen Hero* argues, "is of any value which investigates with the aid of the lantern of tradition."[5] Lawrence makes large and direct claims for literature. "Art-speech is the only truth," he says in *Studies in Classic American Literature*.[6] "Art has two great functions. First, it provides an emotional experience. And then, if we have the courage of our own feelings, it becomes a mine of practical truth" (12). Joyce's claims are only slightly less direct. If Stephen in *A Portrait* dismisses the idea that great art should induce action, he nevertheless makes a lofty claim for art: "The esthetic image in the dramatic form is life purified in and reprojected from the human imagination."[7]

Nearly every term from psychoanalysis with a negative or pejorative connotation potentially conflicts with the revaluation of values found in Lawrence and Joyce. Narcissism and perversion are two examples. A text such as *Women in Love* tests, explores, and redefines received notions of perversity. Rupert Birkin and Ursula Brangwen discover a new relation below the personal, emotional, or even the conventional life of the sensations, by plunging into a "pure Egyptian concentration in darkness,"[8] which numerous commentators have tried to pin down to a specific act of sexual perversity. Rupert also tries to live out a physical and spiritual relation with Gerald. Whereas Freud connects bisexuality and homosexuality to narcissism ("Leonardo da Vinci and a Memory of Childhood"), *Women in Love* experiments with bisexuality and "perversity" as antidotes to the ills of contemporary life and indicts contemporary European society for the narcissism of its superficial and mechanical human relationships and art.[9]

Joyce is perhaps even more at odds with the ethos of psychoanalysis than Lawrence. *Finnegans Wake*, whose style itself many readers find perverse, incorporates various sexual perversities into its text. Narcissism abounds; it is substance, style, and theme. The characters of the *Wake* are each reflections of one subject, H.C.E., who may not even be a character so much as refracted fragments of Joyce. To understand the book's multitude of allusions, a reader needs to learn Joyce's own peculiar interests and follow his researches, the text leading back to the mind of its author. Near the end of his perceptive and sympathetic reading of Joyce, Colin MacCabe throws up his hands declaring that Joyce's work is "narcissistic" and "perverse" (112) because "the effort of reading Joyce is one of imaginary identification" (157) with the author's mind.

Embedded within these kinds of psychoanalytic judgments are not only the conflict in values between literature and psychoanalysis but also the problem of the devaluation of the feminine under patriarchy. According to Freud, the female psyche is more infantile and narcissistic than the male's because in her development the female does not set up as powerful a superego as does the little boy: "The fear of castration being thus excluded in the little girl, a powerful motive also drops out for the setting-up of a super-ego and for the breaking-off of the infantile genital organization" ("The Dissolution of the Oedipus Complex," *SE* 19: 178). Freud's very important 1914 essay "On Narcissism" and his 1917 essay "Mourning and Melancholia" explain identification as a process of secondary narcissism. The person's love for an object ended, she withdraws her libido back into her own ego, but hidden in such a way that it causes her to identify with the lost, abandoned object (*SE* 14: 248–49).

Texts that are self-reflexive or that focus on intersubjective relations, texts that explore sexual perversity, sadomasochistic relations (as *Ulysses*), or mirror relations (as in many of Lawrence's late works and in *Finnegans Wake*) are often viewed through the frame of psychoanalytic discourse and values. Post-Freudian, poststructuralist readers add the frame of Lacanian theory with its emphasis on inscription of the sex/gender system in language. One consequence is that texts with the characteristics of female psychology are often construed as "female discourse." Hence MacCabe suggests that Joyce writes "women's speech" (*JJ and the Revolution of the Word*), while in a later study he qualifies his sexual theme: Joyce writes the male imaginary of woman's speech ("An Introduction to *Finnegans Wake*").

Embracing these "pejorative" characteristics and lauding them as signs of "women's speech" or even as the male imaginary of the female is not, it seems to me, an adequate feminist strategy because it explains away the contradictions of the female position within patriarchy without destabilizing the dominance of that binary system. Categorizing discourse into male (classical, logical, non-Romantic, with characteristics of the male psyche) and female (Romantic, narcissistic, nonauthoritarian, with characteristics of the female psyche) does not solve either the problem of the clash of values between literature and psychoanalysis nor the problem of the devaluation of feminine traits it is meant to shore up.[10]

Too smoothly sliding the terms of psychoanalysis, such as *narcissism* or *perversity*, into literary evaluation overlooks the clashes, disjunctions, and different aims among psychoanalysis, late-Romantic aesthetic theory that shaped the thinking of Lawrence and Joyce, and feminism. I am interested in reading Lawrence and Joyce through all three lenses. Yet the three simply cannot be laid one on top of another, or an ill-defined blur would result.

To call a work "narcissistic," for example, imports a pejorative term from a discourse outside literature into the literary realm. The term's pejorative connotation clashes with the values of the Romantic literary tradition that preceded psychoanalytic discourse. From a psychoanalytic point of view, Keats's "negative capability" does not demonstrate a powerful shift in perception from the cold, aloof dissection of the classical view to imaginative sympathy through identification of the Romantic position. Rather sympathetic identification with others is narcissistic and infantile.

While psychoanalysis has anti-Romantic ethical assumptions, Lawrence and Joyce are heirs to Keats, Blake, and Coleridge, and to Romantic aesthetics. Lawrence reveals his affinity most perhaps in his poetry with its acute sympathetic insight into the otherness of animals and plants. But all his prose is marked by his intensity of sympathy with others—with the position of each character in a story or with the spirit of a place in its material manifestation in his travel writing. Joyce's earliest writings, his "epiphanies," are demonstrations of a kind of "negative capability," the writer willing to give himself up to seeming transparency in order to render the whatness of people, situations, objects.

Both writers also conceive of the power of the imagination in direct descent from Blake and Coleridge. However, in contrast to the dynamic, plastic quality of a Romantic creative imagination, psychoanalysis points to the repressed, hidden forces of the unconscious at the root of human productions.

Gayatri Spivak pries open the gap between the Romantic conception of the imagination and the psychoanalytic as she deconstructs the apparent unity of Coleridge's great I AM. Spivak argues that in *Biographia Literaria* Coleridge everywhere tries to hide "the force that would bring the object and the subject, as well as the divided ground of the self, into unity" (215). Psychoanalysis shows us, Spivak argues, that desire has everything to do with the illusions of the ego, which are fed by the hidden currents of desire, "the desire of the other and the desire to produce the other as well as to appropriate the other" (215).

Lawrence, I believe, sticks to his Romantic roots more than Joyce in the sense that Lawrence presents creativity occurring from union with an Other (whether person or plant or animal or place) and because his characters seem able to experience the unconscious realm partially through their own intent or will. Thus Lawrence is open to charges of appropriation and colonization of the Other, even though union with the Other comes from a kind of dissolution of the self. Though a Lawrentian character has to give up his willful ego to experience otherness, surrender is an action he can practice. In chapter 2 I argue that Lawrence posits a unique, Lawrentian unconscious different from the Freudian. Lawrence's unconscious is a creative, nonhuman substrate, potentially fierce and cruel, but to be respected. As Lawrence presents it, humans must give up intellect (the "dissecting mind," the Romantics might say) to experience the Lawrentian unconscious, and in doing so they discover knowledge unavailable in culture.

In rejecting a mental imagination as the source of creativity, and turning to an unconscious realm of animal existence, Lawrence reveals the influence of late nineteenth- and early twentieth-century materialist theories of evolution. Joyce, on the other hand, embraces twentieth-century notions such as psychoanalysis, relativity, and overdetermination as well as evolutionary thinking. *Finnegans Wake* perhaps out-Freuds Freud.

The Joycean unconscious is a grab bag of history, culture and language fragments, and is sexually overdetermined—that is, all fragments have a sexual foundation. Joyce retains the Romantic emphasis on the mental but also incorporates a modern notion of material and physical determination. To Blake's and Coleridge's mental and eternal imagination, Joyce adds the leavening of the material world—sexuality and broken shards of variously remembered and randomly preserved culture. The universe we can infer from Joyce's texts is not, I think, entirely linguistic, although it is true that the physical and material world is only known as it is filtered through the human mind and not directly. But I am not speaking of idealism. The *Wake* gives us the *material* human mind: the psychical materialism of the unconscious and the physical object of the sleeping brain in a body, which John Bishop so persuasively demonstrates in *Joyce's Book of the Dark*. In chapter 4, I argue that *Finnegans Wake* presents a Freudian unconscious—with the human at bottom bisexual and multiply perverse—as the source of human imagination. Almost a reversal (and yet a double) of Coleridge's eternal I AM, Joyce's text on imagination has no seeming unity and seethes with multiple desires. Thus Joyce is open to the charge of perverse narcissism.

The borders between psychoanalysis and literature are always unstable. I have pointed out how problematic gender issues get smuggled into the narrative of literary evaluation from psychoanalysis. I do not propose to close down the frontiers or put up guards in an attempt to purify one realm or the other. Instead, I believe a feminist reading should move back and forth across the borders of psychoanalysis, literature, feminism, and social history.

Developing a nondominating relation among various discourses is a political and aesthetic practice that models the goals of feminist politics. A feminist politics of reading, of psychoanalysis, and in the social world may make use of gender-specific analysis but must also ultimately resist the pull to thematic representation based on the present dual sex/gender system because as feminists we are not interested in shoring up that system but in understanding and changing it.

TOWARD A FEMINIST PSYCHOANALYTIC PRACTICE—READING PSYCHOANALYSIS, READING TEXTS, READING DIFFERENCES

Since the feminist project entails both setting multiple points of view side by side and also reading the universal female position, a feminist psychoanalytic reading might begin by comparing the differences among psychoanalytic theories, and in particular how they (differently) cast the scene of gender formation, construe gender, and produce psychologies of gender.

We do not yet even know what a Freudian reading is, Shoshana Felman warns, though she suggests it is "not a reading guaranteed by, grounded in, Freud's knowledge," but "a *reading of Freud's 'knowledge,'*" one that "takes its chances" and is "threatened by error" (116, 117; italics in original). Felman's words suggest two directions: a revisionary rereading of Freud and an open, creative "Freudian-like" reading of texts. In the subsequent chapters of this book, I attempt the second kind of reading. My "Freudian-like" reading, however error threatened, is not an originary revising of Freud but a thinking through of the network of relations represented in texts in ways opened up by Freud and the critiques and supplements to Freudianism of the last several decades as well as by other psychoanalytic readings of literary texts. There are three areas of debate that inform my reading: Freudianism's reputed bias against women, its simplification or complete lack of a social theory for the construction of the subject, and its relation to theories of language.

The first problem, whether Freudianism is biased against women, has hardly been perceived as a problem at all in reading Lawrence and Joyce texts, since almost all commentators, until recently, assume both writers replicate Freud's reputed misogyny. Putting aside for the moment Lawrence's and Joyce's attitudes to women, I would like to track how theories of psychoanalysis read family relations and gender formation and thus influence literary interpretations. What are the differences?

FREUD'S OEDIPAL NARRATIVE

For Freud the passage through the Oedipus complex institutes gender identity based on the perception of sexual difference as the result of castration. Freud's Oedipal theory is by no means a seamless narrative, however.[11] He did not express the theory all at once; rather, it developed and changed from his

earliest to his last essays. At first, he called this structuring mechanism "the castration complex," and he imagined that it func-
tioned in the same way for both genders. Only relatively late in
his career did he come to believe that the Oedipal passage might
be different for females.

Starting in the early to mid-twenties, Freud wrote a series
of papers that begin to lay out the different ways that males and
females undergo the Oedipal passage. In "The Dissolution of the
Oedipus Complex" (1924), he unites his theory of the castration
complex and the Oedipus complex. Along the way in explaining
the boy's castration anxiety, Freud raises his own question: How
can women have a castration anxiety when castration (the belief
that the parent may cut off the penis)[12] has always already occurred for women? In two subsequent papers, "Some Psychological Consequences of the Anatomical Distinction between the
Sexes" (1925) and "Female Sexuality" (1931) he follows up his
own questions about female development by rethinking how
women pass through the Oedipus complex.

The first Oedipal narrative and its subsequent refinements
feature the young male child as the universal human. In the pre-
Oedipal period, Freud reasons, the boy and girl child experience
the same relation to the mother. The infant-child is at first help-
less and disorganized, mostly receiving the mother's care. The
child perceives the mother as "phallic" (meaning active). As the
child develops he organizes the libidinal drives he has from birth,
and he begins through the force of his own drives to break up
his passive unity with the mother. Anxiety ensues. Separation
anxiety, which Freud noticed in the repetitive play of his grandson, is one example, and there are others in the years of early
development. These all become consolidated in the Oedipus
complex.

The child comes to realize the father's rivalry; his claims to
the mother have precedence and absolute social authority over
the child's. The mother then comes to be perceived as an object
(passive) of the father's. No longer perceived as active, but as
passive, the mother is perceived as "castrated." Somewhere dur-

ing this time, the child might be warned not to play with his genitals because they will be cut off or fall off, or he might see the female genitals and reach his own conclusions. Freud says the exact mechanism does not matter. What does matter is that from the narcissistic instinct to preserve his own genitals, the boy child gives up his identification with the mother. Viewing himself now as active and his mother as passive, he then perceives the father as rival to himself in his relation to his mother, and he hates his father. Overvaluing his father's power (a reversal of his own hatred), the boy fears the father.

When the Oedipus complex is shattered, the boy will give up his mother as object, turn his hatred for his father to love, identify with the man, and internalize the hated, overvalued father within as superego. He will retain the same aim of his desire. He will desire women as love objects, but simply postpone attaining his goal until adulthood.

How is the female's Oedipal passage different? Freud was not concerned with this question until late in life when it became apparent after listening to many similar problems in female patients that this scenario did not adequately describe female formation. The girl's passage, Freud decides, is more fraught with difficulties, is spread out over a longer span of time, and may never be as completed and dissolved as the boy's. The girl not only has to change the object of her love, away from her mother and women to her father and men, but also her aim. She must convert her active aims to passive ones, seeking the male to substitute for the power (penis envy) she lacks and wishing for the gift of a baby (the substitute phallus). As Freud discovered from his patients, many women (perhaps most) retain ambivalent feelings of love and hatred for their mothers and achieve heterosexuality only at a great cost of "dis-ease" since heterosexuality requires that they identify with femaleness (relationally passive) yet reject and turn away from it to value and desire the male (the active).

The equation of male/active and female/passive, Freud asserts, is not based on biology but is the result of becoming gendered by completing the Oedipal passage. "The antithesis active-passive coalesces later with the antithesis masculine-feminine, which, until this has taken place, has no psychological meaning," Freud writes in his 1915 essay "The Instincts and Their Vicissitudes." "The coupling of activity with masculinity and of passivity with femininity meets us, indeed, as a biological fact; but it is by no means invariably complete and exclusive as we are inclined to assume," he concludes (SE 14: 134).

According to Freud, individuals are born with sexual drives, but infant sexuality is initially undifferentiated, bisexual, polymorphic, and perverse.[13] A person develops by a process of self-differentiating psychical agencies, the formation of which depend on the structuring role of the Oedipus complex. At first Freud thought of psychical development in terms of memory, then in terms of his great discovery, the unconscious. By 1920, Freud adopted the names ego, id, and superego for these psychical agencies; these he calls his "new topography." The Oedipus complex marks the juncture where Freud's theory of the unconscious crosses his theory of sexuality. The result is a theory of the psyche as a dynamic interrelationship of ego, id, and superego.

Not only did the Oedipal narrative and terms for the dynamic parts of the psyche change. Freud's dream theory and theory of the unconscious evolved over time also.[14] Freud thought of the unconscious and the conscious as two systems, each with its own separate laws of regulation. A barrier between the two systems means that a perception is registered in two localities and is different in each. Based on the sexual case histories of his patients, Freud thought of the libido as a psychic element, containing force, operating on the unconscious side of the barrier. The barrier between the two systems is so strong that even in sleep the conscious system represses unconscious material through the censorship of the dream work. Dream interpretation allows the patient and analyst to reconstruct the workings of the libido. Dreams are not, however, equal to or the same as the unconscious but an opening to it, "the royal road."

The forces of the unconscious system are not directly knowable, but only as they take on representation or present themselves. There is representability (*Repräsentanz*) between instinctual force and meaning, between the two systems, the unconscious and the conscious. "[A]n 'instinct' appears to us as a concept on the frontier between the mental and the somatic," Freud writes in "The Instincts and Their Vicissitudes," "as the psychical representative of the stimuli originating from within the organism and reaching the mind, as a measure of the demand made upon the mind for work in consequence of its connection with the body" (*SE* 14: 121–22). The censoring operations of the dreamwork—condensation, displacement, transformation into visual images, replacement, reversal—derive from the basic postulate of representation and from the principle of repression.

The unconscious system is primary. It is indestructible and regulated by the pleasure/unpleasure principle; it does not perceive time, negation, or contradiction. Time operates in the secondary system of consciousness, as does repression, which rationalizes dreams through secondary revision. That is, Freud theorizes that we make narrative sense out of dreams by using the conventions of the conscious world, but that we do so in order to keep the forces of the unconscious from conscious knowledge.

Freud began thinking about psychic activity using the idea of a memory trace. Even though he moved away from a simple genetic equation of "most deeply buried" with actual infant perceptions, terms such as "infantile" retain a pejorative connotation as movement backward to the primary system of pleasure/unpleasure as opposed to the reality principle.

As Freud moves toward the final topography of ego, id, and superego, he explains regression in terms of a dynamic economic exchange within the structures of the primary and secondary systems rather than as a simple return to childhood memory. In the new topography, the ego is not equivalent to consciousness but merely forms the outer surface, the exterior that presents itself to the world. The id has all the aspects of the unconscious— the agency of the instincts, impersonal, timeless, unknown, indestructible—but it is not equivalent to the unconscious. The unconscious is greater than just the id, since "large portions of the ego and superego are unconscious" also (*SE* 22: 69).

The superego is the new, important construct. It is the agency of the suprapersonal, all those elements from parental authority and cultural tradition that the passage through the Oedipus complex institutes inside the individual. Freud's earlier theories about the ideal ego had pointed the way to the notion of the superego, and later Freud would regard the ideal ego as a function of the superego.[15] The superego comes to exist through the dissolution of the Oedipus complex. As a result of the passage through the Oedipal stage, the energies of the id attach themselves to perceived parental authority (greatly magnified in the psyche), giving birth to the superego. Then, in reaction, the superego represses knowledge of the Oedipal situation. From this primary repression of the superego, all later repressions come.

The genesis of the individual occurs from the interrelationship of the three—the ego, id, and superego. But the scheme of the new topography presents a genetic view that is relational and economic, never proportionate. That is, the ego (the self for the outside world) never equals some ratio of superego to id, or authority to instinct. In fact, the superego is closely aligned to the id and arises through the id. Hence, in a radical sense, the ego is irrational.

Joyce, in particular, shares the attitude implicit in Freudianism that "conscience" and authority have an irrational origin. Vicki Mahaffey in *Reauthorizing Joyce* analyzes the multiplication of authorities in *Ulysses*, stating that "Joyce represents authority as inherently double, a doubleness that takes as its two poles an individualistic model of authority on the one hand, and a communal model on the other" (13). Mahaffey's analysis is particularly rich as she follows the figuration of textiles and weaving, long associated in Western culture as woman's domain. As entrapping web or creative activity, weaving stands for the two contrary tensions Mahaffey sees in Joyce's work. She concludes that Joyce "subvert[s] the view that 'female' weaving is in any way inferior to the art of writing" (212). My reading of Joyce complements Mahaffey's, but whereas she examines clothes, figures, and garments, I look underneath, reading the psychic economy of desire in his texts. Similarly, I conclude that Joyce does not validate male over female or vice versa but portrays a continual circulation of desire and movement between those relational poles. Joyce increasingly deconstructs moral categories from *A Portrait* through *Ulysses*, I believe, and in the *Wake* portrays the circulating energy of hidden forces and relations underlying the surface authority of ego, the gendered, daylight world, and Western civilization.

Lawrence's work up through 1920 at least also seems to question received notions of authority, but thereafter Lawrence appears to undergo a turn to authoritarianism. Barbara Mensch in *D. H. Lawrence and the Authoritarian Personality*, measures Lawrence's characters and plots against authoritarian profiles and concludes Lawrence actually remained a liberal cultural critic to the end. On the other side, in *D. H. Lawrence and the Devouring Mother: The Search for a Patriarchal Ideal of Leadership*, Judith Ruderman concludes Lawrence adhered ever more rigidly to a patriarchal ideal because of his fear of the devouring mother. David Holbrook goes further, blaming Frieda for "his seduction" into "amoralism" that turned him "against his own true daemon" (*Where D. H. Lawrence Was Wrong about Woman* 29). I argue that Lawrence's so-called turn to fascistic, patriarchal, or authoritarian ideals in the twenties should not be read in terms of any personal animosity toward women and does not really mark a change from his earlier work. The psychostructural relations in both early and late texts depend upon patriarchy. What is important, I believe, is understanding how both "liberal"- and "authoritarian"-seeming positions equally depend on, and reproduce, the underlying structure/culture of patriarchy.

Both Lawrence and Joyce also explore the role of death within the drives of life, as Freud was to do after World War I. Correcting his theory of instincts, Freud introduces the concept of the death instinct in his 1920 work *Beyond the Pleasure Principle*.

In addition to the sex drive of the libido, he argues, there is another, equally strong instinctual drive—the desire of the organism to return to its original nonliving state.

Freud reached his conclusion only reluctantly after observing the almost manic compulsion to repeat pain in his grandson's game with a spool of thread and the desire to reenact traumas seen in his patients. Freud's revised theory of instincts posits a dualism of drives. Renaming these instincts "Eros" and "Thanatos," he raises them from a mechanical or physiological level to a mythic level.

Each of the psychic agencies can be channels for both drives. In the Oedipal drama, the opposition between two desires (the little boy's desire for his mother as love object and his narcissistic desire to preserve himself and so give her up) propels the individual to create a new structure. But the setting up of the internal agency of the superego does not indicate a new totality achieved from a primary dualism, for, profoundly pessimistic, Freud considers the superego "a pure culture of the death instinct" (*SE* 19: 53). The ego constantly mediates the demands of the id and the superego, and both can be channels of the death instinct. The ego institutes the reality principle only through difficult structural necessity, according to Freud, when it gives up the deviations and autoeroticism of the libido and subordinates libido to genital and specifically procreative sexuality. Freud claims that only the sexual instinct in its desire to join another fights against the conservative pull toward death, and the tragic conflict of Eros and Thanatos is resolved only at the level of the species.

Even though Freud mythifies a conservative ethic of procreative sexuality, his dualism is not a simple dichotomy of life force and death drive but a dynamic dialectical structuring process. In a way similar to Freudianism, Lawrence's and Joyce's texts present creative and destructive forces in dialectical, rather than merely oppositional, relation. *The Rainbow* and *Women in Love* suggest that from destruction or dissolution arises a new growth, which is not a resolution of opposites but something new produced from conflict.

Joyce begins by setting up neat oppositions, by which his characters (like the young Stephen) learn about the world. Stephen gains mastery by categorizing the world in binary sets— red and green brushes, hot and cold, mother and father. Yet as he grows, he realizes the limit of each system of knowledge, learns its contradictions, and thereby deconstructs its authority. While Joyce's interest in Bruno and Vico may seem to suggest that Joyce retains at least the notion of binary opposition as a valid system of meaning, I argue in chapter 4 that *Finnegans Wake* satirically deconstructs even the relation of two, the "mirror stage" in psychoanalysis, showing it to be a "vicious circle." Out of the conflict of twos, embodied in Shem's and Shaun's rivalry, emerges the unfixed dialectical three, which, I argue, has the sexual shape of the human genitals—three times two (3 x 2), bisexual ("bisectualism" of "sixuous parts"—*FW* 524.12, 297.22),[16] female overlaid on male. This bisexual human genital portrait is revealed only in pieces through dream interpretation, since it exists in the unconscious register beneath repression. One counterpart representation in consciousness is the threesome of the Oedipal triangle with its rivalry produced by conventional sex/gender division.

Many readers of the *Wake* claim that the Oedipal drama is presented as an eternally recurring structure and thus that the work upholds essentialist ideas of sexual difference (the eternal male and female) and conventional family form instituted by the son's rivalry with the father and the father's eventual fall. "We distort the *Wake*'s basic aim of the depiction of the family if we look too hard for the unusual or abnormal sexuality which simply does not appear in the narrative," claims Michael Begnal (112). Begnal never specifies the book's "basic aim" in its "depiction of the family" other than asserting it is normative.

I come to quite opposite conclusions. In chapter 4, I explore the sexual pieces beneath the *Wake*'s "words" and "characters," which I believe are composite and interchangeable. The Egyptian material in the *Wake*, as well as the psychoanalytic, suggest that conventional family form, the threesome of the Oedipus complex, is not a necessary shape but only *one* of the representations that unconscious drives (polymorphically perverse) may take in consciousness.

Freud, Lawrence, and Joyce conceive of movement arising from the internal conflict of opposition, so that the stable two is destabilized. During the last ten years of his life, Lawrence railed against women distorting, as he saw it, their innate sexual nature, and Joyce declared openly against feminism in his conversation and letters.[17] Even so, the work of both is inherently interesting to feminist readers and susceptible to feminist analysis because in their work family and gender issues are embedded within destabilized, dialectical structures. "This problem of dealing with differences without constituting an opposition," Jane Gallop remarks in *The Daughter's Seduction,* "may just be what feminism is all about," and she adds parenthetically "(might even be what psychoanalysis is all about)" (93).

In Joyce's texts, dialectical structures destabilize notions of fixed difference. The relation of form to content suggests that Joyce's work can be read as a kind of writing that challenges and breaks down essentialist notions of sexual difference. Although Lawrence's plots return again and again to the moment of perceiving sexual difference, his plots do not come to rest in that moment. Sex difference, in Lawrence's work, is not a fixed, absolute point but momentary, glimpsed fleetingly, relational, tentative, tested and reestablished over and over. Even more destabilized, Joyce constantly transforms gender, giving us womanly men and manly women, and finally transforming even the intact human body into parts, organs, and segments of personality.

While the texts of Lawrence and Joyce share with Freudianism some of the same attitudes to authority, to death, and to dialectical movement caused by conflict, neither Lawrence nor Joyce shares Freud's pragmatic, evolutionary ethic that raises procreative sex to the most moral act. Sex is a central activity in their texts, but for exploration and pleasure, not utilitarian production. Still, I believe both writers are not far from Freud's evolutionary perspective. Just as Freud does, they portray the human against an immense backdrop of a powerful natural world.

All Freud's work bears the stamp of evolutionary thinking. He argues that the development of the individual recapitulates the development of the species. He speculates that the Oedipus complex, now a structuring interrelationship, was probably once an actual event involving mother incest and parricide (*Introductory Lectures* 335 and *Totem and Taboo*). He sees reality as intransigent; for him, it is *Ananke*, necessity. Freud's conception of reality somewhat resembles that of late nineteenth-century Darwinism. His late works assume a hostile environment, stemming both from the natural world and from culture itself, exerting nearly intractable pressure on humans. Freud derives his ethic of procreation from this view of existence. Grounded on the survival of the species, it is an ethic based on the theory of evolution.

Freud privileges genital, procreative sex within the institution of the patriarchal family, raising the nuclear family to the status of the sole purveyor of the life force. Freud substitutes the family for religion. Only Eros sublimated to procreative sexuality holds back those agents of the death instinct, pure culture and nonprocreative libidinal drives.

Lawrence and Joyce most diverge from Freud on this family ethic. While Lawrence's plots begin in the family, they invariably end by moving away, focusing instead on the relation of two. *The Rainbow* suggests, for example, that the old, fixed forms of family are worn out and destructive, especially to the development of women and to relations between the sexes. Joyce's attitude to family, as I interpret it from his texts, is less oppositional than Lawrence's, but Joyce's texts do not, I argue, endorse fixed family form. *Ulysses* and especially *Finnegans Wake* suggest that sexuality and creative, perverse imagination are the purveyors of the life force rather than the family. In *Finnegans Wake*, the family may merely be a representation of the sleeping hero's unconscious drives, and hence from a Freudian point of view the family is a secondary screen formation created by the censoring mechanism of the dream work.

Freud's reputed bias against women is ambiguous. Despite Freud's well-known prejudices against women and despite his famous remark "anatomy is destiny," he seems to have resisted attempts to "sexualize" the psychic system. According to Freud, gender identity is produced by passage through the Oedipus complex; at the earliest stages all individuals are bisexual. Neither gender (male or female) is identical to consciousness, unconsciousness, or repression. There is less severe repression in women, generally, Freud says, because of their less forceful superego formation, yet each individual case differs. Freud's is not a universal symbolic system but an individual as well as cultural process of development. In the course of more than twenty-five years he rejected Jung's revision of the Oedipus complex as symbolic (*SE* 5: 123); it is particular and variable, Freud insists. He rejected Adler's notion of "masculine protest" (5: 354) and Fliess's idea that sexual difference caused repression: "I can only repeat that I do not accept this view: I do not think we are justified in sexualizing repression in this way—that is to say, in explaining it on a biological instead of a purely psychological basis" (5: 355).

These defensive statements are not entirely persuasive, however. For one thing, in each case Freud is more interested in distinguishing himself from his rivals than in making clear distinctions about how the biological and cultural become the psychic and/or how the psychic shapes the cultural and defines what biology is.

A MARXIST CRITICISM: CONSCIOUSNESS AS IDEOLOGY

One problem may be that Freud lacks an adequate theory of the social. This is the beginning point for V. N. Vološinov's (Bakhtin)[18] critique of Freudianism. "*The entire process of character formation*," Vološinov argues, "*runs its course within the confines of the subjective psyche viewed as an isolated entity*" (71–72; italics in original). Vološinov examines the analytic session between psychoanalyst and patient and turns to linguistic theory to correct the Freudian account. "Not a single instance of verbal utterance can be reckoned exclusively to its utterer's account," he argues. "Every utterance is *the product of the interaction between speakers* and the product of the broader context of the whole complex *social situation* in which the utterance emerges" (79; italics in original). Vološinov concludes that the structure of the Oedipus complex is not "natural" or "psychical" but "*a purely ideological formulation*" (82; italics in original). Vološinov equates the human psyche with discourse (83). Discourse is not controlled or even defined by the lone individual but is "the property of his *social group*" (86 italics in original), and "in actual fact there is no fundamental dividing line between the content of the individual psyche and formulated ideology" (87).

Vološinov's linguistic corrective to Freudianism redefines the notions of conscious/unconscious in terms of the language community. Taking very seriously Freud's metaphor of the conscious as a censor, Vološinov equates consciousness with officially accepted discourse and ideology, unconsciousness with "the unofficial" and unacceptable (89). The unconscious, "excluded from the zone of verbalized behavior" becomes "*asocial*" and "animalian" (89; italics in original). When a community is healthy, "there is no discrepancy" between the two, he claims (89). However, when deep contradictions develop between official ideology and "indistinct inner speech," then it is possible that "a struggle with that official ideology" will occur, giving voice to revolutionary ideology (90).

Vološinov's criticism has a somewhat puritanical strain. For example, he complains about Freud's sexual emphasis and indicts Freud for his "*wholesale sexualization of the family*" (90; italics in original). He does not critique Freud on gender at all. Yet, Vološinov offers a powerful critique of the subject and of family, showing how Freudian theory is linked to capitalist ideology and bourgeois family form, and he suggests a theory of the political unconscious that has been developed by Fredric Jameson.[19]

Recent work in Lawrence and Joyce studies take up political

analysis drawing on the narrative theory of the Bakhtin Circle. Nigel Kelsey's *D. H. Lawrence: Sexual Crisis* locates Lawrence's strength as cultural critic in his dialogism. "When Lawrence's writing gives way to dialogism," Kelsey states, "the ideological entanglements and conflictive nature of social change is registered to supreme effect" (184). Richard Pearce in *The Politics of Narration* argues that Joyce's style is political and potentially liberatory. Pearce focuses on the gaps, obscurities, contradictions, and shifts in perspective to show how Joyce's style enacts a dialogic struggle for authority. Joyce's polyphonic texts have the effect, Pearce concludes, of making the reader aware of how narrative establishes and maintains its authority.[20]

Patrick McGee in *Paperspace: Style as Ideology in Joyce's 'Ulysses'* uses theories of Bakhtin and Lacan to tease out the political implications in Joyce's text, concluding that *Ulysses* deconstructs style, revealing it as ideology. *Ulysses*, he states, offers "an implied critique of Western patriarchy under the rule of capital through a parodistic disclosure of the ideology of literary form" (156–57). I find McGee's analysis particularly strong when he adopts the feminist strategy of resistant reading.[21] McGee explains his resistance by reference to Lacan as a "refusal" (*Verwerfung* in Freud, "foreclosure" in Lacan) to accept the politics of patriarchy in Lacan's theory. "My use of 'foreclosure,'" he explains, "is intended to deconstruct rhetorically, even through a sort of parody, that Lacanian apparatus which privileges paternity and legitimates patriarchy by creating the illusion of its historical necessity" (210n3).

I deploy a slightly different reading strategy. I read *Ulysses* in the context of *A Portrait* and *Finnegans Wake*, both as a resistant and compliant reader—that is, reading with as well as against Joyce's texts. McGee places Molly "between male and female" (181); I argue Molly and Poldy embody sex role stereotypes and explode them, uncovering the ideology of gender. My conclusions about desire differ considerably from McGee's. I theorize Joyce's relation to capital and to desire differently too. Whereas

McGee concludes that Molly's monologue "does not represent Joyce's desire for meaning but the breakdown of meaning and the blockage of desire" (188), I argue that the deconstruction of style, systems of meaning, and gender, disclose beneath the surface the fluid, circulating energy of multiform desire. Consumer capitalism depends upon desire's continual displacement onto a series of substitute objects. Joyce, I believe, exposes the deadly forces of capitalism in the commodified object of exchange systems while also appreciating and using those forces through mimicry and parody. In *Finnegans Wake*, I argue, he accelerates this deconstruction of binary oppositions (on which value judgments as well as an exchange economy depend) and unleashes the proliferation of anarchic, multiform, perverse desire.

Vološinov's critical sketch of Freud, published in 1927, was not available in the West, but its influence did spread indirectly through Roman Jakobson and the Prague Linguistic Circle. The work of Jacques Lacan may bear some traces of this linguistic critique, probably because Lacan was influenced by the Russian formalists. But Lacan's linguistic revision of Freudianism has an entirely different aim than Marxist revisions of psychoanalysis. Vološinov is interested in theorizing how the individual's psyche is constituted by the linguistic community and in understanding how ideological shifts come about and where dissonant cells of change lay dormant (in the "unconscious" of the nonverbal substratum officially excluded from discourse). Lacan's theory, on the other hand, emphasizes the structuring authority of patriarchal law in the symbolic system of language and defines mental health as accepting the Law of the Name-of-the-Father. "It is in an accident in this register," Lacan states, referring to the register of the Symbolic in his theory, "and what takes place in it, namely, the foreclosure of the Name-of-the-Father in the place of the Other, and in the failure of the paternal metaphor, that I designate the defect that gives psychosis its essential condition, and the structure that separates it from neurosis" ("On the Possible Treatment of Psychosis," *Ecrits* 215).

THE SUPPLEMENT OF
STRUCTURAL ANTHROPOLOGY

Lacan draws on Saussure's and Jakobson's structural linguistics and on structural anthropology, particularly the theories of Claude Lévi-Strauss.[22] Lévi-Strauss reformulated Freud's haphazard ethnological speculations about incest and parricide into a social theory, rather than the psychoanalytics Freud had presented in *Totem and Taboo*. Lévi-Strauss postulated that the incest taboo and kinship systems—whatever their specific contents—mark the passage into human culture by instituting a system of symbolic exchange, the exchange of women by men, as well as a host of other exchange items. Lacan adapts Lévi-Strauss's method—applying the principles of Saussure's linguistics to material in another field—and the idea that before all other social needs and beneath all social appearances is the organizing field of "the primary classificatory function" which Lacan calls the Law of the Name-of-the-Father (*The Four Fundamental Concepts* 20).

While Freud viewed the Oedipus complex as a universal structuring principle in the genesis of the individual, Freud also believed that the Oedipal drama occurred at the site of each individual and particular family, so that the effects of the passage through the Oedipus complex were specific to each individual. Structuralism, however, shifts the location of the Oedipal drama from the individual subject and family to the structure of the society as a whole. In fact, it is only by choosing to disregard particular social phenomena that structuralists construct a theory of the underlying social exchange system.

In this respect, structuralism reflects a movement even further away than Freudianism from the subject as a personal, volitional entity. Structuralists also draw the boundary line between nature and culture at the moment when kinship systems are instituted, removing from consideration any idea of the "natural" and hence shifting focus away from thinking in terms of conflicts between nature and culture.

Freud's insistence on the importance of prehistory in each individual—that state before the person completes passage through the Oedipus complex—seems to be incompatible with the view that what is human is entirely cultural. The archaic agency of the id is something like the inhuman force of the natural world inscribed within individuals. The id knows no time, no negation, no speech, and is driven solely by the pleasure/unpleasure principle. The id operates before the Oedipus complex, in part triggers the Oedipal drama, and survives after it as "the great reservoir of the libido" ("The Ego and the Id," *SE* 19: 38).

For Freud, the human situation is a continual, precarious clashing not only between "natural" instincts and the demands of human systems but even between the conflicting directions of the instincts themselves, which can and do attach themselves to cultural forms. The death drive desires to return to a previous, inorganic, constant state and the sexual drive wishes to unite. In Freud, "natural" instincts both create culture and threaten to destroy the bonds that tie humans together. Freud locates the structuring mechanism of the Oedipus complex within each individual, as well as the struggle between nature and culture. Structuralism, however, displaces both of these beyond the individual onto the social exchange system itself.

The structuralist maneuver has certain advantages because it shifts the scene for inquiry, interpretation, and explanation from particular individuals to larger forms of social organization. For feminists, in particular, structural analysis reveals the interrelationship of seemingly disparate phenomena (social roles, modes and division of labor, religious prescriptions) as effects of an invisible social and psychological sex/gender system. Many feminists are drawn to the structural psychoanalysis of Jacques Lacan because "what Lacanian feminists have found liberating in this father-dominated narrative," Claire Kahane says, "is Lacan's disclosure of sexual difference as a construction in culture rather than, as in Freud's more conservative moments, as a natural fact that determines history" (29). To Lacan, woman's conflict results from her position in the symbolic order. She is "bound up in an order of exchange in which she is object" ("Sosie," *The Seminar, II*: 262).

Despite its analytical effectiveness, however, a structural approach has difficulty accounting for change. This is the point Jacques Derrida makes in his critique of Lévi-Strauss in "Structure, Sign and Play." Lévi-Strauss must constantly posit ruptures and gaps between structures to explain change. Derrida quotes Lévi-Strauss's "Introduction to the Work of Marcel Mauss" in which Lévi-Strauss speculates that "language could only have been born in one fell swoop" to explain the leap from nature into the human world of the symbolic (291). There "is a risk," Derrida caustically notes, "of falling back into an anhistoricism *[sic]* of a classical type" (*Writing and Difference* 291).[23]

Whereas Lawrence's texts return again and again to the psychic moment of gender division and therefore seem oriented nostalgically toward the past, I think all Joyce's works explore how change comes about. Hence Joyce's texts seem to play across the structuralist, poststructuralist field. Joyce's *Portrait of the Artist* shows how Stephen grows up within a highly structured society. Each system of meaning in Irish life—the Catholic church, English domination, Irish nationalism—arranged like circles around him, Stephen passes from one to the next as he learns to understand, use, and then reach the limits of each system. His progress through each means abandoning the last, as he finally must abandon Ireland herself or risk becoming one of the paralyzed caught within her webs. Between *A Portrait* and *Ulysses*, Joyce seems to pass from a structural to a poststructural view, from satire's analysis of exchange systems to the continual destabilizing of free circulation.

LACAN'S FREUDIAN REVISION

In psychoanalysis, Lacanian theory occupies the structuralist/poststructuralist position.[24] Adapting the linguistic maneuver of Lévi-Strauss, Lacan postulates that "*the unconscious is structured like a language"* (*The Four Fundamental Concepts* 20; italics in original).[25]

Lacan's revision of Freudianism results in a different emphasis than Freudianism or in a different theory, depending upon one's critical point of view. Lacan's notion of desire, for example, is connected to Freud's libido, but whereas Freud thinks of the libido as a primary force, Lacan sees desire as arising from lack. "Desire is situated in dependence on demand—which, by being articulated in signifiers, leaves a metonymic remainder that runs under it," Lacan states. That remainder, he explains, "is not indeterminate, which is a condition, both absolute and unapprehensible, an element necessarily lacking, unsatisfied, impossible, misconstrued *(méconnu)*, an element that is called desire" ("Sexuality in the Defiles of the Signifier," *The Four Fundamental Concepts* 153–54). "Man's desire," as Lacan defines it in another lecture, "is the desire of the Other" ("Of the Subject Who Is Supposed to Know," *The Four Fundamental Concepts* 235).

For Lacan, desire arises because of the need for demand to pass through the limiting system of intersubjective language, where that which comes back from the Other is never adequate. Desire is never satisfied, but in fact is caused by the condition of insatiability. On the other hand, Freud, as Paul Ricoeur points out, "is in line with those thinkers for whom man is desire before being speech" (313).[26]

The radical disproportion of the Freudian ego seems to become in Lacan a series of spatial metaphors. Lacan's various schemata (L, R) for intersubjective relations and the psychical structure imitate the formality of mathematical logic (see "On a Question Preliminary to Any Possible Treatment of Psychosis" *Ecrits* 192–99).[27] In contrast, Freud's topography describes an ego that mediates the demands of the superego and id. Large parts of the ego are themselves unconscious, Freud insists, and he does not suggest that the whole equals some constant proportion of its constituent parts as a geometric figure does.

A great synthesizer, Lacan incorporated ideas and terms from philosophy and literature into his theories. He develops his theory of the gaze, for example, from Sartre ("The Object Relation and the Intersubjective Relation," *The Seminar, I*: 215–25). Lacan's dialectic of the gaze has proved an especially useful notion for feminist thinkers. In Joyce studies, Kimberly Devlin uses Lacan's theory to explore the many ramifications of the act of looking in *Ulysses* and *Finnegans Wake*. She notes that "Joyce revises the sexist myth" by "transforming the reified female object into a critical female subject" as Gerty turns her gaze on Bloom ("See Ourselves" 891).

Connected to the gaze is Lacan's theory of the mirror stage, which I use, along with Freud's 1910 essay "A Special Type of Object Choice," to analyze the dyadic structure of Lawrence's late novella *The Man Who Died*. Lacan's initial theory of the mirror stage reflects the influence of object-relations theory, existentialism, and Gestalt theory of child development, although he adapts each source to his own theory. The mirror stage describes the subject's essentially empty position at the start of life. Looking in a mirror, the child discovers a form in his reflected image that provides him with a corporeal unity he lacks at this stage of his development. This self Lacan calls the *moi* ("Ego-Ideal and Ideal Ego," *The Seminar, I*: 140). The self is initially alienated because it lacks wholeness and correspondence (which it seeks) with the whole image reflected in the mirror. The self will enter into subjectivity later—not by achieving correspondence with the reflected image—but by appropriating language, which is its entry into the symbolic order and subjectivity ("The Mirror Stage," *Ecrits* 1–7). The play of Freud's grandson in throwing out a spool and retrieving it ("gone! there!" *Fort! Da!*) Lacan reads as the "moment in which desire becomes human" and "in which the child is born into language" ("Function and Field of Speech and Language," *Ecrits* 103).

In *Beyond the Pleasure Principle* Freud had interpreted the play of his grandson as an example of repetition compulsion that revealed the death instinct. Lacan reads that play as entry into the universal symbolic system of language, since the child discovers in her repetition of gone! there! the principle of absence/presence by which language operates. An object must be absent for it to be discovered. So too, for Lacan desire is dependent upon the notion of lack.

The mirror stage reveals the self as an imaginary construct and the source of all later identifications ("The Mirror Stage," *Ecrits* 4). Identification for Lacan, as for Freud, reflects narcissism. The mirror stage is Lacan's paradigm for what he calls the Imaginary relationship, as the *Fort! Da!* is his paradigm for the Symbolic.

The site of subject-object discord, the Imaginary is an order of illusion in which the subject posits actual correspondence— for example, between a real referent such as a penis and the symbolic role of the Name-of-the-Father, or between the initially empty self and the whole image reflected in the mirror. Adapting Saussure's linguistics, Lacan claims that one-to-one correspondence is the equivalent of a zero phoneme, which is Lacan's version of Freud's constancy principle, the death instinct. "On the imaginary level," Lacan states, the subject "feels himself to be in disarray in relation" to objects ("The Dream of Irma's Injection," *The Seminar, II*: 169). Aggressivity, narcissism, and masochism are tied up in the Imaginary. Either the subject is alienated from itself and feels lacking in the presence of the object, or the subject wishes to kill the object. "The masochistic outcome," Lacan states, "is located at the juncture between the imaginary and the symbolic," and "primal masochism" develops "around this original murder of the thing" ("The See-saw of Desire," *The Seminar, I*: 172, 174).

The Symbolic order is the order of language, "the determining order of the subject" ("Translator's Note," *Ecrits* ix). The subject recognizes, after necessary "misrecognition" (Lacan's term), that no action, individual, or relationship is symbolic by itself but depends on the third term, the Other, to enter into the intersubjective exchange system of symbol. "The condition of the subject," Lacan says, "is dependent on what is being unfolded in the Other O. What is being unfolded there is articulated like a discourse (the unconscious is the discourse of the Other)"

("On the Possible Treatment of Psychosis," *Ecrits* 193). He also defines the other as the listener in the psychoanalytic relationship.

Lacan's third relationship, the Real, is a function of the relation of the Imaginary and the Symbolic, but it is outside the Symbolic, "that which is foreclosed from the analytic experience" ("Translator's Note," *Ecrits* ix). Lacan's concept of the real changes, but may be similar to Vološinov's idea of that which is not able to enter discourse.

The intention of discourse is to fill the gap caused by the discovery of the primordial lack of object, a condition that causes desire, but a condition that is the *effect* of language, not the result of some existential situation: "desire is an effect in the subject of that condition which is imposed on him by the existence of the discourse, to make his need pass through the defiles of the signifier" ("Direction of Treatment," *Ecrits* 264).

Lacanian theory, then, transposes Freudianism to the field of language and translates Freud's terms to linguistic ones. Lacan renders Freud's *Verschiebung*—or displacement—as metonymy, the perpetual displacement of need upon a chain of signifiers. Freud's *Verdichtung*, condensation, becomes the symptom as metaphor. For Freud's distortion, *Entstellung*, Lacan adopts the linguistic term *glissement*. In a strictly linguistic sense this denotes the changing of meanings in a word during the evolution of a language. But Lacan's use of the term indicates "the sliding of the signified under the signifier, which is always active in discourse (its action, let us note, is unconscious)" ("Agency of the Letter in the Unconscious," *Ecrits* 160). Glimpses of the unconscious, then, can be traced in the play of language beneath intentional control.

Lacan derives his concept of the Name-of-the-Father from Freud's *Totem and Taboo*. The Symbolic father is not a real or imaginary father, but "in so far as he signifies this Law, the dead Father" ("On the Possible Treatment of Psychosis," *Ecrits* 199).

The Name-of-the-Father expresses the very condition of being bound to the rules of signification. The phallus is the signifier of desire, as well as the Law of language, since desire, in its perpetual displacement onto signifiers, generates language to fill the gap caused by the lack of object. For Lacan, the phallus is thus the transcendental signifier that ordains the rules of language that generate meaning and bestow subjectivity. "Freud revealed this imaginary function of the phallus, then, to be the pivot of the symbolic process that completes *in both sexes* the questioning of the sex by the castration complex" ("On the Possible Treatment of Psychosis," *Ecrits* 198; italics in original).

Lacan states variously that the Symbolic father is a myth (*Ecrits* 198–99), that the mother constructs the father's symbolic power (*Ecrits* 218), and the symbolic function is the necessary effect of naming. He denies over and over that he actually refers to a real phallus or an existential condition of phallic dominance, for believing in actual correspondence would be to operate in the Imaginary register.[28]

Actually, though, Lacanian theory makes sense because there has been an actual history of male dominance and widespread, though not universal, teleologies of a Father/God (and of course these references abound in Lacan's lectures). With history restored, rather than "foreclosed" (and here I'm adopting the parody of resistance), then Lacanian theory merely (but boldly) asserts that language bears the history of male dominance, or the mark of the phallus. Language may structure consciousness and the unconscious may be like a language; nevertheless, to be marked by the phallus means that prior, constituting conditions, existential relations of power, production, sexual division of labor, always have preceded and are already inscribed in the language in which the subject must take up her position.

If history always is already inscribed in language, would it mean that history and humanness precede language? Lacan is most contradictory on this point. On the one hand, he declares in "Where is speech? Where is language?" that "language is completely burdened with our history, it is as contingent as this sign, and what is more it is ambiguous" (*The Seminar, II:* 285). On the other, in the same seminar he talks of language as though it were a pure, abstract, closed system that produces humanness. He calls it a "universal machine," stating that "language exists completely independently of us" (284). He ends the seminar by equivocating, "I wasn't trying to tell you that I believed that language was in the beginning—I know nothing of origins" (293). Again, in his 1958 seminar, "The Signification of the Phallus," he reiterates, "it is not a question of the relation between man and language as a social phenomenon" but about "the laws that govern that other scene" whose "effects" are discovered through linguistic operations which he calls "a topology, in the mathematical sense of the term" (*Ecrits* 285).[29]

The privileged position Lacan gives to the Symbolic father as guarantor, or underwriter, so to speak, of the Symbolic order casts discourse as a coterminous, unified totality with patriarchy itself. Lacan's concept of the Symbolic father also results in a different reading of the Oedipal scene, of the family, and of gender identity. Lacan's Oedipal scene recasts the individual sexual rivalry of Freud's Oedipal protagonists into the impersonal roles of "givers and receivers" in a kinship structure. This shift of interest and meaning from particular individuals to symbolic systems extends to the "family constellation" (Lacan's term). Hence the *symbolic* family structures identity, according to Lacan, not actual family relations, which are in the order of the Imaginary, the realm of the illusion of correspondence.

Opposite to Freud, Lacan insists that the passage through the Oedipus complex is relatively easy for girls, but difficult for boys (Wilden 271). The boy must realize that his penis is not the same as the Imaginary phallus, a realization that gives access to the symbolic process, but which the little boy persists in denying. This is his denial of castration, that all subjecthood begins from a lack. The little girl, since she has no penis, simply rejects castration (in Lacan, the Imaginary register, a belief in correspondence) and thus can enter the Symbolic order, where it is understood that the penis as the Imaginary phallus does not equal the Law of the Symbolic father.

In both the Freudian and Lacanian versions of the Oedipal

scene, the penis represents the object of sexual difference, so that female/male are not properly symmetrical terms, each having different content. Rather, one term has no content, so that they form the pair, absence/presence. Sometimes when Lacan writes "the woman" he crosses through "the" to emphasize the relation to absence on which gendering is based. "Woman [La *femme*] doesn't ex-sist," he states (*Television* 38).

Strictly speaking, Lacan's equation of the psychic system and language and of sexual division and linguistic operation (presence/absence) is one of analogy.[30] The analogy derives its persuasive power from the referent it wishes to deny, the historical dominance of men.[31] By concealing the historical reference, Lacanian theory strains toward the mythic, timeless, and universal and so works to preserve patriarchy and male dominance. The Lacanian analogy might be presented like this: psychic system: language :: language : sexuality. Canceling the middle terms uncovers the implicit reduction, the sexual determination of the psychic system. The mediating position of language conceals the unevenness, differences, and contradictions in history and cultures. The equation depends upon an abstract conception of language, erasing the differences among languages and smoothing over the multitude of particular ways in which different languages structure experience. The analogy ignores the role of chance, that disruptive force of nature, making static and formal what is dynamic and discontinuous.

The conservative undercurrents of Lacanian theory exert a pull toward the normative and regulatory, preserving the present binary sex/gender system and myths of gender. Despite this undertow, I have found Lacan's theory of the mirror stage useful in understanding the relations of aggressivity and doubling, especially in *Finnegans Wake*. In reading the *Wake*, I therefore use Lacanian terms, but in resistance, refusing his mythification of language and patriarchy.

Lacanian readings of Joyce texts far outnumber those of Lawrence texts, as a recent issue of *James Joyce Quarterly*, "Joyce Between Genders: Lacanian Views" makes apparent.[32] Lacanian readings of Joyce range from those that flexibly adapt Lacanian theory to more programmatic readings that subsume and merge Joyce and his texts beneath the regulatory and normative terms of Lacan's psychoanalysis.[33]

Lacan's relation to Joyce is a complicated matter. In 1975–76 Lacan gave a series of seminars on Joyce, in which he explores Joyce "as symptom." Lacan learns from Joyce, but to what extent is not yet clear.[34] Joyce, of course, did not know of Lacan, but Joyce did know Freud. Consequently, I construct a reading of *Finnegans Wake* more by reference to Freud's work that Joyce read[35] than to Lacan, although I use some of Lacan's ideas. I do see a relation between Lacan's notion of desire as insatiable and Joyce's unleashing, as I see it, of anarchic, multiform desire, but I believe their directions and values are reversed. Lacan's is arrayed to shore up the necessity of the symbolic, the normative Law of the Name-of-the-Father. Lacan theorizes desire arising from lack and always needing the third term of the Symbolic to put it into play. The word/world scramble of the *Wake,* on the other hand, points in the opposite direction. There, the symbolic, whether language or H.C.E. as father, never operates quite properly. Impropriety is everywhere. Language, fractured and soldered into a contradictory jumble, tries to hide yet cannot help but divulge its underside, its unconscious (as Lacan theorizes). However, the unconscious underworld of the *Wake* is full, teeming with multiple meanings, and is sexually overdetermined. Nearly every word construction discloses anarchic, chaotic sexual desire lurking, not fully articulated, but mumbling and gesturing within. Joyce affirms that underworld—desire, pieces, the presymbolic in unregulated circulation—whereas from the point of view of Lacanian psychoanalysis Joyce's affirmation is "symptomatic" of neurosis or psychosis, a refusal of castration, a fetishization, a perversion.[36]

It is worth noting, too, that Lacan's concept of desire as lack is implicated in capitalism's dependence on a "law" of scarcity, as well as in the Judeo-Christian tradition of a fallen world and an all-powerful God.[37] Economic exchange systems and Western religions rest on the patriarchal structure of sexual division of labor and the exchange of women by men, whose institutions—labor/property/capital and marriage—Joyce resisted. I contend it is this notion of commodified desire, of regulating desire by directing it through the closed system of patriarchal exchange, that Joyce exposes, struggles against, and finally deconstructs. A growing number of Joyce critics—Mahaffey, McGee, Pearce, for example—also read Joyce texts as subversive in their resistance to conventions and institutions.

The smaller number of Lacanian readings of Lawrence tend to be more polyvocal and less regulatory in subsuming Lawrence to Lacanian theory. In "The Familial Isotopy in *The Fox*," Jane Nelson uses theories from Lacan and Kristeva to explore how readers, using details of the story and the Symbolic family constellation, construct different family configurations by which to understand the shifting relations of March, Banford, and Henry. Hilary Simpson in *D. H. Lawrence and Feminism* suggests that Lawrence sometimes uses the term "phallus" in the way Lacan does, as a third term by which sexual difference can be represented (133). I also find Lawrence situated within the field of discourse characterized by the term "difference." The similarities between Lawrence's phallic theorizing and Lacanian theory, I suspect, have less to do with accident or Lawrence's anticipation of Lacan and more to do with the fact that Lawrence (as I would argue Lacan does) remains enmeshed in the binary oppositions of patriarchy even though he opposes its limits.

FEMINIST CRITIQUES: THE DISPUTE
OVER THE MOTHER

Post-Freudian psychoanalytic feminisms debate the extent to which particular history and cultures shape individual psychology or universal symbolic systems hold sway. Feminists dispute too how deeply sexual difference is inscribed within systems of meaning. At one pole, American object-relations psychologists view the psychological formation of the gendered individual more through the effect that particular cultural structures have on the individual. They focus more on the child's earliest relation with the mother than on the later Oedipal formation. At the other pole, European Freudians influenced by Lacan emphasize the importance of woman's relation to the phallus and symbolic relations in structuring the psyche.[38]

Juliet Mitchell, as a post-Freudian Lacanian, insists on the importance of the father, while Madelon Sprengnether, in *The Spectral Mother*, contends that Freud was unable to theorize maternal subjectivity and therefore Freud's Oedipus complex "obscures as much as it illuminates" (4), making a subversive ghost of the mother.

Mitchell argues that Freud's seeming male bias arises from misreading the castration complex, "demoting" it from "its key role in the construction of sexual difference" to a "biological explanation" (*Feminine Sexuality* 19–20). Mitchell, following Lacan, reads the castration complex as the intervening third term, which is necessary in realizing that the self-division in the very construction of a human subject and its relation to an always absent object is not the result of a direct relation to anatomical difference but a relation to absence. "Psychoanalysis is phallocentric," Mitchell argues, because society is "patrocentric. To date, the father stands in the position of the third term that *must* break the asocial dyadic unit of mother and child. We can see this third term will always need to be represented by something or someone" (*Feminine Sexuality* 23).

In her earlier *Psychoanalysis and Feminism*, Mitchell stressed the importance for feminists in Freud's discovery of the asymmetrical nature of gender relations in patriarchy. Instead of criticizing Freud's ideas, Mitchell wrote, women need to understand their full implication, that "under patriarchal order women are oppressed in their very psychologies of femininity" (*Psychoanalysis and Feminism* 414). They are not oppressed because women's values or psychology are inferior to men's (neither is the reverse true; they are not superior). Rather, the asymmetry of psychic relations *reveals* woman's oppression—her asymmetrical and inferior status.

Between *Psychoanalysis and Feminism* of 1974 and *Feminine Sexuality,* coedited with Jacqueline Rose, of 1982, Mitchell slightly shifted her emphasis, from reading psychoanalysis in order to understand woman's oppression to reading Freudianism to explain Lacan's reformulation. My own reading of literary texts has been more strongly influenced by Mitchell's earlier work, especially by the chapter in *Psychoanalysis and Feminism,* "The Cultural Revolution," in which Mitchell links a critique of capitalism to her exposition of the psychology of patriarchy. Mitchell's border crossings between psychoanalysis and feminist critiques of labor and capital provide an exhilarating model of a feminist practice and helped shape my analysis of Lawrence's relation to patriarchy.

Sprengnether objects to Freudianism for valorizing the father as the third term and obliterating the mother. "The Oedipus complex," she states, "like Lacan's choice of the phallus as signifier, both explains and sustains patriarchy" (243). In a close reading of Freud's formative case histories and letters to Fliess, Sprengnether exposes Freud's repression of maternal desire and aggression and his blotting out of the early mother-child relation. Object-relations psychology, she notes, appears to restore interest in the ghostly mother—so called because she haunts Freudianism even though she disappears from view. However, Sprengnether argues, object-relations theory continues, rather than corrects, Freudian bias, since it "reproduces Freud's split conception of the preoedipal mother—as ideally loving and fulfilled by maternity, on the one hand, and as intrusive, overwhelming, or aggressive, on the other" (187). Object-relations theory continues the "desubjectifying" of the mother. That is, the mother is conceptualized in terms of the "good" or "bad" mother rather than as a "fully developed adult personality" (186). Sprengnether suggests the mother's body itself "represents at once the dream of plenitude and the recognition of its impossibility" (230) and argues that "the process of enculturation begins with the onset of life itself" (243) and not with phallic intervention.

Object-relations psychology, developed by Melanie Klein and later carried on by D. W. Winnicott and others, focuses on the pre-Oedipal period of the mother-child relationship that Freud neglected. Whereas Sprengnether criticizes object-relations theory for replicating Freud's problem of the mother, Mitchell and Jacqueline Rose, co-editors of *Feminine Sexuality*, criticize object-relations theory from the standpoint of Lacanian theory. Object-relations theory is mistaken, they contend, because it explains subjectivity arising from the infant's internalized relation *to* an object, rather than to its absence (3n1, 31) and because it presumes the distinction between the sexes from the model of what is already given—women and men (23).[39]

Object-relations theory has informed literary readings, especially readings of Lawrence texts.[40] This theory of the pre-Oedipal period turns our attention to the mother-child relationship and the rich material associated with the primary senses of touch, taste, smell, and hearing and the problems of merging and separation. Too often, though, interpretations of family relations that draw on object-relations theory devolve into accusations of "good" and "bad" mothering (as Sprengnether complains of in psychoanalysis) rather than respecting each family member's subjectivity and analyzing their relations.

I agree with Sprengnether that object-relations theory does not necessarily restore the subjectivity of the mother, since it is a theory of the internalized drive of the infant. For example, the *devouring mother* is a term that expresses the ambivalent desire and fear of the infant in the mother-child relationship. Klein explored the significance of the infant's first object-relation with the breast. The infant's wish to devour this source of pleasure and food expresses the emotion that is generated by one of the infant's first activities in the world. From this relation to the breast and the emotion it brings forth arises the projected fear turned back on itself of being devoured by the mother. Within the *devouring mother* complex lie the issues of separation and

merging that mark the pre-Oedipal stage and that also characterize, according to Freudianism, women's adult relations. In order
to resubjectify the mother, the term *devouring mother* should be
understood as a nexus of multiple relations and subjectivities
and not as a term with an absolute content.

On the one hand, I have tried to restore the mother's and
female's subjectivity by reading relations from multiple points
of view, not just from the infant's, and by reinserting social and
economic relations into psychoanalysis. This would be a reading
against the grain of psychoanalysis. On the other hand, I also
find it useful to read with psychoanalysis and compare Lawrence
and Joyce in terms of their differing interest in pre-Oedipal and
Oedipal material. Lawrence is always interested in the problems
of separating and merging. His plots revolve around twosomes,
and the structure of his stories is often dyadic, suggesting the
pre-Oedipal psychic relation of two. Joyce, on the other hand,
is more concerned with the triadic associated with Oedipal relations.

However, I also find that these neat (perhaps too neat) distinctions are not altogether adequate to describe the complexity
of either writer's texts. For example, despite Lawrence's interest
in questions of boundaries, merging and separation, his plots
always gravitate to a reenactment of the Oedipal moment that
establishes the distinction between the sexes. Joyce's apparent
interest in triangular relations may signal an Oedipal structure,
but I find that in Joyce relations of three transform into twos
and back again. For example, the triadic relation of two men
and a woman, common to *Exiles, Ulysses,* and Shem, Shaun, and
Issy in *Finnegans Wake,* seems on closer examination to suggest
a male/female relation with a doubled male figure—as a sign of,
and defense against, castration perhaps. Lawrence uses doubled
female figures this way. But in *Ulysses,* and even more so in
Finnegans Wake, with its revolving twos and threes, Joyce portrays,
I believe, the bisexuality of humans before or below consciousness entirely.

Nancy Chodorow's *Reproduction of Mothering* is perhaps the

most forceful and systematic feminist view of gender production based on object-relations theory. Sprengnether's complaint that "psychoanalytic feminism to date" does not "critique the Oedipal/preoedipal hierarchy" (186n1) could not properly apply to Chodorow. In *The Reproduction of Mothering*, Chodorow argues that the establishment of gender identity precedes the Oedipus complex (150), that psychical processes are induced through social structuration (7), and that the development of the self is relational (68).

Sprengnether admits Chodorow's account of female development is "appealing" but criticizes her argument for appearing essentialist (190–94). However, Chodorow presents neither a naive mimetic model of social/psychic gender reproduction, nor a mechanistic biological explanation. Instead, she analyzes the contradictions in the sexual division of labor to suggest how they produce in the family a psychology that reproduces the gender system: "That women mother is a fundamental organizational feature of the sex-gender system. It is basic to the sexual division of labor and generates a psychology and ideology of male dominance as well as an ideology about women's capacities and nature" (208).

Chodorow points to well-documented clinical research showing that children assume a fixed gender identity by the age of three. How a child perceives her body, and her experience of other bodies, help shape gender identity. But "its major input," Chodorow argues, is "from social ascription of sex that begins at birth and is cognitively learned concomitantly with language" (150).

Chodorow's analysis of how women reproduce in their mothering the culture of gender offers both a persuasive explanation for the pervasiveness and persistance of patriarchy and the hope of change. Presumably changes in the sexual division of labor will lead to changes in language. As the sex/gender system is modified in labor and language patterns, so too will the internal structure of our psyches change.

Chodorow does not, I think, clearly distinguish what she

believes the roles of language versus labor are in structuring the subject. And it is not clear whether the internal subject arises in direct relation to what precedes it (mother and father) or in relation to an absence. Yet I find her analysis persuasive and powerful. Women produce in their mothering a culture of gender that reproduces the sex/gender system of patriarchy and in particular the woman's conflicted position under patriarchy. She shows how women, intentions notwithstanding, become complicit in the devaluation of the female. Her analysis provides a way of reading the relations of Paul and Mrs. Morel in *Sons and Lovers,* a way that reclaims the subjectivity of the mother and yet does not smooth over the internal conflicts of Mrs. Morel.

One problem of focusing on the mother-child relationship in the pre-Oedipal period is that it may minimize the very real historical role of the father and his powerful symbolic place in psychological structuration. This criticism would apply equally to object-relations theories or to a Freudian "interventionist" perspective such as Sprengnether's. As Maria Ramas argues, object-relations theory may sidestep the critical problem of the woman's relation to the phallus (155–56).

However valid this criticism may be to the field of psychoanalysis, most psychoanalytic readings of literature have erred in the other direction, focusing solely on fathers, on fathers and sons, and, if mothers are mentioned, on the distorted effects (of course on their sons) of their too strong mothering. My strategy has not been to redress this imbalance by focusing exclusively on mothers, but to examine family relations from the perspective of multiple subjectivities.

The pre-Oedipal focus has also been criticized for undervaluing, or entirely dismantling, the notion of an unconscious. Object-relations theorists analyze the construction of the self from relations to part objects (Kleinians) and/or social relations (albeit internalized). Even internalized relations, however, come from the external world first, so the theory does not account for the nonexternal, hidden relations of the Freudian unconscious that knows no time, no negation, no contradiction. The Freudian unconscious is irrational and internally constructed from contradiction and discontinuity. Hence, object-relations theory minimizes the role of conflict stressed by Freud—that libidinal instincts generate conflicting drives and that the subject creates a conscious/unconscious psychological structure to satisfy the drives, retaining the conflict as well as repressing knowledge of it. Or in Lacan's reformulation of Freud, the theory glides over the "rupture, split, the stroke of the opening [which] makes absence emerge" ("The Freudian Unconscious and Ours," *The Four Fundamental Concepts of Psycho-Analysis* 26). That absence Lacan calls "the concept of the lack," a term he develops by wordplay from Freud's *Unbewusste* (unconscious) (see 26n1, trans.).

Sprengnether, however, does not smooth over the notion that the subject is constructed from radical discontinuity. Rather, she proposes a feminine psychic economy, an alternative to the father as third term. "The mother's body," she suggests, "represents estrangement as well as origin" and "provides a paradigm for the construction of the ego, itself a form of memorial, or a presence that enfolds absence" (233–34). However appealing it might seem to locate in the mother's body the model for the construction of the subject through self-division and absence, Sprengnether's suggestion still relies on the concept of modeling, the "paradigm" as she puts it. This argument thus relies on a direct equation between biology (the woman's body) and representation (the psychological structure created). I am as uneasy with this model as with Lacan's father-dominated model, not only because of the seeming biological determination, but also because of the direct relations it assumes between base and superstructure, material world and representation.

FEMINISTS ON THE RELATION TO THE PHALLUS

Julia Kristeva, analyst, theorist, and literary critic, follows Freud in positing a bisexual unconscious but incorporates into her own very original theory the linguistic emphasis of Lacan.

She links the semiotic (in her theory, a system of meaning associated with rhythm, gesture, nuance learned through the mother's body) with the pre-Oedipal stage, and the symbolic with the father (from Lacan's Name-of-the-Father). She emphasizes that Western discourse has obscured the influence of the mother. "No language can sing," she says in "The Novel as Polylogue," "unless it confronts the Phallic Mother" (*Desire in Language* 191).

Kristeva suggests in "Place Names" that the birth of a child might represent the intervening third term. "Love replaces narcissism in a third person that is external to the act of discursive communication," she says, and "loosen[s]" the "death drive" (*Desire in Language* 279). *Finnegans Wake*, I argue in chapter 4, presents a dialectic something like this. But whereas Kristeva finds this idea in the "brilliant inspiration of Christian tradition" (279), Joyce, I argue, turns away from Christianity to Egyptian myth for the figure of the child as intervening third term: "though his heart, soul and spirit turn to pharaoph times, his love, faith and hope stick to futurism" (*FW* 130.36–131.1).

Kristeva resists essentializing the relationship between biology and representation. Though she uses a family figure (the child) to theorize the intervening third term, she also resists the reification of family/psyche/discourse. "When all protagonists in what was the family become functions within the signifying process, and nothing more," she says, "the family loses its reason to exist. It withdraws before something else, something still invisible, an other social space serving the polylogizing subject" ("The Novel as Polylogue," *Desire* 200).

Like Kristeva, Hélène Cixous sees the woman as encoded by patriarchy, as "a body caught in his gaze," as "the colonized body" (*The Newly Born Woman* 67, 68). While Kristeva insists that discourse is androgynous, containing both the semiotic and symbolic impulses, Cixous connects writing ("the passageway, the entrance, the exit, the dwelling place of the other in me" 85–86) to female sexuality. She expresses this as "coming" to writing (69, 88, 90–92). We only know what woman is now, under patriarchy, Cixous argues, and "for historical reasons" woman is bisexual (85). She distinguishes between a bisexuality that denies castration and is "a fantasy of a complete being," a "fantasy of unity," and "the other bisexuality" (84). The other type, which is the woman's location under patriarchy, she defines as "the location within oneself of the presence of both sexes," and "the multiplication of the effect of desire's inscription" (85). This second kind of bisexuality, the presence within of both sexes and the multiplication of desire, runs throughout the text of *Finnegans Wake*, I believe, but I do not believe the *Wake* connects this bisexuality only to women. Cixous suggests that women should abjure a discourse of mastery and instead write a subversive discourse. "Woman must write her body" (94).

Cixous is careful to avoid simple biological equations. However, she often seems to rely on a kind of noble feminine argument. The male, she says, is caught up in a "mirror economy" and "needs to love himself" (94), while the female "launches forth; she seeks to love" (94). Her call for *écriture féminine* is just as ambiguous. She never answers her own question, whether writing is specifically feminine (86), and she admits she uses the language of mastery with students because she refuses "to leave organized discourse entirely in men's power" (136).

The problem is theorizing a third term that escapes the ordering hierarchy of patriarchy, a point Luce Irigaray explicates in *Speculum of the Other Woman*. Irigaray warns against "the impossible regression toward the mother" (346) and reiterates the dream of "going beyond representations themselves" (346). The terms "'mother' and 'father' can no longer copulate," she notes, "because they have already yielded to a genealogy of sameness which makes them substitutable" (346–47). Irigaray's play on copula/copulate underscores her critique of the patriarchal law that has dominated discourse, logic, and desire since Plato. As long as we remain in Plato's cave, the name of the Father will always echo in return, no matter what we call out. Even so, Irigaray emphasizes women's writing as a political act that will reclaim the female body for women's use and subvert patriarchy.

In *This Sex Which Is Not One*, and particularly in the chapter

"When Our Lips Speak Together," Irigaray muses on the dream possibility of a feminine economy figured by the female body. "And don't worry about the 'right' word. There isn't any. No truth between our lips. There is room enough for everything to exist. Everything is worth exchanging, nothing is privileged, nothing is refused. Exchange? Everything is exchanged" (213). The dreamed female economy needs no hardness, rigidity, or divisions. It is fluid, circulating, all in multiplicity, in a subdued light like the amniotic flow, relationship, and light of the fetal world. This dream recalls the fluid, circulatory world of *Finnegans Wake:* "Amnios amnium, fluminiculum flaminulinorum! We seek the Blessed One, the Harbourer-cum-Enheritance" (264.7–9). The tone of the *Wake* text, however, its parody of the Latin *omnia saecula saeculorum* (One God, world without end) substituting *flumen* (river) and *flamen* (priest), sounding like "fulmen" (thunderbolt), and the fact that who's coming is H.C.E., all suggest humorously the futility of the fantasy of returning to the mother without the echo of the father. (This passage occurs in II.2, the children's grammar lesson, where indeed they are trying to figure out the mother).

Irigaray, of course, recognizes that returning to the sign of the woman's body does reinscribe the power of the patriarchal signifying system. Her parting gesture is nevertheless to call for a female aesthetic that writes female desire, even though "female" is of necessity defined by patriarchy.

In *Gender Trouble* Judith Butler credits Irigaray for "broadening the scope of feminist critique" in showing us how logic, law, and desire are structures of "a masculinist signifying economy" (13).[41] However, Butler contends that Irigaray is guilty of the same kind of colonization and appropriation of differences to her single narrative, in her drive to articulate global phallogocentrism, as is the discourse of patriarchy she opposes. Butler questions the "epistemological imperialism" of gender-identity politics (13) and argues that our liberatory task is "a radical proliferation of gender, *to displace* the very gender norms that enable the repetition itself" (148; italics in original). I argue in chapter 4 that "radical proliferation" of gender displacement occurs in *Finnegans Wake,* and moreover that the proliferation of desire works to displace repetition from the compulsory return of the repressed to creative repetition whose sign of promise is the child. In *Wake* language, "We drames our dreams tell Bappy returns. And Sein annews" (*FW* 277.17–18), suggesting that the repetition of dreaming turns Pappy's return (the return of the repressed, the law of the father) into the birthday greeting, "many happy returns," generating the same anew, as being re-news, and is or makes new(s).

REPRESENTATION AND GENDER

Those who believe in a female aesthetic often situate the work of Lawrence and Joyce at opposite poles. In a collectively written feminist essay, "For the Etruscans: Sexual Difference and Artistic Production—The Debate over a Female Aesthetic," Sara Lennox divides modern literature into two camps, one antithetical to a "female aesthetic," the other congruent with the traits of an *écriture féminine.* Lawrence gets put in the "group-against" (150), along with Eliot, Pound, Yeats, and Lewis. Lennox calls these writers "the most problematic nonhegemonic group because they make a conservative, sometimes *fascisante* criticism of bourgeois culture," and advocate a return to a romanticized past based on "peasantry and patriarch" (150). Joyce exemplifies the other, liberated camp, according to Lennox. Along with Williams, Stevens, Levertov, Woolf, Joyce's writing is "characteristic of postmodernism" as is women's writing. Both contain the traits of "inwardness, illumination in the here and now (Levertov); use of the continuous present (Stein); the foregrounding of material (Woolf); the muted, multiple, or absent telos; a fascination with process; a horizontal world; a decentered universe where 'man' (indeed) is no longer privileged" (151). Lennox adds that the similarity of traits among these writers and women's writing is not complete enough in one essential respect. Their works are "politically quietistic" (151), while *"women's writing is, if ambigu-*

ously, (of double [sometimes duplicitous] needs) *nonetheless pro-foundly revolutionary."* Then she adds a contradictory postscript without a pause *"(as are, in their confusing ways, modernism and post-modernism, also written from positions of marginality to the dominant culture)"* (152; italics in original).

The last assertion blurs the distinction of her category, un-derscoring, I think, the uselessness of compiling a list of "female writing" traits. Indeed, Lawrence's writing exemplifies all the traits of the liberated side, as Richard Aldington's famous preface to his 1933 posthumous edition of Lawrence's *Last Poems* empha-sizes. Not a feminist, Aldington also typecasts Lawrence and Joyce but reverses the categories. "At two opposite poles of mod-ern literature stand D. H. Lawrence and James Joyce," Aldington begins. "The contrasts between the work of these two men can be elaborated almost indefinitely. The great difference I want to touch on now is that Joyce's writing is founded on the concep-tion of Being, and Lawrence's on the conception of Becoming" (8). Whereas *"Ulysses* is static and solid, logically planned," he goes on, "Lawrence's work—how fluid, how personal, how im-perfect" (9). Aldington's great dichotomy is as arguable as Len-nox's, for surely his Lawrentian characteristics apply to Joyce's work as well—fluid, personal, and in its own way as "imperfect" as Lawrence's.

If literary texts can "test" theory, then I believe the works of Lawrence and Joyce "test" the notion of gendered discourse and call that theory into question. For it is possible to ascribe a female aesthetic of writing to both writers, just as it is possible to assert its contrary—a male aesthetic—for both writers.

I suspect Lennox's principle of division is actually the stated politics of each writer, rather than his work. And here we enter the labyrinth of women's relation to politics, as well as the relation of literary works and their form to politics. Lennox, as well as Cixous, Irigaray, and other feminists of *écriture féminine,* want women's writing to be revolutionary. Yet the very notion of a form that follows from a biological fact, Logos from phallus or an ambiguous, duplicitous women's writing from the double lips *(labia)*, as Irigaray plays upon, is a profoundly conservative notion of representation, one that also comes perilously close to duplicating an older belief in some kind of "natural" theory of language.

A "natural" theory of representation ignores history, discontinuity, randomness, and diversity of cultures. It assumes a direct relation, rather than an overdetermined and oblique relation, between a writer and her writing. A "natural" theory of representation, based on gender, oversimplifies human sexuality into a fixed binary sex/gender system and ignores the varied relations individuals, especially writers, have to their assigned gender. Further, the theory of gendered discourse mystifies the sex/gender system by claiming gender is an intrinsic quality of the text or of language rather than as the effect of a language practice subject to the vagaries of history. Finally, a theory of gendered discourse explains the multiple formations in a text by a single category, reducing to a single sex/gender issue the many effects of literary convention, politics, culture, economics, history and—yes—gender.

Indeed, I would like to make a case that both Lawrence and Joyce are more politically progressive writers about women's issues than they are usually given credit for, not because of any intrinsic gendered style of their writing, and not because of their overt politics, but because in the works of both writers form and content, taken together, resist, challenge, and contradict the conventions and structure of the binary sex/gender system.

Lawrence is generally considered a politically conservative writer, based on his personal comments, his overtly "apolitical" stance, and the subject matter of his writing. This last category of evidence is particularly problematic because all too often the assumptions of literary analysts about what is "conservative" or "liberal," "political," or "apolitical" are not examined but merely asserted. I do not dispute that Lawrence is a political conservative on broad national-political issues, preferring the individual "great man" and natural aristocrat to the masses. He also *appears* to endorse a conservative view of gender: men should be manly, women should follow men. But then there are the contradictions:

his desire for alternative man-to-man relations and his rendering (even if somewhat negatively) of lesbian desire; his fascination with strong, female protagonists; his fight for the sexual liberation of women; and his plots that disconnect and free women from family. On the surface of Lawrence's work, there are a multitude of contradictions. To explain these contradictions, I have plunged into a deeper analysis of his "politics" of gender and family, examining, in chapter 2, psychostructural relations in Lawrence's three major novels and, in chapter 4, those in his last novella.

The politics of women's issues are not identical to the politics of nations or political parties, although certainly there is overlap. For a very long time, in fact most of the twentieth century, Annette Kuhn reminds us that women's issues were not considered properly a separate formation. There was widespread belief that women's liberation would follow naturally and necessarily from Marxist revolution. In the literary realm, a writer's "revolutionary" position is almost always assessed by reference to political, historical, male-dominated categories. For example, Lawrence shifts very early in *Sons and Lovers* from a social critique to a sexual analysis. This has always been interpreted as a move by Lawrence away from realism, social concerns, and history. I believe women readers, however, find Lawrence's interest in relations of two, and in gender issues, compelling and *political,* because for women gender is a political issue. Women readers are drawn to Lawrence's clear understanding of the destructive elements of bourgeois family relations, of the constraints that middle-class conventions impose upon women and upon sexual relations. Further, even in Lawrence's late period of phallic iconography, his romance quest plots, built on the desire to find a powerful mate in a balanced, exchange relationship, reveal how the heterosexual economy constrains as well as generates desire and produces melancholy.

Since Lawrence's plots reveal the desire to achieve an equal balance in a relation of polar difference, his work remains caught up in notions of sexual *difference.* Paradoxically, then, Lawrence's work has a place in the theoretical field where "difference" is an operative term, joining those promoting a female aesthetic based on the binary sex/gender system.

Lawrence returns again and again to the Oedipal moment when sexual difference is perceived. He reifies exchange with an Other, seeking a balanced sexual exchange system. In a typical Lawrentian plot, the male protagonist *reveals* sexual inequality and the inferiority of the female by his very desire to overcome it, to find a phallic mate (often the doubled female figure). The idea of the perfect, balanced partner at the same time *denies* sexual difference, since it covers up the asymmetry between the sexes. Ambivalently, then, Lawrence's texts assert and deny sexual difference, uncover and conceal the inferiority of the female in the present sex/gender system.

Most psychoanalytic studies of Lawrence would read this ambivalence about sexual difference as evidence of Lawrence's own sexual confusion, revealing his latent homosexual tendencies, failure to be a man, and so on. That kind of explanation assumes without discussion that the present binary sex/gender system is a fixed, unvarying "natural" system that corresponds to a biological truth. This essentialist notion of gender is a position that I believe a feminist psychoanalytic practice constantly must challenge and question.

Lawrence's plots are progressive in that they can offer a potential critique of sex/gender relations. However, my criticism of theories of gendered discourse holds true for Lawrence's texts also. At bottom each is partially conservative in that each relies on a fixed, polar sex/gender system to make its point. For feminists, the question is whether we can actually subvert patriarchy by constantly invoking a category ("difference") that is itself derived from patriarchal structure. As Lawrence does, we may end up making our present binary sex/gender system seem more indomitable than it is.

Just as theories of "difference" deny/assert the gender system, Lawrence asserts/denies gender difference. In a similar way, Lawrence upholds patriarchy not only overtly in his direct statements but also internally in the psychostructure of plots that focus on the Oedipal moment, even though he too wishes to critique and change current forms of patriarchal society. "An artist usually intellectualizes on top, and his dark under-consciousness goes on contradicting him beneath," he writes in *Studies in Classic American Literature* (35). The "dark under-consciousness" in Lawrence's novels, such as in *Sons and Lovers*, is learned through the body, outside of language, suggesting that culture asserts difference, while body experience denies it. But the reverse could just as easily be read: that the biological body is indeed the basis of gender difference, while present culture denies sexual differences. And many do read Lawrence this way. Sometimes, as in "Give Her a Pattern," he even sounds off on this primitive theme.

Reading Joyce against Lawrence, I think, can provide one possible answer to a persistent question about Lawrence's work, namely, why Lawrence changes in the early twenties from exploring new kinds of sexual relation to advocating patriarchal and authoritarian ideals. This shift can and has been explained by reference to Lawrence's own life; Judith Ruderman's thorough and scholarly study of Lawrence's middle period is perhaps the best study of this kind. Yet Lawrence was not the only person to undergo a similar shift in thinking. Is not our desire to understand Lawrence's shift a desire to get beyond the personal, to gain some insight into why this historical shift occurred? Here I am not so much interested in questions (important and connected though they may be) about Lawrence's relation to fascist ideologies as in his shift to a conservative sexual ideology. Historically, after women received the franchise in the teens and early twenties, in Great Britain and the United States, radical women's movements lost popularity and momentum, entering a quiet period that extended through the fifties. Lawrence's shift is thus representative.

Joyce is more revolutionary, I believe, and I would agree with Sara Lennox when she lists him with those writers who share the revolutionary characteristics she would claim for women's writing. But many Joyce readers disagree, finding that his work for all its stylistic experimentation reaffirms male-dominated discourse and upholds patriarchy (see Scott, *Joyce and Feminism,* particularly chap. 6).

I believe Joyce's writing is revolutionary because it moves beyond the impasse of binary oppositions of "difference," in the sex/gender system beyond male and female, and in reasoning beyond contraries such as yes/no and same/different. *Finnegans Wake* offers an explanation for, and critique of, the reciprocal nature of binary logic. Just as Shem and Shaun are mirror twins, locked in the same old vicious circle, Lawrence's reification of sexual "difference" locks him within a binary sex/gender system, so that his flip-flop to reaction against gender experimentation is the "equinoxious points of view" (*FW* 85. 28) implicitly reflected from his starting point.

In *Finnegans Wake* diverse, perverse sexuality, the forces of the unconscious, remnants of civilization and linguistic experimentation of style are all elements, *the material base,* of the overdetermined universe of human imagination. Out of these shards an open-ended dialectics spirals outward. Unlike biological theories of representation with one-to-one correspondence, the *Wake* celebrates the gap between nonmeaning and meaning, between figure and representation. Meaning always must be constructed and therefore is not "natural," self-evident, or primary; nonmeaning always threatens to swamp us. Representation must be constructed from fragments, pieces of bodies, sexual organs, but also a mess of pottage. Too much always threatens; the project of making meaning is discontinuous, in part random, not literal, but littered with leftover bits and pieces, creatively messy. Secondarily, then, the *Wake* implies that the sex/gender system, family, and human thought are unfixed forms, always constructions from a diverse, sexual but ungendered, human, material substrate.

I am not turning either Lawrence or Joyce into a feminist, even though I am claiming that their texts implicitly challenge our thinking on feminist issues such as family form, female sexuality, and gender. Oddly, too, these modernists are situated in a similar relation to "politics" as feminists. Just as Lawrence and Joyce insist on pursuing their own ends in writing, feminists argue from their particular location, constituted as female subjects, and contest totalizing theories that would render them invisible, voiceless, eliding their subjectivities under a "universal" male subject. And both modernist writers and feminists have been accused of narcissism for asserting their own interests apart from traditional, "male-dominated" political concerns.

Neither Lawrence nor Joyce is interested in subordinating his own writing to any end outside itself. In his essay on Benjamin Franklin, Lawrence shouts back to that notable pragmatist, "Benjamin, I will not work. I do not choose to be a free democrat. I am absolutely a servant of my own Holy Ghost" (*Studies in Classic American Literature* 29). Lawrence's refusal is like Stephen Dedalus's *"non serviam,"* a refusal to lend himself to causes outside a writing practice that is continuous with, and produces, the self.

Often at the very moment of asserting this feature of Lawrence and Joyce, the psychoanalytic critic of the past jumped in to pronounce a judgment. "Narcissism!" he might cry, "these modern writers are narcissistic with their self-interest focused on their own lives, their writing, their bodies." And we are back at the psychoanalytic description ("narcissistic") of the female psyche. The feminist's role, as I see it, is to step in at this very moment, to challenge the psychoanalytic value judgment, pointing out that it denigrates the female and is a construction from a patriarchal sex/gender system, one that works to reify that system rather than challenge it.

Further, such a pronouncement fails to illuminate what is revolutionary in the refusal to serve causes outside the self. Women especially have been bound to ideologies of subservience throughout human history, and so refusing to serve the needs of others is for them a profoundly revolutionary act, as it is for all people who are denied full personhood in their cultures. But declaring the primacy of individual freedom and self-fulfillment admittedly still remains perhaps the most difficult and contested step in women's liberation movements because "self" is still cast in binary opposition to the liberation and well-being of the community. Women must refuse this dichotomy, working to make sure that improvement in women's lives means improvement for all people—people of all races and classes, children, women and men.

We are still enmeshed in the psychology that Ibsen's *Doll House* explored more than one hundred years ago.[42] A woman's, and especially a mother's, declaration of an individual right to self-fulfillment is profoundly threatening to our psychological construction of family. Very frequently, historians call upon psychoanalysis when they bemoan the break up of old forms of family and the emergence of new forms, declaring a "new narcissism" and thus repeating the attack audiences and critics waged on the character of Nora Helmer. Psychoanalysis helps us recognize that human reluctance to grant women autonomous lives and the right to self-fulfillment is rooted in our primary infant relationships, in our need for the care and protection of a "good mother" (a selfless caretaker) and a "strong father" (a protective caretaker). But we should also see that viewing "family" as an either/or institution—either families uphold patriarchal form and order, or the breakdown of the old form indicates psychological disease—is a false distinction that really does not include the possibility of new, psychologically healthy family forms emerging. Nor does the old binary opposition grant recognition and respect to alternative family forms that already exist: for example, the blended families of divorce, gay and lesbian families, African American matriarchal, extended families, Native American clans and tribal families. A feminist psychoanalytic reading must resist the pull to reaffirm the patriarchal structure out of which the psychoanalytic narrative is constructed, so it must question and challenge psychoanalytic value judgments. Our defenses against changes in the sex/gender system are so strong because so deeply embedded in earliest experience. We therefore need to read with and against psychoanalysis. A reading against questions the borders and the system of psychoanalysis itself, and a reading with accounts for our present attitudes and defenses by reference to our earliest family relations.

Can a certain kind of writing style—polyphonic, dense, contrapuntal, and opaque—be political? This question has been posed about Joyce's texts for more than forty-five years, and it is relevant to any discussion of *écriture féminine*. Most often literary critics interested in politics attack Joyce for choosing stylistic exfoliation over political message or accessability. That line of attack, however, sets up another false distinction—either form must be a transparent medium through which a political message passes, or form is so opaque that there can be no political implications. Again, this apparent choice is no choice, as Terry Eagleton points out in *Criticism and Ideology,* since it reduces literature's production of meaning to content alone. Yet, insisting that style alone has a political force repeats the same kind of mistake in reverse. If we are to hold that Joyce's writing, or likewise *écriture féminine,* has a political and moral dimension, we must seek to explain that effect through the interaction of form with content. Both Joyce's writing and *écriture féminine,* I believe, use form to increase our resistance to content, to make what the text says a problem, breaking up our perception of any "natural," logical and noncontradictory meaning-of-the-text, and thus deconstructing our illusion that the text neutrally and nonideologically mirrors what we already consider to be true. Eagleton concludes, "'morality' fully emerges as a distinct mode of discourse when historical contradictions sharpen to the point where such relative 'transparency' is unattainable—where the question of the ideological criteria which should govern individual behaviour becomes vexed and recalcitrant, the relations between individual behavior and social function indecipherable and opaque" (182).

I have been arguing against a theory of representation based on gender because such a theory ultimately rests on a simple "transparent" notion of representation. However, I believe the contemporary movement in feminist theory and women's writing, loosely gathered under the title a "female aesthetic," is carrying out an important and effective critique of assumptions about literature and politics, revising and challenging how we think of writing as an activity.

The traditional categories of active and passive, materialist and idealist pursuits are beginning to change. Many feminists no longer accept the judgment that difficult, condensed writing is a quietistic, apolitical activity. Two effects of their aesthetic revision are to reclaim the material body of writing (its textuality) for political analysis and to recast as political practice a certain kind of writing that is recalcitrant, opaque, and resistent to transparency, a writing distinctly modern.

Lawrence and Joyce texts are most often read on issues of gender and family form as if their aesthetic production were transparently conceived, even though we know each writer produced his work from a consciously experimental aesthetic denying transparency. In the following chapters I analyze family and gender in the work of Lawrence and Joyce, beginning with the assumption that their texts resist a transparent reading. Indeed, because gender and family issues are embedded within recalcitrant and opaque experimental form, such as Lawrence's shifting omniscient points of view and Joyce's condensations, and because interpreting family and gender issues depends upon cultural and psychological ideologies, I turn to a feminist psychoanalytic analysis. From my point of view, family form, family relations, and gender roles are not "natural" categories against which literary interpretation takes place but cultural constructions that literature in part appropriates, in part helps to construct, and in part challenges by internal contradiction as well as by authorial intent.

2

D. H. Lawrence: The Sexual Struggle Displaces the Class Struggle

Everything that has beauty has a body, and is a body;
everything that has being has being in the flesh:
and dreams are only drawn from the bodies that are.

—D. H. Lawrence, "Bodiless God," *Last Poems*

As Sophocles' *Oedipus Rex* is to psychoanalysis, so Lawrence's *Sons and Lovers* is to psychoanalytic criticism: an "*Ur*-text," as one critic has called it (Adamowski 70). Published on May 29, 1913, Lawrence's third novel inaugurated the Freudian analysis of family relations in modern literature as critics immediately discussed Paul Morel's "mother problem" in terms of Freud's Oedipus complex, as in the anonymous 1916 review "*Sons and Lovers*: A Freudian Appreciation." Later, postwar interest in psychoanalysis and biography in the fifties led to the probing of the text for insights into the development and failures of the writer himself, and there are now beginning to appear studies that connect psychoanalytic textual analysis with Lawrence's formal experimentation.[1] *Sons and Lovers* can serve as a paradigm for the ways that psychoanalysis and literature have come together—as another "ism" to interpret a text and its author or, more recently, as a formal and analogical method of analyzing stylistics.

My interest in psychoanalysis and literature has a slightly different focus. I am interested in analyzing the interplay of form and content and in exploring the contradictions between family relations and the formation of the gendered individual rather than in pure stylistic analysis or psychoanalysis of the author. I start from what I see as the major contradictions in Lawrence's work that have made themselves apparent to many readers over time. These are, first, the conflicts between social and class analysis on the one hand and gender critique on the other. Second, and perhaps the most interesting paradox to women readers, is the contradiction between Lawrence's interest in, and understanding of, central female characters and his growing phallic ideology. What accounts for Lawrence's continuing appeal to women readers despite this phallic ideology?[2]

I believe the answer can be found in the psychostructural relations of his texts. Although Lawrence appears to turn abruptly against women after World War I, both early and late plots are built on surprisingly similar psychostructural relations of family and gender. Judith Ruderman also sees a similarity of attitude in Lawrence's early and late works but explains Lawrence's swerve after World War I toward authoritarian and phallic idolatry as the result of his mother problem and increasing hatred of women. While Lawrence may well have come to hate women, and there is conflicting evidence on this point, I believe that the major contradictions about women in his work, seen in the relations of family and the psychology of gender embedded in his plots, show that Lawrence chafes at the constraints of patriarchy yet depends upon its binary oppositions. Indeed, Lawrence's very contradictions confirm and reveal how deeply involved he is in the psychology of patriarchy. This kind of ambivalence goes beyond being a merely personal problem of Lawrence's. The desire to preserve and at the same time to deny unequal gender relations is a distinguishing feature of patriarchy itself—and of all hegemonic rationales of "separate but equal."

SONS AND LOVERS

Sons and Lovers, like the later *Rainbow* and *Women in Love,* contains both social and sexual analysis in an unusual and typically Lawrentian amalgam, so that "social grievances" have a way of turning into "sexual frustrations" (Sanders 24). Critics often see this transformation of the one into the other as a flaw or even a failure, calling Lawrence's realism incomplete and romantic and his sexual swerve mythic but alienating and isolating. "The most interesting contradiction in Lawrence's art," writes Graham Holderness, is "between his impulse to write social tragedy and his impulse to evade or transcend it" (159).

Lawrence's own comments about *Sons and Lovers*, such as those in his famous letter to Edward Garnett, make clear that from the start he conceived of his story both as a cultural critique of the social relations that shape mental and sexual life and as an uncovering of the hidden, mythic relations that construct the gendered subject. Whether or not Lawrence knew much of Freud during the three years he was writing the novel, when he invokes the Oedipus analogy "as the great tragedy of thousands of young men in England" (*Letters* I: 477), he sounds very like early Freudians who often made simple analogies and sweeping generalizations.

Although there is no hard evidence that Lawrence knew much specifically about Freud as he was writing the draft of the novel, we do know that Frieda influenced his extensive revision of it during their honeymoon abroad in 1912.[3] Frieda was a self-proclaimed admirer of Freud. Before she met Lawrence she had had a love affair with Otto Gross, a peripheral psychoanalytic figure and free-love advocate (Smith, "A New Adam" 27). Had Lawrence become acquainted with Freudian ideas through her, they would almost certainly have been Freud's early theories of sexuality (1905) and earliest version of the Oedipus complex (set out in "The Interpretation of Dreams" [1900]).

On the other hand, Lawrence may have arrived at his mother-son ideas independently of Freud. "A Checklist of Lawrence's Reading" shows that in March 1911, a full year before he met Frieda Weekly, he read *Oedipus Tyrannus* (Burwell 75). At that time he was working on early drafts of the novel. Furthermore, in 1910–13 Lawrence could not have been familiar with Freud's theory of the unconscious, which appeared in 1915, yet a Lawrentian theory of the unconscious takes shape in *Sons and Lovers*.

In some ways the novel resembles nineteenth-century realism, beginning with the marriage of the Morels, tracing the birth and growth of the protagonist amid family conflicts, and ending with his eventual flight from home to the larger world. Yet, as many have noted, the novel moves away from the rendering of social history from an external point of view ("'The Bottoms' succeeded to 'Hell Row'")[4] toward the presentation of subjective experience from an internal point of view. This shift is often viewed as a defect, a common judgment being that Lawrence was writing himself into twentieth century subjectivity as he developed his story.

Rather than a shift or a defect, however, Lawrence's narrative style fuses both social history and psychological exploration, just as his letter to Garnett indicated. The narration combines both omniscient point of view and subjectivity, resulting in a textual voice that authorizes each character's experiences as equally legitimate, presenting competing centers of "authenticity" of "felt life," to borrow a term from Henry James. However, it is precisely a belief in the unified and autonomous self that the text will also undo. Unlike a nineteenth-century novel, *Sons and Lovers* does not focus mostly on its hero. In fact, the focus is squarely on Mrs. Morel for all of the six chapters of part one. In part two Paul must wrestle with Mrs. Morel for dominance until the last chapter. The novel presents the growth of a subject as a struggle-in-relation, where the outcome is never assured, and the very concept of "self" is built out of conflict with another. In fact, many readers doubt whether Paul has truly achieved freedom at the end.[5]

The struggle of selfhood occurs for each character, too, though the novel dwells mostly on the struggles of Mrs. Morel and Paul. The family relations that affect each Morel are both psychic and material. The psychical is made material, and the material conditions are rendered psychically. The narrative style fuses both the subjective and objective, by rendering inner, nonverbal feeling from the outside in the third person, or by using psychologically imbued symbolism to present an objective correlative to a psychic state.

When I use the word "material" here, I mean physical reality, the external world including living organisms, and external relations, as opposed to psychical relations and inner states of mind. When Lawrence uses the word "material," he usually means dead matter, as opposed to living organisms. In "The Individual Consciousness v. The Social Consciousness," an essay unpublished in his life but collected in *Phoenix,* Lawrence gives his definition of materialism, equating it with his often invoked image of an empty shell or husk.

In chapter 1, "The Early Married Life of the Morels," Mrs. Morel sits waiting for her husband to return late at night: "When the light was fading, and Mrs. Morel could see no more to sew, she rose and went to the door" (13). She sees the world from her vantage point as a woman, mother, and working-class wife: "women were coming home from the wakes, the children hugging a white lamb with green legs, or a wooden horse. Occasionally a man lurched past, almost as full as he could carry. Sometimes a good husband came alone with his family, peacefully. But usually the women and children were alone" (13).

Her values, isolation, and sense of injustice permeate her perceptions. Women and children are innocent ("hugging a lamb"); men are stupid brutes ("lurching"). Men and women are divided, and she is isolated: "Mrs. Morel was alone, but she was used to it. Her son and her little girl slept upstairs; so, it seemed, her home was there behind her, fixed and stable" (13). The cause of her alienation is her very condition as a woman, being dependent, a mother with too many children and not enough money, with no life but poverty and childbearing. Her children literally weigh her down, for she is pregnant. "But for herself, nothing but this dreary endurance—till the children grew up. And the children! She could not afford to have this third. She did not want it. The father was serving beer in a public house, swilling himself drunk" (13).

Such a passage renders an interrelation of structures in concrete, objective terms: the social history of the Erewash valley, the sexual division of its culture, the drinking of the husbands. It presents Mrs. Morel's values (a "good" husband comes home peacefully—submissively?—with his family). It also suggests her alienation from her husband ("the father"), her ambivalent attitude to her children (by turns, innocent victims, mere signs of her own identity, or unwanted burdens), and her denigration of Morel, who remains unnamed, uncalled for, but resented. He is not enjoying the fruits of his labor by sharing a convivial drink with his mates, but from her point of view he is "swilling" himself drunk.

The passage presents social history *from* Mrs. Morel's position as a subject in a network of relations. Chief among these are the sexual division of labor and the Protestant and capitalist ideology of individualism and social advancement. The novel does not suggest or point to an essential self that transcends a network of relations, as in the Cartesian notion of the *cogito*. Rather she exists as a subject from within these relations, within her "fixed and stable" home. From it, she views the returning miners only as wage earners and supporters of their families, or as she more often sees them, as violent, irresponsible threats to the well-being of women and children. In either case, she perceives them as commodities, calculating their economic costs and benefits, reckoned from the particular point of view of a working-class woman, dependent upon the labor of men. She seems to have no interest in the miners themselves—in their working conditions in the mines or as an exploited class. Neither does she have any feeling of solidarity with them. She views herself apart from the community. She is a bitter individualist and an adversary to her husband.

Why is she alienated and what explains her lack of class consciousness? Paul might answer by saying that she really does not belong to the working class. Mrs. Morel identifies herself with the middle-class rank she assigns to her father, and Paul concurs. She considers herself better educated, more refined in taste, and more ambitious than Morel, and she always stands in judgment over him.

Actually, though, as a woman in late nineteenth-century patriarchal capitalism, Mrs. Morel does not really inhabit any class on her own. If she actually were a member of the bourgeoisie before marriage, she would have pulled her husband up to her class level. However, as a woman she can never be a class member in her own right, so at marriage she is pulled down into the working class. She resents having been dragged down in class. In many respects, the conflicts between Mr. and Mrs. Morel are the result of the clash of different class values. Because Mrs. Morel, as a woman, cannot independently attain a class, these conflicts turn into sexual ones. Put differently, Mrs. Morel's predicament would never be the same for a son because a man could inherit as well as attain class rank and therefore sustain his own inherited position or move up in class.

The novel itself does not "correct" Mrs. Morel's "false" perception, as a progressive nineteenth century novel might by developing a class critique that reveals not Morel, not the miners, but social ills themselves as the cause of her alienation. Neither does *Sons and Lovers* reaffirm a conventional relation between a husband and a wife by any reversal of attitude in Mrs. Morel, for instance by her learning to appreciate unseen virtues in Morel or by learning a lesson of Christian love.

Throughout the novel, even when Paul takes up the action in the second half, values and attitudes reflect the mother's experience. By this I mean that the point of view of the two main characters as well as the plot of the novel are rooted in the psychological, social, and economic contradictions of the female subject. For the female subject under patriarchy, the sexual struggle and the sexual relation to power are primary and displace class struggle and class relations, which she secures only through an intermediary.[6]

Social critics frequently denounce Lawrence's turning of social relations into sexual relations as a flight to the personal. Psychoanalytic critics always question Lawrence's own masculinity in light of this central female focus. However, women readers recognize in his novels a compelling representation of the woman's relation to the world even as his phallic theories seem objectionable.

Lawrence elucidates the hidden relations between men and women—what is not talked about, only dimly perceived, or even not understood. He brings forward all that is repressed by means of original presentational techniques and an original idea of the unconscious. In scenes suffused with sensuous images, he dramatizes what is essentially inarticulate and nonconceptual knowledge repressed by culture. This is the original, Lawrentian unconscious. The contrast between the experience of the unconscious and the daily struggle of family and social relations reveals to a character the structures of culture that yoke, alienate, imprison, and that the struggling "self" must constantly throw off to grow. One of those imprisoning structures is gender itself. ("Self" is a paradoxical notion, however, since outside of culture, the individual melts away.)

In a scene from "The Early Married Life of the Morels," Mr. and Mrs. Morel have had a violent fight about his spending money on drink, and Morel lashes out at her: "'It's ma as brings th' money whoam, not thee. It's my house, not thine. Then ger out on't—ger out on't!'" (33). Within her "fixed and stable home," Mrs. Morel has a location and even a powerful role in the structure of family relations, but she occupies that position by virtue of the husband-relation, and not on her own. Cast out, she goes into the garden under the "high and magnificent" August moon (33) and there "lost herself awhile" (34):

She did not know what she thought. Except for a slight feeling of sickness, and her consciousness in the child, her self melted out like scent into the shiny, pale air. After a time the child, too, melted with her in the mixing-pot of moonlight, and she rested with the hills and lilies and houses, all swum together in a kind of swoon. (34)

Morel's drunken words have ripped through the veil of illusion. Her earlier identification with the house itself destroyed, she understands with a sick feeling that what so recently had seemed her "fixed and stable" position in a concrete and unalterable social network was merely an illusion, not reality. Because she is a woman, Morel controls her identity, despite her education or former social level, no matter how much she believes in "individual effort." He is leased the home and has the paying job, even if she actually makes the home and judiciously distributes the money. At their marginal level of existence, the sexual inequality of power is both more apparent and can potentially produce real hardship and suffering. This goes a long way toward explaining Mrs. Morel's hatred of her husband. Even worse than the financial threat, however, is that he (and principally as a husband-relation, not because of his personal volition) robs her of independent identity.

Fleeing to the garden, Mrs. Morel experiences a sensual union with nature and even with her unborn child: "after a time the child, too, melted with her in the mixing-pot of moonlight" (34). From the loss of her identity and place in family relations there flows a kind of genderless sexuality that is only available to Lawrence's characters outside of culture. This experience leaves her feeling "invigorated" though "forlorn" (35) in relation to the mystery and infinite vastness of the night sky. The child within her is, in fact, Paul, whose incestuous relationship with his mother we could say precedes even his own birth and extends beyond her actual death. At the end of the novel, her death for Paul is "the tear in the veil, through which his life seemed to drift slowly, as if he were drawn towards death" (451). Morel rips away the veil of illusion for Mrs. Morel, and she does the same for Paul when she dies.

To anyone who has read much of Lawrence's work, here is the familiar convergence of sexuality, loss of selfhood, and a Keatsian swoon of "easeful" death. This ecstasy dissolves the conscious shell of the human being into the great, unconscious flow of nature. Later in *Sons and Lovers* Paul Morel experiences this in sexual intercourse with Clara Dawes. Afterward, they return to the world at "rest within themselves," having experi-

enced the "grains in the tremendous heave that lifted every grass-
blade its little height" (398).

There is also another kind of unconscious moment portrayed in *Sons and Lovers*. This is the unconscious as creative. It
is intimately connected to the mother, "her warmth inside him
like strength," and to woman, as Paul takes his creative production to Miriam "who stimulated [him] into knowledge of the work
he had produced unconsciously" (190).

> "I can do my best things when you sit there in your rocking-chair,
> mother," he said.
> "I'm sure!" she exclaimed, sniffing with mock scepticism. But she
> felt it was so, and her heart quivered with brightness. For many hours
> she sat still, slightly conscious of him labouring away, whilst she worked
> or read her book. And he, with all his soul's intensity directing his pencil,
> could feel her warmth inside him like strength. They were both very
> happy so, and both unconscious of it. These times, that meant so much,
> and which were real living, they almost ignored. (190)

Both the first kind, participation in the unconscious flow of
nature, and the second, participation in the creative unconscious,
are described as authentic experience in contrast to the falseness
of daily life. For Paul and Clara, from the first emanated "their
belief in life" (398), and Paul calls the second kind "real living"
(190). The text portrays the first kind of unconscious experience
often occurring during sexual union, but it also occurs during
"intercourse with flowers," as one critic has aptly named what
Mrs. Morel, Paul, and even Miriam sometime experience in nature.[7] By the feeling of wholeness with the universe it provides,
this experience heals and soothes the tormented individual
locked into adversarial subjecthood and gender. But wholeness
is purchased at a cost, as human proportion is reduced to the
infinitesimal against the potency and giganticism of the natural
world. Thus the feeling of merging with the universe can also
cross over into "the drift toward death" (Lawrence, *Letters* I: 477).

The explicit phallic images Lawrence uses to render the
natural world *seem* to suggest that the unconscious experience

of nature is aligned with the male. In Mrs. Morel's garden "the tall white lilies were reeling in the moonlight, and the air was charged with their perfume, as with a presence. Mrs. Morel gasped slightly in fear. She touched the big, pallid flowers on their petals, then shivered. They seemed to be stretching in the moonlight" (34). As Paul and Clara make love, they join "the tremendous heave that lifted every grass-blade its little height" (398). I will return to this passage later, however, to discuss other details that complicate the gender of the imagery.

The female, particularly the mother, presides over participation in the creative unconscious. The feeling of wholeness achieved in moments of the close mother/child relationship induces the creative experience. This experience does not generate peace but "stimulate[s]" "knowledge" and leads outward to the world (Miriam as Paul's audience, for example) and to critical thought: "A sketch finished, he always wanted to take it to Miriam. Then he was stimulated into knowledge of the work he had produced unconsciously. In contact with Miriam he gained insight, his vision went deeper" (190).

Not only are the two forms of unconscious experience apparently related to different genders, but each form also seems to correspond to the particular characteristics of the father and the mother in the novel. Unschooled and uninterested in bourgeois striving, Morel is associated with the natural world. "He loved the early morning" (38), walking across the fields, looking out for mushrooms. "So he appeared at the pit top, often with a stalk from the hedge between his teeth, which he chewed all day to keep his mouth moist, down the mine, feeling quite as happy as when he was in th field" (38–39). At home, Morel resembles a child or household pet. He is inarticulate and clumsily tender, yet capable of sudden violence or rage, and just as suddenly he returns to quiet contentment with a warm fire, food, or household repairs to make. "Not knowing what he was doing—he often did the right thing by instinct" (18).

If Morel is aligned with nature, instinct, and the pleasure of labor in itself, Mrs. Morel stands firmly on the side of culture, will ("I *shall* have my own way" 36) and the competitive product. She exercises her critical faculty. She remains at a distance from her husband and neighbors. She strives for the advancement of her children, focusing all her energy on them as if they were products to be successfully traded in the marketplace of life, primarily conceived by her in terms of the proper marriage.

Although Mrs. Morel represents culture, she is not cut off from nature. In fact, she is extremely sensitive to the natural world. She retreats to it for consolation and nurture, seeks it to restore the battered self in its worldly clashing, and returns from it reinvigorated for competitive battle. Thus Mrs. Morel has access to both kinds of unconscious experience, even though she is portrayed as warped by her defense of culture. While the novel is rooted in her perspective, the novel criticizes her, showing that she is alienated from her labor (as housewife and mother) and alienated from her community. Her consciousness is "reified," to use the term of Adorno, in that she perceives a characteristic (such as Morel's distrust of learning) as an inevitable property of him himself rather than as an effect of social institutions and relations of production. As she pushes her children, especially Paul, toward "refined" and "cultured" values, she also exhibits the reified consciousness of capitalism in that she believes cultural forms exist and have absolute value severed from social institutions.[8] Lawrence's later writing suggests that he is critical of this view. In *Women in Love,* Lawrence criticizes Loerke's aesthetic view that art should have "no relation to anything outside that work of art" (430).

The two kinds of unconscious experience, linked to characteristics of the father and the mother, might suggest two gendered forces somewhat like animus and anima. Sometimes too the description of the unconscious experience suggests a kind of Platonic scheme of essences, as the following passage from "The Test on Miriam" (chap. 11) seems to describe:

To [Paul] now, life seemed a shadow, day a white shadow, night, and death, and stillness, and inaction, this seemed like *being.* To be alive, to be urgent, and insistent, that was *not-to-be*. The highest of all was, to melt out into the darkness and sway there, identified with the great Being. (331)

But the two kinds of unconscious experience described in the novel also suggest the pre-Oedipal and Oedipal stages of development *for the female subject*. The creative type of unconscious experience is like the pre-Oedipal stage, marked by the child's attachment to the mother. The boundaries between self and Other may be blurry, and the child is typically seen as narcissistic, selfish, willful, not yet having recognized the separateness of the other. But for the girl child, there is a wholeness and validation of identity in the pre-Oedipal stage, girl child reflecting woman-mother (he "could feel her warmth inside him like strength" 190) that she will become alienated from as she passes through the Oedipus complex.

For the female, completing passage through the Oedipus complex is not easy. Freud addressed this problem late in his career when he noticed that many women never successfully completed their Oedipal project because, like Paul Morel, they had life long difficulty in resolving conflicts with the mother and completely separating from her.[9]

What the female has to do in the Oedipal stage is at first what the male has to do, give up the mother as love object, develop appropriate heterosexuality, transforming narcissism into eros. The boy gives up the mother through fear of the father as sexual rival (castration fear). Then the boy identifies with that very same phallic power, internalizes it, and takes it on as his own, turning away from the family to other women as mother substitutes.

The girl, however, has to turn away from women entirely and thus be partly alienated from herself to reach heterosexuality. As Juliet Mitchell explains in *Psychoanalysis and Feminism*, the passage through the Oedipus complex is a confirmation of the first love object for the boy but a contradiction for the girl (111). A girl is driven to turn away from the mother as she recognizes the male power the mother lacks (symbolized by the penis). The girl must give up the woman as love object and convert her active aims to passive ones, as she seeks the male to substitute for the power she herself as a female lacks (penis envy) and comes to wish for the gift of a baby (the substitute phallus). The girl must identify with, and yet be alienated from, womanhood to develop to heterosexuality.

If she does complete the typical passage to gender identity by uneasily identifying with, and rejecting, the female, she accepts her submission to male dominance and so becomes defined by her reproductive sexual role. She must sublimate her independent, willful self to become the nurturing mother for others. She takes on sexuality but she loses absolute selfhood in that her identity is now gender-relational and negative (she who is not male). In that she submits to male dominance and control, her selfhood is also alienated.

To pass through the Oedipal stage is finally to turn away from the pleasure principle to the reality principle, to face the threat of death and to survive by repression. In associating sexuality, death, and swooning or lapse of consciousness with phallic images, the first kind of unconscious experience in the novel (the one I have described as joining the flow of nature) resembles the father-dominated Oedipal stage in Freudianism, if a moment can be imagined just before repression, when the subject submits himself to sexuality and death, led by the pleasure principle rather than the reality principle.

While the two kinds of unconscious experience might suggest male and female essences, they could also be considered as different modes along one continuum of a nongendered unconscious. The description of the unconscious in *Sons and Lovers* seems then perched between these two poles: on the one hand, an archetypal view of male and female essences; on the other, a developmental, cultural, and biological view of the psyche.

The unconscious experience of the flow of nature (perhaps "male") and the unconscious experience of creativity (perhaps "female") do not get equal play in the novel. Only Paul experiences participation in creativity, while Paul and Mrs. Morel, Miriam and Clara, to varying degrees, participate in the ecstatic flow of nature. These characters are able to leave behind a differentiated mature self (described very often as a shell) and return to ("melt" into) early developmental stages of being, those preceding repression at the moment just before submission to the Oedipus complex. If we think of the Lawrentian unconscious in this way, gender itself is tragic, just as consciousness is. In consciousness is selfhood, but it is willful, alienated, and problematically sexual or even nonsexual. In unconscious moments selfhood melts away as characters reexperience the blissful and creative intimacy of the pre-Oedipal stage (the mother mode) or surrender to a fully experienced sensuality (the father mode)—experiences that are paradoxically genderless. Of course, that space before or beyond gender and selfhood is very close to death's realm. Likewise, if the Lawrentian unconscious is a transcendent, archetypal realm of sexual essence, as some passages seem to suggest, then gender distinction in the quotidian world is also false, a pale shadow.

Since 1916 critics have argued that Paul Morel somehow fails in his Oedipal development. Either, it is argued, he never passes beyond the stage of desiring the mother and wishing to kill the father, or as another argument goes, he gets stuck in the negative phase of the Oedipus complex, where "the son seeks to become the object of paternal love by accepting for himself a 'feminine' or 'passive' attitude toward his father" (Adamowski 75).[10]

Clearly, however, readers ignore the evidence to the contrary. Paul develops heterosexually. Paul seems reconciled to his father by the time of his mother's death, and there is no indication that he desires to be his father's love object or even to be admired by his father ("The Release" pt. 2, chap. 14), as say Stephen desires fame and recognition at the end of *A Portrait of the Artist*. Often Paul's relationship with Baxter Dawes is cited as a substitute father relation, and it is true that the Clara and Baxter Dawes interlude works as a kind of Family Romance.

Paul makes love to Clara, realizing his sexuality and thereby validating hers. When he fights with Dawes and loses, he renews Dawes's sense of potency and restores the marriage. This is just the kind of heroic role a child of divorcing parents might imagine for himself, the child-lover who restores his parents' sexuality and reunites them.

Paul does achieve an intimacy with Dawes based on the sharing of the same lover, and this kind of relationship is of interest to Lawrence, as it is to Joyce. In the Freudian scheme of things, both interpretive and ethical, this kind of interest is generally thought to indicate perversity and latent homosexuality, the shared female substituting for the other male, standing in for the phallus of her lover. In this scheme, she herself is a cipher, naught.

In *Sons and Lovers,* though, Clara is a much more distinct character than her husband. She gets in the last words, and her function seems to be as another, external critical view of Paul. After Paul and Baxter Dawes fight, Paul becomes "small and mean" (450) in her eyes. "There was something evanescent about Morel, she thought, something shifting and false. He would never make sure ground for any woman to stand on" (450). The Clara and Baxter Dawes interlude suggests more the shifting, relative nature of relationships rather than any underlying male-to-male bond. Her last comments also take up and repeat the narrative momentum of diminishment in Paul's size and value that occurs near the end of the novel as a result of Mrs. Morel's death. At the very end, he becomes a mere speck in the universe.

But perhaps Paul's connection with Baxter Dawes does indicate a hidden desire for man-to-man relations too. If so, his impulse is bisexual rather than incestuous, however, since it occurs after a turn outward from the family unit and after passage through the Oedipus complex.

Juliet Mitchell argues that when Freud described the Oedipus complex, he discovered and described the unconscious, internal law of patriarchy (413). Mitchell reminds us that Freud describes the typical, not the invariable; men or women "can go through the Oedipus complex, or come out of it, in a way more typically feminine and vice versa" (112).

Paul passes through the Oedipus complex mostly in the way a boy does. He retains women as love objects. He does not convert his active aims to the passive wish to be desired and to be given the gift of a child. He pursues first Miriam and then Clara, desiring impersonal sexual relation, not wishing to be the object of their spiritual love.

Paul's incestuous drive is surely connected to his mother, not to his father. Paul has separated from his mother and developed to male heterosexuality, and yet, like a woman, he also retains deep connections to his mother. Like a woman, Paul has extreme difficulty resolving his ambivalent feelings and conflicts with his mother, even as he does complete the stages of the Oedipal project more or less successfully. He resembles those perplexing cases Freud faced at the end of his career, women who felt both extreme love for and resentment of their mothers.

In some respects the path to manhood is as tortuous for Paul as her path is for a woman. Just as a woman develops to heterosexuality from a contradictory relation to womanhood, Paul develops his own male-gendered identity amid contradictory relations to manhood. Through his deep mother connection, Paul internalizes many of her views and at least partially rejects identification with patriarchy—specifically understood from the feminist perspective to be the unequal social and psychological construction and valuation of gender. Believing his mother superior to his father, he inwardly suffers the injustice of her position.

Before Paul is born, as an infant, and as a child, he learns male dominance and violence. As a very young child, he clings to his mother, following her around, becoming his mother's little lover. Freud described the little girl as a "little man" in that stage where she is intimately connected to the mother, before her turn to the father. And Paul fits this description too because he is his mother's little man through sympathy for and identification with her rather than through any identification on his part with his father's role.

In fact, Mrs. Morel is the one who substitutes her sons for her husband, first in "The Casting Off of Morel—The Taking on of William" (pt. 1, chap. 3) and then, when William dies, in the substituting of Paul. Here the mother, not the child, is the seducer. From a Freudian point of view, however, Paul (or Lawrence) is still the seducer, for according to Freud the child screens out the memory of his own sexual drive by reversing the roles. The Freudian scheme allows only a passive role for the mother in the drama of family relations and so neglects the tragic actions of that bitter, disappointed woman—Mrs. Morel.

Paul is literally baptized in the blood of patriarchy, the relation of power between the sexes, when his father in a rage throws a drawer at the mother and her blood drips onto the infant Paul. But the baptismal mark is ambivalent. If the blood dropping on the child's head marks patriarchy, it is also her blood that bonds him into a kind of blood sisterhood with her. In later childhood we see Paul acting out, and thus taking on, the role of male power in the game he initiates of burning the doll Arabella. Like Morel before him, Paul turns violently against a feminine image he had hurt unintentionally through blundering, and then he rejoices in his power of domination. According to Freud, "flame is always a male genital" (*Introductory Lectures* 162). Paul's play acts out his completion of the Oedipal stage. As he takes pleasure in his violence upon the female image of the doll, he confuses and frightens his sister. Yet through his deep mother connection, Paul also partially rejects patriarchy. Gender identity, then, is a battle ground of conflicting loyalties, at the same time as it constructs the identity of the self.

To say that Paul experiences the same ambivalent feelings toward his mother that women experience, or that he develops toward heterosexuality in the same problematic relationship to the sexual relations of power as do women is not the same as saying Paul fails to negotiate the male version of the Oedipus complex (a case many psychoanalytic critics have made). Labeling Paul's predicament "a failure to be a man" cancels any notion of a distinct women's experience. In that line of thinking, to be a failed man is to be like a woman, and to be a woman is to be a failed man. Again, the woman's position is a cipher in an all-male narrative.

Lawrence paid more attention to women than did Freud (at least until Freud turned to the problem of women in the 1920s and 1930s). As Freud did, Lawrence saw reality as tragic, but his ideas about the unconscious are quite different from Freud's. From his later books *Psychoanalysis and the Unconscious* (1921) and *Fantasia of the Unconscious* (1922) we know that Lawrence thought of the unconscious as material and biological; that is, as a force outside of the subjectivity of individuals.[11] He felt Freud's psychic system was too idealistic, a mental projection rather than an empirical finding (Hinz 252, 254). For Lawrence, the unconscious was a source of creativity from which precognitive experience of the world provided an "uncerebral" but rational "form of knowledge" (Hinz 255).

The later discursive treatment in these two books matches what the earlier *Sons and Lovers* presents in fictional form. The unconscious, in both its forms, is available to experience, yet is an experience outside of the ego (Mrs. Morel in the garden). Participation in it offers a kind of knowledge that is universally true yet subjectively experienced (Paul's and Clara's participation in the organic rhythms of the universe). It is the source of creativity (Paul's creative production under the influence of the shared unconscious of the mother).

In contrast, the Freudian unconscious cannot be thought of as directly available to experience. In Freudianism, the unconscious is that which can never be approached directly, but is only interpreted indirectly through the distortions that our censorship imposes, as in dreams. Nor would Freud speak of the unconscious as an experience outside the ego because he considered large parts of the ego to lie in the realm of the unconscious.

Beyond these elemental differences, Lawrence and Freud also part ways on the issue of gender and sexuality. Remember that for Freud, gender is produced by the successful passage of the individual through the Oedipus complex, so that the ego created by that structuring process is a gendered ego. Before the passage through the Oedipus complex, or in the submerged realm of the unconscious, polymorphic sexuality reigns, the unconscious following only the regulation of the pleasure/unpleasure principle. But in Freudianism there is no crossing over at will, no going back to an earlier state, that is not the result of being driven by a neurosis. So genderless sexuality, bisexual experiences, and polymorphic sexuality all are archaic traces pointing to failure at completing the Oedipal passage.

A Freudian analysis, then, of *Sons and Lovers* usually points to Paul Morel's failure to resolve his Oedipal conflicts and cites the moon/swoon passages, not as evidence of a unique Lawrentian concept of the unconscious, but as examples of infantile narcissism, the regressive desire to join with the mother in the pre-Oedipal bliss of dissolved boundaries. And what Lawrence valued—the knowledge gained through experience of the unconscious—becomes devalued. Also lost is the nuanced difference suggested in *Sons and Lovers* between the pre-Oedipal unconscious experience (mother-dominated and creative) and the Oedipal unconscious experience (father-dominated and sexual).

When Lawrence is measured by Freud, Lawrence's narrative experimentation of presenting subjectivity in objective discourse (as quoted earlier in the example of Mrs. Morel) is seen as a failure—the result of Lawrence's inability to distance himself sufficiently from his mother and proof of the author's unresolved Oedipal conflicts. "Because Lawrence is not emotionally removed from the narrative experience," argues Daniel Schwarz, "his superego has not grown sufficiently beyond the experience to evaluate and control his own mother-love" (257). This kind of criticism ultimately leads to accusations that Lawrence himself was bisexual or homosexual, as we get further and further away from understanding how the text portrays family relations and gender formation.

When the conflicts in Lawrence's texts are read in the context of a rigid Freudian ethos, the "woman's voice" in his texts is not allowed to speak, because her experience is outside the early

Freud's male narrative. Or "her" voice is relegated to the personal failure of Lawrence to be a real man. Yet clearly Freud seems the psychoanalytic thinker most applicable to Lawrence's work, since Lawrence viewed himself as a "corrector" of Freud in writing his own two works of the psyche.

Current feminist psychoanalysis builds upon Freud's findings but fills in the missing female narrative. As I discussed in chapter 1, Juliet Mitchell's *Psychoanalysis and Feminism* and Nancy Chodorow's *Reproduction of Mothering* offer a revision of Freud that opens up a space for women in the male drama of the formation of the psyche. *Sons and Lovers* complicates the early Freudian account of family relations in a way, I believe, that anticipates the later Freud's rethinking of female sexuality, that account which some feminists have turned to in theorizing how the psychology of patriarchy is reproduced internally.

Using objects-relation psychology informed by structuralism and feminism, Chodorow argues that both male and female children initially identify with the mother so that her figure is perceived as the universally human. "But, because men have power and cultural hegemony in our society," Chodorow comments, "a notable thing happens" ("Gender" 15):

Both in everyday life and in theoretical and intellectual formulations, men have come to define maleness as that which is basically human, and to define women as not-men. This transformation is first learned in, and helps to constitute, the Oedipal transition—the cultural, affective and sexual learnings of the meaning and valuation of sex differences. ("Gender" 15)

In "The Young Life of Paul" (pt. 1, chap. 4) we can see that as a child Paul already perceives the world divided by gender through perceptions made in the pre-Oedipal period. He identifies the mother with the human, the father with the untamed world beyond the circle of the home. The home and the hearth are warm and filled with light, the province of the mother, whereas Mr. Morel is separate and outside the family circle. "The family life withdrew, shrank away, and became hushed as he

entered. But he cared no longer about his alienation" (56). Morel
is portrayed often as an intruder from the night and the darkness
outside whose presence bespeaks violence and danger (87). From
the standpoint of women and children in a patriarchal society,
sexuality is often frightening and violent. Paul perceives the
father from this perspective, showing that while he comprehends
the world divided according to gender (mother-hearth and fa-
ther-outside night), he has not yet identified with the father's
location. "There was a feeling of horror, a kind of bristling in
the darkness, and a sense of blood" (85). Thus, he internalizes
gender *before* he has completed his own Oedipal passage. In
short, gender and sexuality are presented as separate, the first
a cultural product that literally divides the sexes, the second an
achieved state of genderless sensuality that can only be reached
by developing beyond (shrugging off) the confines of culture—
by turning away from the human to the nonhuman, outside of
the house, with the father, in the darkness.

In the female sphere within the home, Mrs. Morel has "authority" (74). Having no power outside of her location as wife
and over the potentially violent husband, she nevertheless is the
one who passes on to her children the devaluation of the female.
She unwittingly promotes the conflict between the sexes in gender division and reproduces the laws of patriarchy in her mothering. This is of course exactly the process Chodorow describes
in *The Reproduction of Mothering* whereby the family—and paradoxically strong mothers—reproduce a culture of male dominance and the ideology of gender in the unconscious from generation to generation (*Reproduction* 190).

First to William and later to Paul, Mrs. Morel preaches
against the encroachment of women. "But one day you'll find a
string around your neck, that you can't pull off" (80), she says,
and she warns William against the conniving of young women
who "flatter" his vanity (80). Mrs. Morel, not Mr. Morel, teaches
her sons the "meaning and valuation of sex differences" under
patriarchy, including the deep distrust of the female.[12] At the
same time the relations of power in which they all live, both

concretely and psychically real, teach the children to fear and hate the absolute power of patriarchy because it divides the parents, introduces conflict into the home, and threatens to bring economic ruin down on them. In the complex web of psychic and economic family relations, the mother is both victim and betrayer, the father both cruel and innocent.

The place free of the conflict of gender division is the Lawrentian unconscious. Experience of the unconscious reveals to characters the nonhuman elements of existence—the material, organic, evolutionary substrate beneath personality that culture represses. We could say the Lawrentian unconscious is the feminine if we used the terms of Chodorow, who argues that under male hegemony the female becomes identified with the nonhuman. We could also say the Lawrentian unconscious is female if we adopt the terms of theorists such as Lacan or some feminists who equate patriarchy with *logos* and a nonconceptual "flow" with the feminine.[13]

But for Lawrence the nonhuman is specifically and consistently allied with the father, with the male, although it is also, paradoxically, beyond or before gender. For this reason, I think we should not categorize simply as "pre-Oedipal" the urge to melt, to join, to merge, so typical in Lawrence's texts. That label ignores the role of the father-nuanced form of unconscious experience. In *Sons and Lovers* the female is the purveyor of imprisoning culture, though she is its victim too, escaping culture and gender division through experience of the unconscious. Lawrence's notion of the unconscious is probably closest to Freud's earliest and most original idea, drawn from observing hysterical patients—that the unconscious is the body speaking.[14]

Returning to that early scene of *Sons and Lovers* when Mrs. Morel retreats to the garden, we see how Lawrence in fact mixes sexual imagery derived from both the male and the female body and from myth to present what is genderless and before and beyond language and culture. The usually female moon is described phallically. The "high and magnificent moon" dominates the setting (33). "The moon streaming high in face of her *[sic]*, the moonlight standing up from the hills in front, and filling the valley where the Bottoms crouched, almost blindingly" (34). Mythically female, the moonlight is here active and penetrating on a male ("hills") and female ("valley") landscape below. And how do we categorize the gender of those "crouching Bottoms"?

The description of the flowers renders a similar sensual mix of genders: "The tall white lilies were reeling in the moonlight" (34). Although the lilies are phallic in their shape, they are white like the moon and associated with virgins, as well as Christ (a male/female symbol Lawrence likes). Mrs. Morel becomes the sexual aggressor. She is "seared with passion" (33); she touches the "big, pallid flowers" (34) stroking them and shivering as they seem to stretch. She dips her hands into "one white bin" (34). Protean and changeable, the flower image now evokes a female shape, and Mrs. Morel acts out the role of the male. After this metaphor of the sexual act, Mrs. Morel "lost herself awhile" (34). The sexual imagery applied to her unconscious experience of the natural world deconstructs the myth of fixed gender division as it renders a sexually charged physical world by intermixing male and female imagery.

Through such experiences of the unconscious, the characters in Lawrence's novels encounter the reality of the material body of existence that is repressed by the mental dominance of culture. After this experience, Mrs. Morel found "the night was very large, and very strange, stretching its hoary distances infinitely" (35). Like Paul at the end of the novel, the single individual realizes her own smallness in relation to the infinite universe, feels the fragility and miracle of human life in the vast cosmos.

At the end of the novel, a transformation and reversal occurs in the images associated with the mother and the father. In death, Mrs. Morel joins the nonhuman realm of darkness and terror, the realm that the child Paul had associated with the male. Paradoxically, then, Paul's intense mother love that nearly pulls him toward an "embrace" with death (464) in his desire to be near her also draws him toward an identification with the nonhuman sphere, "the vastness and terror of the immense night" (464), revealed to him at the end as the absolute power of death. Paul's confrontation with, and powerlessness over, death is a kind of castration experience ("himself, infinitesimal, at the core a nothingness, and yet not nothing" 464) from which the gendered man emerges, "one tiny upright speck of flesh" (464). Thus at the conclusion of the novel the mother in death has crossed over into and joined the nonhuman, formerly perceived by Paul as the male realm.

Paul should next identify the father as human, if his developmental pattern followed the typical course according to Chodorow. And Paul does turn away from the pull of his mother and the darkness, toward the city. But there is no identification of the city or culture with the father or male, nor is his turn terribly convincing. That is because "the faintly humming, glowing town" (464) seems nearly as small as he in the vast panorama of this last psychic scene where reality reveals itself to Paul as an "immense night" of "eternal," silent "Space" (464), in which there is no time and no distinct, gendered self. His mother is "intermingled" (464), and he is "at the core a nothingness" (420).

A Freudian analysis might equate the fear of being lost in space with fear of women (the fear of the penis being lost within the vagina during intercourse). Yet in the book's own terms, the night and nature recall the father. Mrs. Morel joins and becomes "intermingled" with the natural universe, so once again male and female imagery become mixed.

The natural universe is gigantic, powerful, and indifferent. Humanity is relational, not absolute, and arises from and flows back into the inhuman substrate of a material world. This final vision is particularly modern. Oddly enough, despite the fact that Lawrence accused Freud of building a pseudoscience out of projected ideas, Freud makes the same point that the modern picture of reality strikes a psychic blow to our "*naive* self-love" (*Introductory Lectures* 284) when we learn that "our earth [is] not the centre of the universe but only a tiny fragment of a cosmic system of scarcely imaginable vastness" (284), when we realize we do not occupy a "privileged place in creation" but are descended from other life forms (285), and when we face the Freudian claim that the "ego is not even master in its own house" (285). *Sons and Lovers* dismantles the old, comfortable ego in its own way, a way that differs from, but also shares affinities with, Freudianism.

When Freud dramatizes the conflicts that produce the development of the psyche by using the Oedipus myth, he presents the structuring process from the point of view of the child who stars in the lead role, and so Freud's account can be seen as a kind of "Family Romance." Of course, Family Romance is a particular term Freud invented for the common childhood fantasy of imagining that one's "real" parents are royal or noble (*SE* 9: 237). Freud himself would not say that his description of the formation of the personality is a romance. But in both, the child's drives shape the narrative of development—in the first, through the child's fantasy; in the second, through unconscious, instinctual drives.

Sons and Lovers is an anti-Romantic text because it raises questions about the validity of the Family Romance as both a psychic and economic fantasy. Whereas in Freud the Family Romance expresses the child's drives, in *Sons and Lovers* parent and child struggle to wrest control of the narrative; the plot endorses neither but moves back and forth. Paul "wins" only because he outlives his mother.

The Family Romance can also be seen as deeply rooted in capitalist ideology, in the myth of each generation doing better than the last, in some sense making up in this new (imagined) family for the defects in the previous one. Mrs. Morel herself seems deeply involved in such fantasy. She wishes for her sons what she cannot achieve on her own because she is a woman. In her wishes, she substitutes their success for hers. The fact that she conceives of their improvement in terms of proper marriage reveals all the more that her desire is a female version of Family Romance, since it is only through marriage that women secure an identity. As Juliet Mitchell points out, "men enter into the class-dominated structures of history while women (as women, whatever their actual work in production) remain defined by the kinship patterns of organization" (*Psychoanalysis and Feminism* 406). Mrs. Morel projects this female location of identity (in marriage) on Paul.

The male version of the Family Romance fantasy, on the other hand, would be some version of moving up from one class to another through labor. This myth of self-improvement relies on the myth of individuality and the repression of community ties. The young striver must rely on the sturdy self to work hard, repress any thoughts of extrapersonal, structural impediments to his success (or else he might become embittered and disillusioned), and not hold too dear the ties of the old community from which he will cut loose to enter the next class. William is the perfect example of the bourgeoisie, and William dies.

Paul is a mixed case. He does repress community, and so takes on some of the myth of individualism advocated in his mother's preaching. Paul hates and fears going out in public places. He does not seek the conviviality of other young men, but instead seeks out solitary relations with girls. With Mrs. Morel, he shares a certain disdain for the miners. But Paul rejects both the male version (social advancement through labor) and the female version (through marriage) of the Family Romance.

When he and Miriam finally consummate their relationship, they mimic a bourgeois marriage, though they are not married. They stay in a little cottage; she cooks for him: "It was their cottage for the day, and they were man and wife" (332). Paul clearly rejects this option in his rejection of Miriam and further repudiates marriage in his relations with Clara Dawes who, already married, can provide sex without the threat of marriage.

Paul complains that his mother gets between him and the women he is interested in. She does manipulate his romantic affairs, disparaging Miriam and endorsing Clara, steering her son away from the pitfalls of marriage but toward sexual satisfaction. Why does she? Many readers have believed that she does so because she selfishly wants her son all to herself. Having emotionally separated herself from her husband, she will substitute the son for the husband. Lawrence's letter to Edward Garnett confirms that Lawrence himself believed this.

Another way to explain Mrs. Morel, however, is to see that she projects onto Paul her own desires, the female version of the Family Romance. She does not push him particularly to compete as a worker, the male's role in Family Romance. She does not see him as a substitute husband but as a substitute of herself. She projects onto him the female's psychic location under patriarchy and in late nineteenth-century capitalism.

For a woman of the late nineteenth century, the period of courtship and early marriage, before children arrive, represents the completely achieved moment of independent identity. Before the marriageable age, the woman is the property of her parents, especially her father. She cannot act on her own and does not even have title to her own sexuality. Once married, she gains independence from her parents. She can be sexual, and she can act independently, as the example of Clara Dawes shows. However, once children arrive, she becomes the producer and nurturer of others and all too quickly loses title to herself as individual once again. The addition of children also shifts the symmetry between husband and wife. Sexual relations once more give way to the unequal power relations of patriarchy. Mrs. Morel encourages Paul to seek suitable mates but to postpone actual marriage and so to prolong and suspend the courting/early marriage period, a space of freedom for a woman of her era.

Paul believes his mother's motives are to drive off female competition. He resents the strength of her influence over him, her iron will, and even her refusal to die. When she controls his relations with women, Paul experiences himself as a commodity, very much as a woman of that era might feel like an "object" to be married off to the most suitable bidder. To free himself from her intense attachment, he hastens her end. But the novel's end does not make clear whether or not his beliefs are "correct" or "mature." Rather the novel ends with Mrs. Morel's dissolution into the nonhuman world and suggests Paul's continuing struggle in life. *Sons and Lovers* does not so much resolve the issue of

Family Romance—that desire to imagine more perfect family relations—as it delays or suspends the reproduction of family relations (just as Mrs. Morel had wished).

THE RAINBOW

One way to look at Lawrence's next novel, *The Rainbow* (1915), is as an experiment in imagining a new kind of Family Romance. I believe this novel sets out to try to preserve Family Romance by shifting to an exploration of sexuality in marriage and by trying to distribute the power between the sexes more evenly. In order to render the men and women characters as equals, the focus has to be close range, showing them as individuals stripped of class and historic concreteness. Any portrayal of real historical community would lead back to actual class conflicts—like those of the Morels—and the resultant inequality, conflict, and tragedy between the sexes of the kind that emerged in *Sons and Lovers*.

The novel portrays three generations, each "tied by interior bonds to its parents and yet," as Terry Eagleton says, "external, even alien, to them" (*Exiles* 200). Each married couple is pitted, man against woman, in an equal struggle toward selfhood and knowledge. From these generational struggles and sexual battles, there emerges the growth of the individual consciousness, and she is female. As Carol Dix notes, "the whole novel is a quest for the coming out of feminine consciousness" (15). Thus this experiment in Family Romance leads to the birth of the female as hero, but with the consequent rejection of family altogether. While the novel preserves the notion of marriage, it redefines marriage as an arena of sexual struggle towards knowledge, rather than as the location for reproduction.

Although earlier critics such as F. R. Leavis praised *The Rainbow* as a historic novel, the current view generally is that the novel romanticizes the past. Holderness argues that the novel refuses the possibility of change, that it presents no rural community of the past but merely "The Family" floating free of history

(183–84). Ideology is not "set into conflictual relationship with history," he concludes, but is "offered as an alternative to history" (175). "Within the course of *The Rainbow*," Scott Sanders remarks, "Lawrence shifted from the first perspective [initiation into society] to the second," what Sanders describes as "escape from the world into pre-social, pre-human mysteries" (15).

The movement backward to a precapitalist, idealized past can be seen as a way to reformulate the relation between the sexes free from the conflicts that arise from class differences. However, such a move ignores or represses the role of patriarchy in sexual relations. The struggle of domination and submission plays itself out in the novel as an "equal" game in the relations between individuals, and specifically between the sexes, rather than between classes.

In this idealized version of the past, women have a certain moral authority and power in the home, and men work hard in the fields, their senses filled and turned inward with generation ("How Tom Brangwen Married a Polish Lady" chap. 1). The novel starts with roughly the same associations of gender characteristics as *Sons and Lovers,* but all presented positively at the start.

The first Brangwen wife exemplifies the unrealistic rendering both of sex and class. She is a Polish widow with a young child, yet she is accepted with little comment by the provincial yeomen of rural England. From her perspective it is just as strange that the widow of an aristocrat would marry down in class. Her easy assimilation into rural English society is totally unrealistic. The plot ignores religious differences, English snobbery against foreigners, as well as the inherent class conflict of aristocrat and small farmer.

Her possession of a child by her previous marriage does not introduce any problems into the community or home (say in assimilation, conflicts of loyalty, religion, patrimony) but instead gives her added substance. As alien and other, she carries a certain mystery. All these features make her more attractive to Tom Brangwen. Their match is oddly *unequal* in two extremely different ways. On the one hand, her aristocratic status suggests that "the common English man is fit for the finest European aristocrat." On other the hand, measuring the balance of power between them suggests another equation: "it takes a foreign woman as well as a child to equal one English man."

This unlikely threesome regroups into a family by giving up their individual wills to "the swift, unseen threshing of the night" (77 ["They Live at the Marsh" chap. 2]).[15] The novel portrays the transformation of the individual self into a relational existence through physical connection. "She did not know him as himself. But she knew him as the man. She looked at him as a woman in childbirth looks at the man who begot the child in her: an impersonal look, in the extreme hour, female to male" (77).

Stripped of specific individualism and historical connection, the men and women characters might at first seem to be mere renderings of sexual essences, the women living to bear children, and the men to work and make love and be mystified by the women. Yet gender characteristics change over three generations. Ursula, a female, becomes the inheritor of the Brangwen traits. Hence the novel presents gender assumptions as formations, rather than essences.

In a moment of weakness, Ursula is tempted to accept the life society prescribes for women and which her mother had lived, the life of the body alone. Her mother had worked hard to reach a state of contentment in the strength of body knowledge and body fulfillment. But the novel makes clear that when Ursula almost accepts this for herself, she is capitulating, opting for an "easy" solution to her dilemma about whether or not to marry Skrebensky. Such a solution would not be a form of growth for her, as it had been for her mother:

What did the self, the form of life, matter? Only the living from day to day mattered, the beloved existence in the body, rich, peaceful, complete, with no beyond, no further trouble, no further complication. She had been wrong, she had been arrogant and wicked, wanting that other thing, that fantastic freedom, the illusory, conceited fulfilment which she had imagined she could not have with Skrebensky. Who was she to be wanting some fantastic fulfilment in her life? Was it not enough that she had her man, her children, her place of shelter under the sun? Was it not enough for her, as it had been for her mother? (448–49)

She writes to Skrebensky in a joyous self-abnegation ("For what had a woman but to submit?" 450) that is ironic. She does not know he has already married to escape her. If her mother Anna Brangwen might seem to epitomize an essentialist view of femaleness, Ursula as counterweight and final hero suggests that the novel as a whole does not endorse essentialism of gender. Instead, it portrays gender forms evolving over generations and arising relationally.

The novel denies to Ursula the old, worn-out role for women. Sinking into the old role would spell defeat for her, indicating backward regression. Instead the end ushers in an apocalyptic birth of a new order in the startling image of the thunderous horses. Inhuman and yet organic and material, they seem to gallop across the threshold between the unconscious and conscious to deliver their message. As in *Sons and Lovers,* the unconscious knowledge that flows from the natural world can be associated, at least symbolically, with the male. Horses do, after all, seem phallic, and certainly they do here in their fearful power. They seem to deliver to Ursula knowledge of phallic power—its potential destructiveness and brutality as well as beauty.

Ursula does not achieve new knowledge through her body in the experience of childbirth, as her mother had. Instead, quite brutally, from the miscarriage and death of the fetus comes the birth of her independent self in a new world order, whose form is the arch. She will seek the unknown Other rather than the old Adam ("He was that which is known" 457). No virgin, she will be the unknown and free Other, rather than the old Eve.

The symbol of the rainbow projects this relational connection. The image aspires upward but is not entirely phallic, incorporating the female circle. Its arch is anchored in the earth at each end, as befits a material and evolutionary sign. The symbol of the rainbow also recalls primitive societies and future promises in the same way that the novel looks backward into an idealized past and ends with a utopian thrust forward.

The symbol of the rainbow also carries along its span in the novel the transformation of the Family Romance from its old to its new form. The first Brangwens find fulfillment in the successful relations of family, the mother and father arching over and protecting the children. In the first generation, the child

Anna's soul was put at peace between them. She looked from one to the other, and she saw them established to her safety, and she was free. She played between the pillar of fire and the pillar of cloud in confidence, having the assurance on her right hand and the assurance on her left. She was no longer called upon to uphold with her childish might the broken end of the arch. Her father and her mother now met to the span of the heavens, and she, the child, was free to play in the space beneath, between. (91)

This passage illustrates how the traditional Family Romance is a child's construction. The child fantasizes the form of the family with herself at the center and the parents above and around drawing a secure boundary. The values expressed in the image are peace, safety, confidence, and assurance, values most important to a child.

By the time the Brangwen generations evolve to Ursula, the symbol of the rainbow evolves from a static picture, like a child's watercolor, to a vibrant modernist image of organic transformation:

And the rainbow stood on the earth. She knew that the sordid people who crept hard-scaled and separate on the face of the world's corruption were living still, that the rainbow was arched in their blood and would quiver to life in their spirit, that they would cast off their horny covering of disintegration, that new, clean, naked bodies would issue to a new germination, to a new growth, rising to the light and the wind and the clean rain of heaven. She saw in the rainbow the earth's new architecture, the old, brittle corruption of houses and factories swept away, the world built up in a living fabric of Truth, fitting to the over-arching heaven. (458–59)

Although the language, images, and tone are biblical and apocalyptic, they are also organic and evolutionary but not human
centered. New life forms will be born out of old ones, but the
birth may be bloody. There is no safe spot underneath the arch,
as new life rises up and the old is swept away. Rather than
rendering the childhood fantasy of sanctuary within the family,
the symbol of the rainbow becomes the sign of upheaval and
change as it retains the mythic association of promise.

The sweep of Ursula's utopian vision at the end of *The
Rainbow* extends all the way from the individual ("new, clean
naked bodies" 459) to the social and historical ("the old, brittle
corruption of houses and factories" 459), but since the historically
concrete has been repressed throughout the novel, it is hard to
imagine just how a "world built up in a living fabric of Truth"
(459) will "quiver to life" (459) from her new consciousness.
Whenever we try to get hold of the connection between individual
consciousness and social forms in *The Rainbow,* the link seems to
dissolve, whereas in *Sons and Lovers* concrete class differences
produced different psychological formations. Since *The Rainbow*
ignores class conflict, we might wonder what element does cause
the struggle between the sexes, the battles of domination and
submission. If the novel endorses Ursula's development to new
forms of womanhood, then it moves away from an essentialist
view of gender difference. But if the novel presents sexual roles
and gender assumptions as formations, we might well ask what
they are formed by, since *The Rainbow*, like *Sons and Lovers*, deconstructs notions of individual agency—that old ego Lawrence was
indicting.

Although class conflict and class relations are not allowed
much force in the novel, the relations of patriarchy permeate it.
And since the relations of patriarchy occur in, and are part of,
concrete history, their presence introduces the shadow of the
real world into the novel. The division of labor according to the
sexes, the division of the spheres of life between the home and
the fields and later between home and workshop and cathedral,
all are historical structures based on patriarchy. More deeply

implicated still is the entire generational plot, the *Brangwensaga,* based as it is on a patriarchal notion of a family unit and patrilinear inheritance.

The novel evades and yet depends upon patriarchy, but paradoxically it also challenges male dominance in its final vision. Had Ursula married Skrebensky and actually given birth to his child she was carrying, she would have gone to live the colonial life in India. However, forced toward change by physical event and spiritual rupture, Ursula throws off the old pattern of marriage, submission to the man, and childbearing. Perhaps not incidentally she avoids collusion with imperialism. It is the institution of patriarchy, more than any other specific historical form, that the end of the novel implicitly repudiates.

Patriarchy structures the relationship of individuals in *The Rainbow.* The novel both builds its plot on this hidden structure and criticizes it at the same time. For example, the marriage of Winifred Inger, the lesbian schoolteacher, to Uncle Tom Brangwen, the pit manager, is an ironic homage to the force of patriarchy that, the novel seems to suggest, spawns the deadly forces of capitalism as well as the mechanical reproduction of the social unit, and decadent, "perverted" sexuality too.

Lawrence's treatment of lesbian desire is surely radical for his time. Although Winifred is portrayed somewhat negatively, she is important to Ursula's development, introducing her to the women's movement, broadening her thinking on religion, helping her to move away from provincial life ("Shame" 316–18). The text suggests that it is not so much lesbian desire that is perverted but the will to dominate, a characteristic Winifred shares with Uncle Tom Brangwen. Although Winifred gets "punished" by ending up in a bad marriage, Lawrence uses the occasion to attack the way desire can become an instrument of male hegemony in a heterosexual marriage:

Brangwen and Winifred Inger continued engaged for another term. Then they married. Brangwen had reached the age when he wanted children. He wanted children. Neither marriage nor the domestic establishment meant anything to him. He wanted to propagate himself. He knew what he was doing. He had the instinct of a growing inertia, of a thing that chooses its place of rest in which to lapse into apathy, complete, profound indifference. He would let the machinery carry him: husband, father, pit-manager, warm clay lifted through the recurrent action of day after day by the great machine from which it derived its motion. (326–27)

The passage emphasizes his "thingness," a commodity in an age of mass reproduction. His desire for propagation is another form of the machine working itself. The traditional family is not a haven from the sickness and mechanism of modern society, not a refuge or moral center exempt from corruption. The tone of the passage emphasizes that desire for family can also become, has become, warped and distorted.

Unlike Winifred Inger, however, Ursula does free herself from the machine of patriarchal structure at the end of *The Rainbow* by *not* marrying and *not* having a child. The open ending of *The Rainbow* projects the possibility of change. Since Ursula achieves her new insight by the physical crisis of miscarriage and by saying no to marriage, the ending sets the stage for the negative dialectic of *Women in Love*.

WOMEN IN LOVE

The issues of patriarchy continue to haunt *Women in Love* (1920), but the desolate tone suggests that the possibility for change has become drastically reduced. Readers have recognized that the novel addresses issues of patriarchy directly, even as they often underrate how the novel's critique of patriarchy provides thematic unity as well as sophisticated social analysis of the relations of power both at the level of the individual and among societies. Readers understand that the novel criticizes Gerald Crich's patriarchal relationship with his workers (Sanders 112), and that Gerald's failure is meant to be more than mere personal failure. Lawrence intends Gerald's failure to be emblematic of the "last days" of European culture. In focusing on patriarchy, however, Lawrence has been accused of ignoring the role of the worker in history and of reducing historical forces to personal interactions (see Sanders and Holderness) and of rejecting any notion of community.

Oddly, the same readers also observe that *Women in Love* furthers the attack on the old personal ego. It "engages liberal humanism" (Holderness 210) and reveals the contradictions in the ideologies of rugged individualism, entrepreneurial energy, capitalism, and democracy. Birkin and Ursula survive and achieve the limited approval of the novel by establishing their love on an "impersonal plane, mystic and physical, below the surface of personal emotions" (Vitoux 828).

On the one hand, the novel appears to explain the decay of the largest social structures (culture, industry) in terms of the personal and subjective relations of industrialists such as the Crich family. Yet, in apparent contradiction, the novel also suggests that a cure for social ills can begin when individuals discover the deep, impersonal plane on which to establish a new kind of relationship. This is exactly the reverse of the familiar twentieth-century idea that social structures arise from, and are driven by, impersonal forces, while the relations of individuals are exclusively fueled by personal sentiment.

Until recently the common notion of patriarchy was of a social organization fixed by God and nature (descent through the male line) that was unremarkable and unimportant as a formative structure. Freud emphasized the crucial role of the father in the psychological formation of the individual, his notion of patriarchy being influenced by the conservative social bent of his ideas. On the one hand, Freud's description of the formation of the individual psyche posits family relations as structural (functional and relational) rather than literal and personal. On the other hand, Freud never imagined any change in family structure. In fact he bases his descriptions of neuroses against a fixed *norm* of family relations and gender roles. Freud also personalized social history whenever he ventured outside of psychoanalysis. For example, he reduced the historical and anthropological to the personal and psychological in *Totem and Taboo*, and he often explained away revolutionary ferment in terms of disobedience to the father. Social critics have attacked Lawrence's indictment of patriarchy in the same way they criticize Freudianism: as a simplistic and apolitical analysis of social organization based on a theory of personal relations.[16]

Only since the rise of structural anthropology and recent feminist theory has patriarchy been seen as a specific form of social organization. Patriarchy is a social organization that is neither fixed and inevitable nor personal but a changing system of male dominance that permeates and affects all other social formations. According to Gerda Lerner in *The Creation of Patriarchy*, the control of women's reproductive capacity by the tribal exchange of women and the division of labor for reproductive purposes created the first class distinctions. Her idea reverses the famous dictum of Engels. Property relations did not produce sexual inequality, but instead sexual dominance set the stage for the class dominance and conflict that emerge later. Today, of course, most Marxists acknowledge that unequal sexual relations and male dominance survive and in fact thrive in Communist societies, so that the early twentieth-century hope that sexual equality would be achieved in a classless society has not become reality.

A feminist views patriarchy as a political as well as personal structure. Feminist psychoanalysts such as Juliet Mitchell explain how the ideology of patriarchy is passed on from generation to generation through the unconscious. Feminist historians, like Gerda Lerner, reconstruct a specific history of the operations of patriarchy.

From a feminist point of view, Lawrence is far more radical in *Women in Love* than he often gets credit for. *Women in Love* presents patriarchy as the connecting link between the sexual, the personal, and larger social forces. The novel shows how structures of thought and relations produced by patriarchy permeate all levels of culture from the relations between individuals to those between worker and manager, from the ethos of the traditional schoolroom to the newest, avant-garde theories of art. The disease of modern civilization does not originate in material conditions or in ideas, the novel suggests, but from a worn out structure of relations between the sexes marked by the hegemony of Western "male" values and "male" thought processes (understood as a relational term denoting a specific historical pattern of dominant ideology).

Rupert Birkin and Ursula Brangwen struggle to achieve a new kind of sexuality. Their new sexual relation will not be based on the old stereotypes of gender and sex roles. It will be polar rather than hegemonic and bring unconscious body knowledge of the Other into relationship, not merely their sentimental egos. The struggle to achieve this new kind of marriage is dead serious and life threatening, as the image of the drowned Diana Crich and her new husband, arms entwined and choking each other, renders so visibly. The new marriage will not lead to a permanent abode and the reproduction of the social unit. It will not be a phallic marriage, but one founded on exploring alternative physical relations. As the chapter "Excurse" makes clear, Ursula found a "rich new circuit" of connection at the base of Birkin's back (314).[17] But such a new marriage does not mark the withdrawal from community; it is not solipsistic or narcissistic. Instead it marks a tentative new community of two, based on equality, not dominance. However, the fragility of this new community and the long odds against its success are evident in the last chapters of the novel.

Gender and desire are at the radical center of *Women in Love,* as Lawrence's suppressed prologue makes clear. At the start of the novel Birkin is split: he wants to love women but cannot will himself to desire them. And he perceives women as split into two groups, those whose souls are high, but for whom he has no passion, and those whose bodies he responds to but who have no souls. He finds himself desiring anonymous men he sees around him: "So he went on, month after month, year after year, divided against himself, striving for the day when the beauty of men should not be so acutely attractive to him, when the beauty of woman should move him instead" (*Women in Love*, Appendix 2: 504).

The novel thoroughly rejects all the old forms of social organization, including fixed notions of sexuality. Birkin does not will himself to be bisexual; in fact, he fights the pull in him toward other men, though the novel never suggests that Birkin's feelings or impulses are immoral. To the contrary, Birkin's sense of profound loss at Gerald's death reinforces the legitimacy of his attempt to establish a new kind of intimacy with another man. He has to be content with only a partial solution to a new kind of society in his marriage to Ursula. The kind of intimacy Birkin seeks and finds with Ursula is at bottom not sexual but rather an acknowledgement of the deep otherness of the Other at its vital life source.[18]

Birkin seeks an intimate relationship with an Other as an antidote to the mechanical relationships of the modern world—the commodity relations of producer and laborer, and the commodity relationship of the modern bourgeois family. On the one hand, people are transformed into things (worker, reproducer). On the other, they make up for the lack of deep, impersonal relations with each other with superficial silly sentiment that is the by-product of the mass-produced era.[19]

There are no real bonds between men like Gerald and his workers, only the pseudoemotional, and so men have no relation to one another. Hence Birkin's great need for, and sense of loss of, man-to-man relationship. The primacy of sexual sensation over other kinds of individual bonds also comes from the severing of older forms of community ties (such as religious ritual), leaving only the nuclear family relationship in modern, atomistic society. And although Birkin is a prophet of a new kind of sexuality, he criticizes the merely sensational. So Birkin's desire for relationship with men is sexual, but it is also deeper, the need for some genuine exchange with another who is male. Finally, too, as all elements of life become commodities for exchange, they become objects, severed from their relationship with a context.[20] Like Mrs. Morel in *Sons and Lovers*, the modern, young people at the

Pompadour Cafe in London or Loerke in the Swiss Alps believe in a free-floating art that is formal and self-referential, an absolute object apart from the community that produced it.

The novel describes this as a kind of "phallic" art whose spirit is mechanical, formal, and dehumanized. This is the art for art's sake of Loerke. His is an art of death, an art that cuts off all connections with the relations out of which it grew. Not surprisingly, his sculpture is of a giant phallic horse upon which is perched a frail girl.

Women in Love links all these elements—the mechanical reproduction of human relations in late industrialism, the spiritual malaise of the modern era, and the impossibility of deep relation with another—with the structure of patriarchy. The images of coldness, whiteness, and snow convey its killing properties. Patriarchy spawns a deathly ideology, exemplified by Gerald's state of mind, a hyperconsciousness based on the need to control and dominate. Gudrun and Gerald are doomed by these qualities, which the novel presents not so much as personal flaws in their characters that seal their fate but as impersonal forces of Western civilization to which they succumb. "For Gudrun herself, she seemed to pass altogether into the whiteness of the snow, she became a pure, thoughtless crystal" (420). So too Birkin and Ursula survive by submitting themselves to the impersonal, dark forces, associated in "Excurse" with the ancient, secret Egyptian culture of the East.

If we interpret Birkin's desire for male relationship along the lines of a typical Freudian reading, we lose the sense the novel imparts of a world malaise. Then, instead of portraying how impersonal forces shape the thought and desire of individuals, the novel merely chronicles a character's personal failure to complete the Oedipal passage "normally." Rather than the personal, the novel portrays a cultural crisis of desire resulting from the decay and dissolution of the "old, fulfilled, obsolete idea," that is the spirit of the time (*Women in Love*, Appendix 2: 495). This is not to deny that *Women in Love* speaks for homoeroticism; surely it does. However, the novel suggests that our frame for considering healthy and unhealthy sexuality is worn out, spent.

Whereas *Sons and Lovers* delays the reproduction of family relations, and *The Rainbow* asserts the independence of the woman from reproductive functions, *Women in Love* assaults our deepest-held notions about gender. A Freudian interpretation works least well with *Women in Love* because the novel questions the very ground of Freudianism—fixed notions of gender and the inevitability of the family as an institution.

After *Women in Love*, Lawrence increasingly seems to turn to the worship of male power. Lawrence seems only too eager to cast his thought in terms of fixed essences of gender and to preach the Lawrentian gospel of "phallic" marriage in some of his later writing. What he means by "phallic" is not entirely clear, however.

In the late essay "Apropos of *Lady Chatterley's Lover*" (1930) Lawrence defines "true marriage" as the phallic marriage, a heterosexual relationship that "set[s]" the man and woman "in relationship to the rhythmic cosmos" (*Phoenix II*: 509). In this essay, he carefully places the relation of sexual exchange at the center of human development. Marriage is not a matter of property relations, he says, specifically referring to bolshevism (502). Further, humans need "no Word, no Logos, no Utterance" (510) but the "deed of a woman's life at one with a man's" (510). Birkin declares to Gerald in *Women in Love*, "because the relation between man and woman is made the supreme and exclusive relationship, that's where all the tightness and meanness and insufficiency comes in" (352). Either Lawrence completely reversed this critique of marriage between 1920 and 1930, or he means something different in "Apropos of *Lady Chatterley's Lover*" by "phallic marriage" than the "tightness," "meanness," and supremely foolish egocentric institution he attacked in *Women in Love*.

A 1928 essay "Matriarchy" repeats the warning in *Women in Love* against tightness:

Let us drift back to matriarchy. Let the woman take the children and give them her name—it's a wise child that knows its own father. Let the woman take the property—what has a man to do with inheriting or bequeathing a grandfather's clock! Let the women form themselves into a great clan, for the preservation of themselves and their children. It is nothing but just.

And so, let men get free again, free from the tight littleness of family and family possessions. Give woman her full independence, and with it, the full responsibility of her independence. (*Phoenix II*: 552)

This passage suggests that Lawrence, late in his writing career, makes the same gender associations he made in *Sons and Lovers*: the woman inside the circle of domestic light, associated with mother, child, culture, and property; the man outside in the dark and sensual night. He also still asserts independence for women, however ironically and negatively tinged here by her control of, and responsibility for, property.

As for men, "give the men a new forgathering ground, where they can meet and satisfy their deep social needs," he says, "deep as religion in a man. It is necessary for the life of society, to keep us organically vital, to save us from the mess of industrial chaos and industrial revolt" (*Phoenix II*: 552).

When Lawrence puts heterosexual marriage at the center, as in "Apropos of *Lady Chatterley's Lover*," he sounds like the rigid Gerald Crich. His thinking sounds like the very thinking Birkin attacks in *Women in Love*. Yet all three pieces of writing—*Women in Love*, "Matriarchy," and "Apropos"—reiterate the same points about the proper Lawrentian marriage: it should be "committing" oneself "into a relationship," not an "accept[ance] of the established order" (*Women in Love* 353). Marriage is not an institution but a relationship of exchange.

Because Lawrence places exchange with an Other at the center, he often sounds as though he upholds a fixed, essentialist sex/gender system. The same predicament occurs, I think, for feminists who reify notions of sexual "difference" by calling upon a special "female consciousness." Even when their goal is to subvert male thinking and hegemony, as Christine Mackward warns, "the theory of femininity," used as a starting point for argument, "is dangerously close to repeating in 'deconstructive' language the traditional assumptions on femininity and female creativity" (96).

Lawrence falls into this same problem, except reversed. In the twenties Lawrence focuses more and more on the condition of male consciousness. In "Matriarchy," for example, he is more concerned about the relation of men to men than with definitions of marriage. Then, in "Apropos of *Lady Chatterley's Lover*," Lawrence ends by praising the "phallic" marriage, by which I think he really means "phallic consciousness." In using this term I mean to point out that Lawrence seeks roughly the same goal as proponents of a "feminine consciousness": to subvert and dismantle the present thought systems of dominance and control. Lawrence wants to revivify those aspects of consciousness that modern, Western life represses in *men*: a sensual, intuitive, nonrational living.

In Lawrence's texts, but particularly in *Women in Love*, sexual identity is a burden that limits. Because of his sex/gender identity Birkin can have no intimate relationship with Gerald. Yet Lawrence makes a fixed, binary sex/gender system necessary for the exchange with the Other that Lawrence values as the basis for all authentic social relations. Thus, by grounding social and philosophical critiques in sexual identity, Lawrence inevitably upholds the sex/gender system he wishes to change.

Insofar as the world rendered in Lawrence's novels is dynamic, discontinuous, and frustrating, as it is in *Women in Love*, Lawrence avoids casting his vision of new relations into a frozen scheme that upholds essentialism of gender. Lawrence himself paid homage to this negative or unfinished aspect in his important essay "The Novel" (1925): "the novel is a great discovery: far greater than Galileo's telescope or somebody else's wireless. The novel is the highest form of human expression so far attained. Why? Because it is so incapable of the absolute" (*Phoenix II*: 416).

So oddly enough, Birkin's failure to achieve a new kind of relationship with Gerald keeps open the possibility of intimate relations of a new kind by postponing them. In a way, each of the three novels ends by a postponement that further reverses the usual progression of the Family Romance. *Sons and Lovers* ends with the delaying of marriage and the extension of the courtship period. *The Rainbow* ends by rupturing the usual progression for a woman from sexual knowledge to marriage and childbirth. In *Women in Love*, marriage finally is sanctioned, but there are no children, and the new male relationship, dreamed of, is unfulfilled.

From the Family Romance narrative, Lawrence retains only marriage, and the marriage he ends up advocating looks back to the quest romance more than it suggests the family plot of psychoanalysis or the contractual relations of economic life. There are no children, no reproduction of the social unit in a community. Marriage is not even undertaken to preserve property rights or inheritance. Instead the Lawrentian marriage is an adventure in the soul's growth, bringing the individuals into relation with the cosmos, not with their neighbors. The marriage quest may replace the religious quest in the modern era of worn-out religion, but in Lawrence it is a pagan religious quest, for his new religion of marriage bears little resemblance to the Christian sacrament. Ironically, this is a free-floating marriage, which could only take place in modern times, when communal ties have been broken or confounded by mass markets, where technology has freed many from the constraints of childbirth, a fixed residence, or the need to work at a subsistence level. Severed from the connections to an earlier meaning, marriage becomes a free-floating signifier, making it a suitable vehicle for a quest. While in his later writing Lawrence decries the lack of connection with meaningful ritual and community in the modern world and seeks models of primitive societies that bond individuals, all his writing reaffirms the need to cut, dissolve, and let go in the difficult process of change. Lawrence preaches a noninstitutional, self-referential form of marriage, clearer in what it is not than in what it is, a definition of marriage suitable to the negative phase of change.

The bisexuality of human nature runs through all three novels. In *Sons and Lovers,* Paul has great empathy for his mother's position. He develops in his relation to patriarchy in some respects as a woman does, even though I think the novel shows he completes his male Oedipal passage. *The Rainbow* includes female bisexuality in the relationship between Winifred Inger and Ursula but ultimately disparages Winifred's lesbian desire by equating it with the desire to control, manifested most purely in the culture of the machine: "She, too, Winifred, worshipped the impure abstraction, the mechanisms of matter. There, in the monstrous mechanism that held all matter, living or dead, in its service, did she achieve her consummation and her perfect unison, her immortality" (325). As a negative character, Winifred Inger marries and is pulled into the machine of mechanical reproduction under patriarchy.

Male bisexuality comes to the forefront in *Women in Love* in the male quest for a new kind of relationship with another man and with a woman. Birkin achieves a healthy heterosexual relationship in his star polarity with Ursula but fails to find the way to a living relationship with Gerald. *Women in Love* praises marriage as an adventure of two souls but is wary of hunger for power and control.[21]

From a Freudian point of view bisexuality is infantile. Desire for new kinds of intimate relations that do not conform to procreative heterosexuality shows the subject's failure to complete the Oedipal project and submit his drives to the reality principle. Leaving aside the ethical judgments and normative direction of Freudianism, we can see that the bisexual impulse might also indicate that the subject internalizes both the mother and the father without the dominance of one over the other. Could we call this the possibility of a post-Oedipal and postpatriarchal bisexuality?

To redefine bisexuality psychoanalytically, as I just did above, is a kind of a Lawrentian operation because to let the term evolve in meaning requires us to cut off the connections our culture usually makes. In a similar manuever, Lawrence redefines marriage, severing its connection to an economic and cultural base (as property relations or location for reproduction of the worker or location for reproduction of the subject). Under Lawrence's redefinition, marriage only produces the self evolving toward consciousness. If we were truly Lawrentian in our thinking, however, we would have to remind ourselves of the danger of "pure, unconnected will," as he describes Loerke in *Women in Love* (427). So we should, as Lawrence also does, criticize our new definitions set loose from cultural constraints.

Freudian analysis can explain Lawrence's swerve to phallic worship in terms of Lawrence's own early childhood, and biographers can point to Lawrence's life on the wing with Frieda after World War I. As they fought and traveled, they cut ties to any single community and witnessed worldwide social unrest and upheaval, even as they found beautiful hideouts from the twentieth century in places like Taos and Taormina. While I do not dispute these explanations, I think the great paradox of Lawrence's work is left unexplained. That is, what is the relation between his deconstructing of gender and patriarchy while increasingly affirming male power and relying on patriarchal plots?

I believe Lawrence's ambivalent relation to patriarchy can account for this paradox. He resists the ideology of patriarchy, as in *Women in Love,* and gender definitions under patriarchy. He experiments with bisexual desires and points of view. All three major novels locate the woman within culture, the man outside, as does his late essay "Matriarchy." Chodorow reminds us that under patriarchy, the female typically represents the body, the male, culture. So Lawrence "speaks like a woman," in that he sees the female as a cultural sign. Whereas from the ideology of patriarchy women are seen as an embodiment of nature (or gender differences are seen as truthful reflections of biological essences), feminists themselves understand that to be "female" means to represent (to be a sign of, for the male) a set of cultural constructions.

Yet Lawrence is also caught up in the very structure of patriarchy that he resists because he locates the sex/gender system and sexual relations at the center of his philosophy. Because he values exchange with an Other as the most important relation, he depends upon a binary sex/gender system. When he gravitates toward phallic ideology in the mid-1920s, he brings out this paradoxical dependence.

Some Neo-Freudian theories depend on the same kind of paradoxical relation to the phallus as does Lawrence's work. Jacques Lacan, for example, emphasizes the "scandal" of phallic symbolism (it is everywhere; the phallus is the Transcendent Signifier). Lacan also analyzes the cultural construction of gender (through language), as discussed in chapter 1. Some feminists influenced by Lacan, such as Luce Irigaray, Hélène Cixous, or Julia Kristeva, discuss the "phallic" nature of all Western culture created by the structure of patriarchy inherent in language itself. They explore the possibility of new forms of culture variously described as "the feminine" or "the bisexual" that would not be based on dominance and mastery but on multiplicity, contradiction, eroticism. They connect consciousness and control with male hegemony, logos, and the rule of the father; unconsciousness and pre-linguistic knowledge with the pre-Oedipal stage of attachment to the mother's body.

Lawrence may appear to anticipate feminists who use the present sex/gender system, often reifying the notion of "difference," to attack Western logic and male hegemony. In *Sons and Lovers* the creative unconscious is associated with the pre-Oedipal relation of mother and child. In Julia Kristeva's theory, the pre-Oedipal relation is also creative and yet prelinguistic. Kristeva calls pre-Oedipal knowledge "semiotic" (in contrast to the "symbolic" knowledge of the Oedipal, father-dominated relation, according to Kristeva). However, Lawrence's other kind of unconscious experience, the more frequently invoked submission to the dark and sensual forces of nature (associated with the father in Lawrence), also yields precognitive knowledge of the body below and before speech. In these kinds of unconscious experiences, Lawrence values all that is typically repressed by Western rationality. *Women in Love* suggests the same kind of dichotomy made by contemporary feminists between female intuition and male logic in the mysterious force of dissolution associated with Egypt, contrasted with the ice cold light of Western reason connected to Gerald.[22]

However, Lawrence's conception of gender and the unconscious differs in important ways from contemporary theorists of "difference." First, Lawrence often portrays consciousness evolving from unconsciousness like thought evolving from experience of the body in the way that a tree's trunk and branches grow from its roots. Lawrence never suggests that consciousness is a function of, or delimited by, language. In Lacan, language institutes both desire and the unconscious, and there can be no direct "experience" of the unconscious, except interpreted through the lapses and doubleness of language. For Lawrence, however, "desire, in any shape or form, is primal" (*Women in Love*, Appendix 2: 500).

Further, Lawrence does not "genderize" experiences of the unconscious or the freedom from repression he seeks. The two kinds of experience of the unconscious rendered in *Sons and Lovers* are indeed associated with the mother and with the father, but to experience the unconscious is to be free of gender, if only briefly. That experience is available and necessary for members of both sexes in all three novels. In this respect, Lawrence's work shows affinity with Freud, who despite his male bias argued against attempts by other psychoanalysts such as Jung and Adler to "sexual[ize] repression" (*SE* 5: 355).

Lawrence's attitude to capitalism is like his contradictory relation to patriarchy. He criticizes it, but he also appreciates its progressive possibilities. While the modern era causes "industrial chaos and industrial revolt" ("Matriarchy"), the resulting fragmentation is like the negative moment of change in *Women in Love,* allowing us to "see" institutions such as gender division, sex roles, and marriage as cultural formations rather than essences.

The "authentic" exchange with another that Lawrence values can be seen as the narrative embodiment of the Oedipal passage. To pass through the Oedipus complex means to understand all that gender division means in culture. When a character perceives the otherness of the Other, he "sees," or perceives, gender difference, and when he merges with the Other, losing his boundaries, he retreats to that "pre-Oedipal" bliss before differentiation. (We should remember that in Lawrence the pre-Oedipal has both a mother mode and a father mode.) Lawrence's plots, I believe, hover around and replay the moment of the Oedipal passage. In chapter 4, I will return to Lawrence's late work, *The Escaped Cock* or *The Man Who Died*, to look more closely at the dynamics of this kind of plot. Even in this "Oedipal" plot, however, Lawrence retains the associations set out in *Sons and Lovers:* the woman, the priestess of Isis, within culture, attached to her abode; the man outside, unattached, in the night.

In the next chapter, I turn to Joyce's *Portrait of the Artist, Dubliners,* and *Ulysses.* Joyce, I believe, starts from the opposite extreme. *A Portrait* portrays women and men from the point of view of patriarchy. But as Joyce begins to deconstruct received systems, he moves progressively beyond the ground of patriarchy. Lawrence's work remains grounded throughout his writing career in a perspective that both resists and upholds patriarchy. Joyce, in contrast, starts by representing woman as body and ends with her as disembodied voice, literally, as Anna Livia Plurabelle dissolves into the sea.

3

James Joyce: Overdetermination Replaces Cause and Effect

This exists that isits after having been said we know.

—*Finnegans Wake*

Reading Joyce is often a case of reading backward because of the seemingly intense drive to totality in each of his works, separately, and in all of them taken together. Post-Wakean readings of *Dubliners* abound.[1] Conversely, the *Wake*'s enigmas are often decoded by the light of Joyce's earlier work. Such reciprocal reading enriches our appreciation of Joyce's texts and certainly is warranted by the condensations, self-referential parody, and circular design of the *Wake*, that "collupsus of his back promises" (5.27–28). Yet Joyce constantly warns about revisionary danger, too, lest like Stephen, we may prove "by algebra that Hamlet's grandson is Shakespeare's grandfather and that he himself is the ghost of his own father" (*U* 1.555–57).[2] Therefore, while we need to connect Joyce's early and late fiction, we also need to distinguish each work and the changes Joyce's thinking underwent over the course of thirty-five years.

Uneasy, even rebellious, as Joyce was with systems of authority, I believe Joyce begins writing from within a traditional, patriarchal point of view. Joyce then submits that view to criticism, breaking up his and our perception of a single, seamless reality into its anarchic, diverse pieces. In the early fiction, whether irony is intended or not, women represent the body, men spirit. Joyce expresses the tentativeness with which he held this view in *Stephen Hero:* "He toyed also with a theory of dualism which

117

would symbolise the twin eternities of spirit and nature in the twin eternities of male and female and even thought of explaining the audacities of his verse as symbolical allusions" (210).

Determining whether or not Joyce moves on from this traditional patriarchal view is of utmost importance, I believe, in reading Joyce's more difficult texts. Some readers argue that Joyce's attitude does not change and claim that *Ulysses* and *Finnegans Wake* present eternal male and female principles, therefore conserving traditional patriarchal structure (see van Boheemen on *Ulysses* and Norris on *Finnegans Wake*). Colin MacCabe argues that Joyce's extreme focus on language is the same in *A Portrait* and the *Wake* ("Introduction to *Finnegans Wake* 30). Stephen Heath, on the other hand, argues that Joyce's work is not "univocal." "Joyce himself often insisted forcefully on the breaks between his various works," Heath notes, "and that insistence deserves to be remembered" ("Ambiviolences" 34).

Yet what makes determining the changes in Joyce's views difficult is that so many fine-tuned details replay themselves over and over. In a surviving manuscript fragment of *Stephen Hero*, for example, Stephen witnesses the body of a dead woman discovered in the canal: "A pace or two from the brink of the water a thing was lying on the bank partly covered by a brown sack. It was the body of a woman" (252). Fascinated and horrified, he gazes "into the canal near the feet of the body, looking at a fragment of paper" (252) floating in the water. There is an integrity of image here that surely returns in *Finnegans Wake*. The thingness of the woman's body, in conjunction with a mysterious, torn, partial message, all floating on the water, reappears in somewhat altered disguise as A.L.P., who digs up a jumbled, mostly undiscernible message and ends by turning into things (stone and trees and river) as she flows out to the sea (*FW* 103 and 628).

Since images such as this one and Joyce's unique symbols (umbrella, nannygoat, plums, to name a few) return again and again, they resemble overdetermined symptoms of the artist's or the text's unconscious. Psychoanalyzing the text or author, we might say that the constant reappearance of symbols signals the "return of the repressed" (as does MacCabe in *JJ and the Revolution of the Word*).

However, like Lawrence, Joyce argues directly against the value judgments of psychoanalysis. Whereas Lawrence rewrites Freud, Joyce takes on the terms of psychoanalysis both in self-conscious parody and in acceptance of their validity (with a Joycean twist). Whereas Lawrence focuses on the exchange relation of adults, Joyce expresses the desire to cast off all repression and to assert in place of the "return of the repressed," unrestrained free circulation and recirculation. From a psychoanalytic point of view, such desire is infantile. Joyce does not argue, but indeed concurs, exulting in his own language and vision of babes happily engaged in their "infantile sexual researches" (Freud's term) in a Joycean "babalong" (*FW* 103.11).

Joyce's knowledge of Freud ran deeper than scholars used to acknowledge. Anderson speculates that Joyce first heard of Freud from conversations with medical students in 1904 in Dublin and possibly in Paris. Tracing internal evidence in *Ulysses*, Anderson concludes that "Joyce includes references to every chapter" (24) of Freud's *Psychopathology of Everyday Life* in "Lestrygonians." Ellmann reports that Joyce knew and read Freud but believes Joyce's disclaimers that he was not interested in, or influenced by, Freud (340n).

When Joyce lived in Trieste, he may have discussed psychoanalysis with his friend Ettore Schmitz, "whose nephew, Dr. Edoardo Weiss, introduced psychoanalysis into Italy in 1910" (Ellmann 340n). Anderson adds that Joyce probably also talked psychoanalysis with Oscar Schwarz in 1914. In his Trieste library, Joyce owned Freud's "Leonardo da Vinci and a Memory of Childhood," Ernest Jones's *Problem of Hamlet and the Oedipus Complex*, and Jung's *Significance of the Father in the Destiny of the Individual*, all in German editions of the 1909 to 1911 period (see Ellmann 340n; Gillespie; Kimball). Kimball also argues that Joyce had specific knowledge of Otto Rank's *Incest Motif in Poetry and Saga* (1912) and that Joyce had read of Freud's Family Romance in Rank's *Myth of the Birth of a Hero* (1909).

Freud's influence on Joyce was deep, but I think it accrued slowly over time, as Joyce adapted Freudian ideas to his own material, symbols, and favorite thinkers such as Vico. "We can now be absolutely certain," Daniel Ferrer writes, that by the time Joyce began writing *Finnegans Wake,* he read, took notes on, and used material from Freud's case studies of "Little Hans" and "The Wolf Man," and other Freud case studies "passed through his hands" (367). In particular, I believe Freud's essay on Leonardo had a more significant influence on *Finnegans Wake* than has heretofore been recognized, and I will return to discuss their relation in chapter 4. I think it is fair to say that while we can no longer blithely accept Joyce's word that Freud did not influence him, we can agree with his disclaimer for his earliest works, *Stephen Hero* (the unfinished draft of *A Portrait*), *Dubliners,* and *A Portrait* itself.

ANALYSIS INTERMINABLE: THE LIMITS OF PORTRAITURE

Both *Dubliners* and *A Portrait of the Artist as a Young Man* came out in 1914, after Lawrence's *Sons and Lovers.* However, they were written over a period that began about six to eight years before Lawrence started to compose his family novel. In 1904 Joyce began writing the short stories that *Dubliners* would comprise, although several were based on epiphanies he had experienced and recorded earlier (see Ellmann 84). At the end of *A Portrait* Joyce gave the dates 1904–14 for its composition, although he probably began work that led to the novel earlier. Theodore Spencer, in his introduction to the unfinished manuscript of *Stephen Hero,* offers the dates 1901–2 for notes and fragments that would become the unfinished first draft. After considering the fact that Sylvia Beach catalogued the manuscript as work from 1903, Spencer argues that Joyce wrote the narrative of the aborted draft between 1904–6 (8–9). "We can think of the manuscript as representing the work of the years 1901–1906," he concludes (9). Joyce scrapped this early draft, compressing the narrative of the university years that it had covered and expanding the scope of his novel to encompass the entire growth of the artist from his earliest memories and perceptions of the world. He continued to revise *A Portrait* until publication in 1914 (Ellmann 350).

Traditionally the canon of Joyce's fiction begins with *Dubliners*. The anonymous boy in the first three stories is often considered a prototype of the young Stephen. Nevertheless, *A Portrait* had its genesis before or at least at the same time as *Dubliners*. It also stands apart from the other three major texts in form. *Dubliners*, *Ulysses*, and *Finnegans Wake* all share structural similarities. They are episodic, ironic, and focus for the most part on male characters. Each ends with a shift to a female focus and then to a dissolving away at the end—Gretta Conroy and the dissolution of personality into the covering of snow in "The Dead," Molly Bloom and the dissolving of consciousness into sleep at the end of *Ulysses*, and A.L.P. and the dissolving of the river into the sea at the end of the *Wake*.

On the other hand, the *Portrait* focuses tightly on the formation of one male personality. It is organized by the principle of human development in ever-widening spheres from the most basic sense perceptions of earliest childhood, through conventional education of mind and body, then to intellectual rebellion that leads to the very opposite of dissolution of personality—the assertion of the isolated individual in self-creation. The single-minded focus of *A Portrait* is even more apparent when it is compared with the draft novel *Stephen Hero*. In the early version, other characters had independent and developed existences apart from Stephen. He seemed more adolescent and vulnerable, less absolute, whereas *A Portrait* progressively and relentlessly obliterates the Other as an obstacle to the expression of the self.

In *A Portrait* "Cranly, Lynch and the rest" become, as Spencer points out, remembered fragments of conversation and diary entries, "items, so to speak, in Stephen's mind" (12).

Sons and Lovers begins before Paul's birth. The narrative tells of the early married life of the Morels from the subjective point of view of Mrs. Morel, whose consciousness is in conflict with her husband's. Thereafter, the children struggle to come into focus, Paul gaining the center of the narrative focus when William dies. Holding the center is a struggle, too, pitting mother against son. Paul only wins his independence when his mother dies, and even then he is merely "one tiny upright speck of flesh" (420). *Sons and Lovers* questions the validity of Family Romance by presenting the conflicting drives of mother and son to write the shape of the future and by delaying or suspending the reproduction of family relations both in their female (marriage) and male (career) forms.

In contrast, *A Portrait* begins with Stephen already at the center of a romance. He is already the hero of a story. He is baby tuckoo, securely positioned at the center of a symmetrical family. Father tells stories and looks at him through a glass. Mother ministers to his body, smells nice, and plays music. Uncle Charles and Dante mirror this balanced world, as do Dante's two brushes.

Stephen has already interpreted patterns of binary structure, gender differences, and family structure. Father controls the specular eye (I) and narrative; mother, feeling and sound, as MacCabe points out ("An Introduction to *Finnegans Wake*" 31). Stephen has already passed through the Oedipal moment and organizes the future by projecting the structural rules of similarity and variation he has mastered. When he grows up he is going to marry Eileen Vance, who has a different father and mother.

A Portrait begins with the personality consolidated and organized by and in a field. It presents a view of the formation and perception of the human subject remarkably similar to Gestalt theory proposed by Wertheimer in 1912. According to Gestalt theory, the organization necessary for and constituent of perception originates in the human mind, not in the world of experience (though the reality of experience is not doubted). Although the theory is a type of idealism, Gestalt theorists believe that the structure and function of the physical brain underlie mental organization, and they have conducted scientific research to support this view. So it is often called an objective idealism. According to Gestalt theory, perceived symmetry means there is a functional interrelation of the underlying process. During primary organization, the mind learns processes and relations that the mind then uses to organize experience. In perception, Gestalt psychology maintains, the mind actually perceives relationships, and in memory recalls by means of the underlying relations rather than by classic associationist principles of mere contiguity.

Stephen organizes his perceptions in a developmental progression of complexity according to the structure and symmetry he perceives in the world of experience. In the earliest stage, he perceives the interrelationship of Irish political and religious issues by a concrete image from his family life. "Dante had two brushes in her press. The brush with the maroon velvet back was for Michael Davitt and the brush with the green velvet back was for Parnell" (7).

The neat divisions the very young Stephen makes, however, break down. Home from school, participating in his first grownup Christmas, the house decorated in "holly and ivy, green and red, twined round the chandeliers" (20), Stephen watches as the men and women at the Christmas table argue politics and religion. The simple division between maroon brush and green brush becomes confused. He understands that the women, mother and Dante, side with the church; the men with the politicians. The women are also patriots, though, championing the anticlerical Michael Davitt's genuine land reform even as they excoriate Parnell's personal sinfulness. Women are associated with land, the peasants, and the church, the gentle moral concern of Mrs. Dedalus, as well as the rigid piety of Irish peasants. Dante defends the priests whose sermons betray reform. As for the

men, they may side with Parnell the betrayed and represent the
political world, but their rhetoric, so much hot air, often supports
the claims of nationalism as well as unpredictably shifting to
betray it in excessive sentimentality and drunkenness. If the
maroon brush stands for the genuine land reform movement of
Michael Davitt, red is also the color of Catholic cardinals and so
recalls the rigid piety of Irish peasants, women, and priests—a
piety that when applied to Irish politics often betrays land reform. If the green brush stands for Parnell the martyred re-
former, green is also associated with the Irish state, political
betrayal, and Mr. Dedalus, whose rhetoric gives life but also leads
to insolvency, drunkenness, and violence, betraying the family.

Stephen organizes his world through unified concrete images that are a kind of shorthand for the underlying relations
he perceives. As a very young child, he is not yet aware of all
the elements in the conflicts contained in the concrete image of
the two brushes, but as he grows, his grasp of the complexities
expands according to the perceptual system he has mastered as
a child. There is no sense in *A Portrait* that Stephen arbitrarily
projects meaning upon the world he is born into. In fact, he
uses concrete images such as the two brushes to learn about the
coincident similarity of unrelated phenomena. When his school-
mate Fleming colors the picture on the first page of his geography
book in green and maroon, Stephen relates the color scheme to
his own system and yet also understands that Fleming's choice
is arbitrary and unrelated to Dante's two brushes (*P* 15). Stephen
compares the systems in his world—family, school, religion, politics—and seeks correspondences to test whether their similarities
are essential or arbitrary. At Christmas dinner, he wonders to
himself "Why did Mr Barrett in Clongowes call his pandybat a
turkey?" (*P* 30).

According to Gestalt psychology, the symmetry of our perceptions is matched by a symmetry of underlying relations. When
a human hears a series of discrete musical tones or reads a series
of words or sees a series of events, he or she actually perceives
the underlying connections, although it appears that only the

disconnected fragments are available to experience. I do not wish to make either Joyce or Stephen into a Gestalt psychologist. Nor, as far as I can discover, did Joyce ever read any specific text associated with this psychology.[3] What I want to stress are the affinities to Neo-Kantian, empirical, and positivist philosophies and to structuralism in *A Portrait of the Artist as a Young Man*. When Stephen retailors Thomas Aquinas for his romantic, aestheticist theory of art, his theory is really a theory of perception, indeed, a Gestalt theory.

Stephen redirects the question of beauty from the old categories of the external and unchanging to the mind of the perceiver. Rejecting Plato (*P* 208), he turns to the psychology of Aristotle for the concept of the continuity of the perceiving subject:

Aristotle's entire system of philosophy rests upon his book of psychology and that, I think, rests on his statement that the same attribute cannot at the same time and in the same connection belong to and not belong to the same subject. The first step in the direction of the beauty is to understand the frame and scope of the imagination, to comprehend the act itself of esthetic apprehension. (*P* 208)

According to Aquinas, Stephen argues, wholeness, harmony, and radiance are necessary for beauty. Stephen then proceeds to locate each of these qualities in the mind of the perceiver. Like Gestalt theorists, he argues that "the first phase of apprehension" (*P* 212) is to perceive an image as "selfbounded and selfcontained" (*P* 212), to perceive wholeness. Next, "you feel the rhythm of its structure" (*P* 212). Last, "you see that it is that thing which it is and no other" (*P* 213); that is, you recognize "the *whatness* of a thing" (*P* 213).

Gestaltists argue against the view that experience is made up of individual sensation units, a stream of undifferentiated and fragmented sense perceptions.[4] Rather humans perceive unified whole objects, through structural relations (not as individual sense perceptions). What we perceive retains such a measure of constancy that the phenomenal fact (the whole, unified shape) supercedes other conflicting evidence. That is, we always experience phenomena as concrete unities first, as in experiments with figure and ground patterns where humans will always see a unique grouping first.

A *Portrait* similarly points to the primacy of the concrete image and primary rules of organization in the shaping of the individual and even his perception. That is, received culture and its systems (the phenomenal facts) supercede nature. Stephen cannot encounter "nature" or "reality" directly. For Stephen, development is a struggle to understand the categories and structures in which he is already enmeshed and then to free himself from them by understanding their internal relations and then moving beyond.[5] He fixes on concrete images that call up the structuring institutions: particular words, taxonomies, riddles, songs. "Words which he did not understand he said over and over to himself till he had learned them by heart: and through them he had glimpses of the real world about him" (*P* 62). As he gets older, he organizes his understanding by recalling literature, history, and the dogma and rituals of the Catholic church. For example, when Stephen experiments with sexuality, he perceives his own actions *from* the perspective of Catholic doctrine. He "wanders" from the moral path; he "revolts" as Satan did. When he "sins" sexually, he sees other deadly sins—gluttony, sloth, pride, despair (see *P* chap. 3)—rising up in himself, just as Medieval theologians taught. Rebelling from his religion, then, is no simple task of merely walking away from its control, since religion structures his thought so completely and pervasively. Instead he must penetrate its core, nearly becoming a priest before he can free himself from the priesthood—if he ever can be free of it.

In Lawrence's portrait of the young artist growing up, the struggle toward selfhood is a struggle with an Other, and that other is generally of the other sex (Mrs. Morel vs. Mr. Morel, Paul vs. Mrs. Morel, Paul vs. Miriam, and so on). The individual arises from the conflict between self and other and from the conflict of gender division. To lapse out of conscious selfhood, however, is to encounter reality, "real living" (*Sons and Lovers* 158), which is direct knowledge of the material substrate of the body. Lawrentian characters can experience this "unconscious" state directly in creativity and in sexuality, usually accompanied by another (although characters can also "melt" into nature alone).

For Stephen, on the other hand, any direct encounter with reality is solitary and elusive. Reality is mediated by the conceptual relations of institutions, internalized in the mind of the perceiver. At the end of *A Portrait* Stephen goes to encounter reality for "the millionth time" (253), suggesting that searching for reality is a never-ending, never attainable task. He is alone and in exile because he must position himself outside the field in order to gain any critical perspective on it, since the field itself organizes perception.

It is a commonplace in current Joyce criticism to claim that Joyce is interested in language as production rather than as expression, and that his "real" subject is writing (see *Post-structuralist Joyce*). Some readers believe that *A Portrait* presents language as the primary means of organizing experience and perception. The novel begins with a story and a lyric. Stephen fixes upon words throughout as upon mysterious objects, exploring whether they convey color or sound or emotion. On the other hand, the beginning also includes primary feeling ("When you wet the bed first it is warm then it gets cold" 7) and rhythmic sound ("Tralala lala" 7) that is not language.

I think it is more accurate to say that at first Stephen finds strength and shelter in the power of the mind: "He felt small and weak. When would he be like the fellows in poetry and rhetoric? They had big voices and big boots and they studied trigonometry" (*P* 17). Certainly irony is intended in the parallel structure and yoking of voice, boots, and the study of trigonometry. As Stephen grows up, he finds just as often that the mind provides only an illusion of power.

He is frequently deceived by language. For example, he is initially deceived by similarities between words that he later discovers have disparate meanings, such as his musings on "turkey." He admires Eileen Vance, and he is attracted by the sensual feel of the touch of her hand and the sight of her streaming hair. He organizes this new feeling in terms of a system he knows, relating Eileen to the words of the litany of the Blessed Virgin (35). *"Tower of Ivory. House of Gold.* By thinking of things you could understand them" (*P* 43). But again Stephen's understanding surely is meant to be ironic because he does not at that moment understand the nature of his own attraction to Eileen or how his adolescent sexual yearning differs from the church's Mariology. Another level of irony, of course, turns back on church doctrine, since the imagery of the litany for the Blessed Virgin originates in "The Song of Solomon" (7:4).

Irony is further compounded by the fact that Stephen associates Eileen Vance with Parnell. Dante disapproved of his friendship with Eileen, just as she disapproved of Parnell because both were Protestants. Dante tells Stephen that when she was a child, Protestant children made fun of the litany. Stephen might also associate the terms with Parnell's mistress, repressing any awareness of the passion in the words of the litany and of the sexual nature of Parnell's misdeed. When Parnell fell, Stephen heard "the moan of sorrow from the people" (35). When Stephen declares that "by thinking of things you understand them," what actually is apparent are all the connections to the words that he represses or does not yet understand.

A Portrait does not privilege language over other mental powers, although Stephen surely is partial to language. Rather the novel shows the young man organizing and understanding experience by constructing mental relationships. He finds that his mental ability does not give him power and control but an ironic, negative, and dialectical capability. For Stephen's increasing mental progress through and beyond the formative structures of his society cancels out his former certainties. Irony accrues indirectly and retrospectively, since he must move through and beyond a system to criticize it.[6] The paradoxical result is that as he develops, he moves from a unified personality to a subject increasingly stripped bare of certainties, even as he arrogantly asserts his autonomy.

Finally, *A Portrait* questions the very notion of continuous self-identity. As Stephen and Cranly are talking, Cranly asks him if he were not happier when he believed in religion. "Often happy, Stephen said, and often unhappy. I was someone else then" (*P* 240). Cranly asks him what he means. "I mean, said Stephen, that I was not myself as I am now, as I had to become" (*P* 240). Here, Stephen moves beyond even his aesthetic theory, which he had predicated on a continuous perceiver. The final portrait of the individual presented here is a claim for a self-discontinuous determined formation ("as I had to become"), not an eternal soul with free will, but a changing individual shaped by psychological and physical circumstances. He seeks freedom by exile from external determining structures: "To discover the mode of life or of art whereby your spirit could express itself in unfettered freedom" (*P* 246).

Stephen's proclamation of discontinuity is an expression of his desire for freedom from the formative and imprisoning structures of family, church, and state. Stephen's desire cannot be taken as a condition of the "real," however, since the entire novel has repudiated the real as directly approachable. Instead discontinuity is an hypothesis, "the mode . . . whereby your spirit *could* . . ."

The desire to fly off to freedom and to be one's own uncreated creator is a male form of the Family Romance. The dream of flying, Freud says in "Symbolism in Dreams," is a male erection dream. As rightful inheritor of patriarchal structure, Stephen invokes its power ("Old father, old artificer" *P* 253) to see him through the creation of a new, better, improved human story. Stephen's version of the romance is not an achievement of marriage or material success but a spiritual improvement. His is a spiritual quest.

If we were to translate the psychic Family Romance into economic terms and ignore Stephen's exaltation of art, we might see that he is embarking on the male version of improvement through a "career." (I realize I am taking some liberty here in comparing Stephen's artistic vocation to a career, but the point is to pierce his pretensions, recognizing his flight as a form of class mobility.) Indeed, a flight into exile was the typical and expected pattern for young Irish men. The economic outlook was so bleak in Ireland that continual emigration reduced the country's population from 8.3 million in 1845 to 4 million in 1905. Of course, Stephen goes to Paris not to Boston (as Joyce's brother did for a time), and he does not flee to seek work or money. He seeks a space, a perspective outside, from which to write.

Stephen's compressed and elliptic diary entries at the end of the novel repress the practical reasons for leaving and the actual conditions he flees. In his entries of 20 March, 24 March, and 6 April he muses on parents, and especially, mothers and their children, revealing his own close relationship with his mother. His brief imagined portrait of Cranly's parents in the 20 March entry and the figure of the old man from the west of Ireland of the 14 April entry both harbor in their descriptions something of the poverty and insularity of the Irish people that Stephen fears. He fears the emotional connections, poverty, and parochial thinking that, if he stays, threaten to drag him down or co-opt his independence and creativity. From a psychological point of view, his flight from material conditions of Ireland, from women and families, from emotional bonds and affiliation can be seen as an expression of male castration fear.

Traditionally, women represent body, flesh, and matter. Stephen, organized by, and in, traditional family structure, associates his mother with feeling and touch. Stephen does not criticize family structure, gender stereotypes, and patriarchy. He inherits and refracts them, bending these systems to his own ends. He toys with the image of the Irish peasant woman, for example, which he puts together from Davin's story (182), from the received misogyny of his culture and religion, and from the Celtic twilight mysticism of Yeatsian nationalism that he, in fact, distrusts. The peasant woman is a symbolic accretion that he has made from found systems, with the added special twist of his own sexual desires: "a type of her race and his own, a batlike soul waking to the consciousness of itself in darkness and secrecy and loneliness and, through the eyes and voice and gesture of a woman without guile, calling the stranger to her bed" (*P* 183).

The novel as a whole does not repress physical sensations of the material world or the female. It gives the reader the cold, sour smell of the ditch and the feel of the pandy bat on small knuckles. The novel contains the decline of Mrs. Dedalus from constant childbearing, from poverty, and from the ill treatment of her husband. However, the book embeds the female within the male narrative and point of view and "codes 'the other' by means of sexual difference," as Christine van Boheemen notes (42). Women are presented through the controlling structures of patriarchy in which the female is feared as castrated and castrator. To see woman as matter, Gea the earth mother,[7] and man as spirit is to deny that man also is matter, to deny he is also castrated, since he is born and must die. Metaphors drawn from gender stereotypes (woman/matter, man/spirit) of patriarchy may express the male's psychological defense against death.

The story of Stephen's growth to individuality is a male narrative, unlike Paul Morel's, whose story is somewhat "like a woman speaking" because of Paul's deep empathy with his mother, and because he grows to manhood in a conflicted relation to patriarchy and to his own gender as a woman does to hers. *Sons and Lovers* ends with Paul facing the reality of his mother's death, diminished to a speck under the vast, lonely universe. At the end of *A Portrait* Stephen has not yet faced death, loss, and failure. Although he may see failure in his countrymen around him, he is still arrogant and detached. Nothing touches him. He is Icarus before his fall to the sea. In his next-to-last diary entry, he relates that his mother prays "that I may learn in my own life and away from home and friends what the heart is and what it feels" (*P* 252), a lesson associated with the female in the gender-divided world of the book.

To say that *A Portrait of the Artist as a Young Man* describes the formation of a male personality under patriarchy is not necessarily to argue that Joyce participates in misogyny or values ste-

reotypical gender roles and male domination. These are important issues, but there are two problems with abstracting Joyce's
attitudes directly from his fiction.[8] First, *A Portrait* presents a
process of individualization in which the subject organizes a unified self starting from the structures around him. Then, by constant displacement and exchange of systems through growth,
experience, and education, the individual becomes progressively
destabilized and discontinuous. This view of human personality
makes a theory of expressionism difficult, because, as Stephen
says to Cranly, "I was not myself as I am now."

Second, there is the problem in Joyce's work of pinning
down a critical position. This problem is related to the structural
view of personality, where the subject is everywhere and arises
from his or her position and function within a system, but strictly
speaking is also nowhere except as an internal relation of a
structure.

The apparent lack of a critical perspective in Joyce's work
has been noted by many critics. Georg Lukács's attack is the most
famous and sets the terms of the debate. Lukács argues in *Realism
in Our Time* that *Ulysses* privileges the private, subjective moment
and thereby ignores the objective social interactions of reality
(26). A stream of sense perceptions, as in *Ulysses*, cannot convey
a "hierarchy of significance" (34) and thus there is no critical
perspective necessary for historicity.

Lukács's criticism somewhat obscures the positivist and empirical thrust of *A Portrait, Dubliners,* and even large parts of
Ulysses itself. In fact, I believe these texts reveal the author's desire
to render an objective truth presented through a succession of
character "types." Joyce embeds "reality"—defined as the structure of relations that shape individuals, and then asks the reader
to find and decode these relations. Pound recognized this element in Joyce's writing when he first read it. Pound praised the
empirical qualities he was to champion all his life. Joyce's writing,
he declared, has a "freedom from sloppiness." It is a "clear, hard
prose." Joyce "does not sentimentalize." Above all, Pound praised

the "rigorous selection of the presented detail" (*JJ: The Critical Heritage* 66–68).

It is true, though, as Lukács declares, that Joyce's work does not present a single hierarchy of significance in which a reader can discover a fixed context for judgment. Despite the concretely rendered social relations, Stephen flees the physical world, perceiving social relations as effects of institutional structures and systems of thought. No system (such as socialism, for example, as Lukács desires) is given a privileged critical edge. Stephen juxtaposes each formative system with the next, not choosing between them, but rather casting off each in a continual act of freeing the self from all limiting structures.

Stephen's aesthetic is structural and psychological. He values art as a self-contained structure, disconnected from the material concerns of everyday life. Rather than Lynch's pragmatism, Stephen values a static art that allows intellectual contemplation of the relations of truth and the aesthetic contemplation of the relations of beauty (*P* 208–9). His personal relationships with people are presented structurally also. That is, others are only relevant to him in terms of their position and function within systems he is trying to learn. No other character threatens to take over the narrative focus, as Mrs. Morel does in *Sons and Lovers*.

Stephen's relationship to his father demonstrates both the structurality of the father character and how interest in structures can also be a psychological defense. When Stephen goes on the trip to Cork with his father, both Simon Dedalus' symbolic position as father (as begetter, namer, and one to be replaced in generation) and his personal failure as father are apparent. Simon is a braggart and a drunk. They go to Cork to sell the family inheritance. At this important juncture in a young boy's life, Stephen withdraws from personal fellowship with his father. He is "without sympathy"; he "heard but could feel no pity" (*P* 87). In fact, at the same time that Stephen so clearly sees a lack, an incapacity, in his father, he begins to understand the symbolic relations of fatherhood as well. He also begins his initiation into the male fellowship of sexual bragging. Mr. Dedalus and his cronies make frequent jokes about Simon's sexual capacity and compare Stephen with his father. Stephen is shocked by the real and physical dimension of generation. He registers shock when he sees "foetus" carved on a desk because the word reveals the same sexual instincts, which he secretly harbors, in his father's generation of schoolboys.

Clearly, Stephen distances himself from personal emotion to defend against the increasing and real impoverishment of his life. So he prefers to "see" the typical and symbolic in father figures rather than the real, desperate father he has, whom he emotionally shuts off. Of course, all children normally go through a stage of denying or feeling very uneasy about their parents' sexuality. During adolescence, they often are emotionally distant with their parents. Thus Stephen's retreat from real family relations to the world of symbol is also a realistic psychological portrait. The novel insists on both.

In *Sons and Lovers*, Paul found "reality" hidden underneath the daily life of the individual in culture. Paul calls the melting away of consciousness in creativity or sexuality, "real living." He experiences this and is renewed by it. In contrast, Stephen has a problem with reality. He can never get to it directly or easily. Sometimes words give him "glimpses of the real world about him" (62). More often, they get in the way, and he can "call forth" "only names" (*P* 93). He views his secret, sexual urges as "monstrous" and "beyond the limits of reality" (*P* 92). He is always trying to "encounter" reality, but when he sees "foetus" carved in a desk, "it shocked him to find in the outer world a trace of what he had deemed till then a brutish and individual malady of his own mind" (*P* 90).

His difficulty making contact with, or finding, reality lasts through the end of the novel. So part of Stephen's quest is a search for the real. He declares that he goes to encounter reality. However, the end leaves the reader with the question of whether or not the novel endorses Stephen's notion of "the real," the spiritual male quest to forge the uncreated conscience of his race, or whether we are meant to read the end ironically. An ironic reading suggests that "the real" is that which Stephen excludes, the subordinated female elements of body, sound, touch, materiality. A third possibility might also be that the unstable irony of *A Portrait* extends beyond even this sexual division, implying that "the real" might be something beyond these old categories of sexual division and mind/body duality.

The Lawrentian experience of the unconscious cannot be characterized as either male or female, because it occurs before or below the level of gender difference. Lawrence more frequently associates characteristics of the father with nature and those of the mother with culture. Hence, while the Lawrentian experience of the unconscious resembles what we traditionally associate with female qualities (pre-Oedipal loss of boundaries, for example), it distorts Lawrence's work to call his unconscious "female."

Stephen's world is overly mental. Although he eventually experiments sexually with prostitutes, he thinks of his sexual awakening first as a "malady of his own mind." Everything in the novel appears through Stephen's perception, no matter how simple the organizing principle is at first (as in Dante's two brushes). The view of the individual as composed entirely of conscious mind reflects the traditional notion of *cogito*. It also reflects the child's desire for mastery. "I am afraid of strange feelings and loud sounds," the child might reason, "but they are only in my mind. They are not real." The child believes that when she grows up, she will have full mastery over them because she will be fully in possession of herself.

A Portrait of the Artist as A Young Man shows a Family Romance constructed from the point of view of a young, immature man who rejects the body, materiality, the female and seeks mastery in an isolated spiritual quest for the real. Equating Ireland to an old woman, he also rejects the social and political problems of his homeland when he flees.

However, because of the unstable irony caused by the continual displacement of ordering systems, this "portrait" also contains its negation. It is a kind of "doriangrayer" (*FW* 186.8) portrait, itself and its shadow. This ironic structure suggests that behind the veil of the conscious world lies the shadow world of the unconscious.

Although the hidden forces of the unconscious have no concrete representation in *A Portrait*, we can reconstruct Stephen's repressions through the self-contradictions revealed in "the rigorous selection of presented detail," to use Pound's phrase. For example, standing outside the library Stephen catches a glimpse of E. C. and begins freely musing on his attraction to her. As his thoughts become more frankly physical, his attention shifts to a louse biting his neck (233–34). The "tickling of the skin of his neck made his mind raw and red" (234). We see Stephen censoring his fantasy, then admitting that physical reality (the lice) affects mental categories. Just as quickly he changes the direction of this thought, once more reestablishing the primacy of the mental. Immediately reversing his thinking, he concludes, "his mind bred vermin" (234). Struggling to free himself from the paralytic web of imprisoning cultural structures, Stephen tries to repress all contradictions that might reveal the fragility of his mental mastery. Ironically, in the very process he shows how thoroughly his thinking has been conditioned by his culture, as he equates sexual thoughts to "vermin."

Stephen rejects the path of the other young students, to stay and try to change Ireland. He perceives that staying will mean getting dragged into the systems of paralysis. Changing Irish society will require changing the ways its dominant institutions (the Catholic church, English rulers, and Irish nationalists) shape thinking. These institutions breed petty jealousy, internecine squabbling, passivity, ineffectual romanticism, and narrow and mean-spirited parochialism. What often occurs is not true change but merely an exchange of one master for another, for example, casting off English imperialism for the new tyranny of Irish nationalism.

The novel presents Stephen's first shadowy musings on this paradox. Stephen associates nationalism with incest. This analogy suggests that he thinks of nationalism as a misdirected passion, desire turned inward. The analogy also discloses how he will rationalize his own flight; exile becomes associated with desire turned outward in exogamy. Coming out of the library into a gray, misty light, Stephen thinks of a Yeatsian scene, "wet silent tree" (228), swans. His mental image of a brother and sister incestuously embracing turns into an image of Davin, the Irish nationalist. No nationalist himself, Stephen asserts his right of individuality. He will not try to save Ireland, but Ireland will become famous because of him. Even though this is a narcissistic assertion, he cunningly frames his flight (against the backdrop of the incest associations) as though it were a "healthy," heterosexual movement outward.

Stephen desires change, yet rejects political engagement or a politically engaged art. Valuing the contemplative in art, he sees his flight as an heroic act. If his desires and actions are not entirely contradictory, they at least suggest immaturity. Yet the novel's shadow world of ironic negation suggests another, different portrait of the self.

In this shadow portrait, unconscious mental processes constantly threaten self-mastery, but flight is not a running away from the female, the body, and Ireland. Indeed, flight may instead signal the continual transformation and freedom from limits necessary for creative change. Free circulation, theme and style in Joyce texts from *Ulysses* onward, may be a positive alternative to merely sterile exchanging of one worn out category for another.

Dubliners, written nearly at the same point in Joyce's life as *A Portrait,* presents a picture of social paralysis similar to that in *A Portrait.* The same movement of negative dialectic informs its series of stories, and there is the same problem of interpreting its unstable irony. Kenneth Burke calls this dialectical form "the narrative equivalent of a Platonic dialogue" (Scholes and Litz 413), noting that a character like Gabriel Conroy progresses through a series of disclosures that reverse his expectations but never reaches the essence he seeks.

The family relations portrayed in *Dubliners* are bleak and, Florence Walzl argues, render a "typical," "comprehensive" and accurate picture of Irish life of 1904 ("*Dubliners*: Women in Irish Society" 31). Men prey upon women, mothers upon their children; men are weak and violent, women weak and domineering. Although the book is made up of separate short stories, with a few told from the point of view of a central female character, Walzl argues that the whole "results in a prevailingly masculine viewpoint" (53). Even the sympathetic female characters are presented from within an encoded system of sex role stereotypes and are types more than individual characters. For example, Maria in "Clay" is presented from within the convention of the good-hearted Irish spinster. She is physically plain, emotionally simple and good-hearted. She works hard in a laundry, proud of her small accomplishments and her meager independence. She raised her charges, is known as the peacemaker, and is thankful for any crumbs of love and friendship the Donnelly family offers. Her interiority remains opaque, however. She is a narrative instrument. In her pathetic, sweet eagerness to be a part of the Donnelly family, she reveals the hollowness within conventional family relations—male violence and drunkenness, family feuding, mawkish nostalgia, and the dismal prospects for women in Ireland.

Just how far "The Dead," the last story in *Dubliners*, challenges the predominant vision of controlling male consciousness and spiritual paralysis has been widely disputed. The essays included in the Scholes and Litz critical edition of the book give a representative sample of readings of "The Dead." Florence Walzl surveys the differences in interpretation, noting that when the story is read as the conclusion to the series of Dublin stories, readers tend to consider Gabriel's epiphany as "a recognition that he is a dead member of a dead society" (424). "But when 'The Dead' is read as short story unrelated to *Dubliners*, the effect is different: the story seems one of spiritual development and the final vision a redemption" (424). Walzl reviews the composition history and arrangement of the first 14 stories of *Dubliners* in 1906

("The Dead" was written later in 1907), analyzes their thematic interconnections and symmetry, and concludes that the final story utilizes "a pattern of ambivalent symbols" to embody "a great final ambiguity" (443). Gabriel's vision is a renunciation of self-preoccupation, marked by selfish attitudes of ownership and possession, signaling his great love for his wife, final transcendence of self, and love for all humanity. Gabriel's final illumination is also that he is dead in that he wants to be covered up and dissolve away. Like "the snow that covers all Ireland," Gabriel "images the deadly inertia of the nation" (442). The portrait of Gabriel is, like Stephen's at the end of *A Portrait,* "doriangrayer."

In one respect *Dubliners* differs from *A Portrait;* it is not a romance (or a shadow antiromance). Its form is episodic, and its focus is transindividual. The stories do not portray the reality of one individual personality but render a medley of types and a network of interrelationships within a community. Irony is more direct and apparent, less dialectical than in *A Portrait* (perhaps with the exception of "The Dead"). *Ulysses* begins from both starting points, displaying the unfolding negative dialectical movement of *A Portrait* and the episodic, transindividual structure of *Dubliners.*

CIRCULATION AND DESIRE IN *ULYSSES*

Joyce began *Ulysses* in Trieste sometime in 1914. By June 30, 1915, he had written the first two episodes (Ellmann 779n16). Joyce wrote the bulk of the book in Zurich, where he found a safe haven from the war, completing "Circe" and the last three episodes after his move to Paris in 1920 (Ellmann 486). Like *The Rainbow* and *Women in Love,* Joyce's novel seemingly ignores the Great War raging outside its pages. Like Lawrence's novels, *Ulysses* focuses on the "private" concerns of its characters, especially extending and challenging the conventions of how a family can be portrayed in fiction.

While the families in *Ulysses* take conventional outward forms, both families we see close up suffer. Stephen's family has been wracked by increasing poverty and degradation and demoralized further by the recent death of Stephen's mother. His young sisters struggle to stay together, even to have enough to eat, evoking a deep pathos. Stephen, arrogant, isolated, and troubled by his mother's ghost, remains aloof. The Blooms harbor secret grief and a secret, unusual marital arrangement. For the last ten years, five months and eighteen days (*U* 17.2282), since their eleven-day-old son Rudy died, the Blooms have not had conventional sexual relations.

The novel presents the inside of families, private peculiarities underneath conventional form, portraying interior experience at the perceptual level. The focus is on the moment when the mind shapes conscious thought and when repression (faint traces from "that other world," as Martha Clifford, Bloom's correspondent, says in a slip of the pen *U* 5.245) may be glimpsed. The particular moment the novel focuses on is neither psychic nor emotional but between the two. *Sons and Lovers* renders psychic relations before or beyond language and culture, and it portrays the emotional bonds of conscious, everyday life—the two levels of experience producing conflict. But *Ulysses* renders a single reality, albeit one still composed of repressed conflicts, remembered sweetness, failed desires, and faint traces of hidden, unconscious life.

The plot develops around the inner conflicts and failures of the characters in their family relations. Stephen mourns his mother, mulling over the conflicts among love and thought and action that make him feel guilty at her death. Leopold tries to repress any awareness of Molly's adultery and may repress consciousness of his own failure as a husband. The book does not include a happy ending with the righting of inner psychology or external action. Externally, the conventional family remains at the end; internally, the end suggests that desire arises each day, is partly satisfied, and partly frustrated each day too.

The form, plot, and subject matter disrupt the conventions of Family Romance. Christine van Boheemen's *Novel as Family Romance* provides a useful summary of recent literary theories that conceptualize the novel's form through psychology. She calls *Ulysses* a "deconstruction of the family romance" (171) not only because it presents a portrait of a family in disarray but also because of its movement by displacement and its episodic structure.

According to van Boheemen, belief in the novel functions like a fetish if it "attributes to the image reflected in the medium a deeper truth, a brighter vitality, and a greater intensity than to reality itself" (20). She notes that Lawrence's insistence on the importance of the novel ("Why the Novel Matters") shows that the novel may also function like a "transitional object," those security blankets that help us adjust to the absence of the mother (20). Lawrence, like Lukács, values the novel because it totalizes experience. But van Boheemen reminds us that the novel's unity may well be a projection of human desire for "a transcendent design of the self" (22) rather than a reflection of any reality. The novel serves the function of the Family Romance, she concludes, manifesting the child's desire to replace his real family by imagining a better or nobler one.

A closely related form of prose fiction prizes real above ideal relations and does not seek to represent more perfect family relations or to totalize experience. We might think of this other kind of writing as a family antiromance, a writing bound up with the relations of family, but one that does not insist on establishing a new set of "ideal" relations. The psychological analogy above suggests that a family antiromance is connected to the pre-Oedipal relation to the mother.

Imagine that the child chooses not to separate from the mother by adopting a transitional object (in our case the form of the novel). Then the child stays attached to the mother, writes the mother. And the antiromance displays the qualities of the pre-Oedipal stage of existence: narcissism, fragmentation, dissolving of boundaries, and so on.

Rejecting the Family Romance also means rejecting the point of view and values of patriarchy that Freud claimed in *Beyond the Pleasure Principle* had to be accepted if humans were to face reality. These are gender differences, the organization and sub-ordination of drives to heterosexuality and reproduction and especially the absolute value of reproductive sexuality. Many contemporary critics consider Joyce's texts as examples of a kind of writing that rejects these values. They argue that Joyce's texts write the desire of the mother, or female desire, or perhaps are examples of bisexual writing (Cixous; Kristeva; MacCabe), or as David Hayman claims in *The Wake in Transit,* Joyce increasingly portrays "female consciousness" (156).

Not all readers sensitive to psychostructural issues agree that *Ulysses* presents an alternative to phallic dominance in its vision and form. While Colin MacCabe suggests that in "Penelope" Molly slays the fetish of the penis (*JJ and the Revolution of the Word* 125–26), Stephen Heath argues that any feminine alternative she might represent comes from the male point of view, "a perverse assumption of the imaginary of the woman" ("Joyce in Language" 137). Christine van Boheemen disagrees with MacCabe too, not-ing that Molly's position (at home, in bed, and in the last position in a series) renders her "an emblem of original presence" (178), a mythic female Other that "invertedly continu[es] the practice of Western metaphysics" (179). She concludes that *Ulysses'* episodic displacement through stylistic parody does not really constitute a new form that replaces the old conventions of the novel. *Ulysses* depends upon and reaffirms the psychic themes of the Family Romance, van Boheemen argues, because the last chapter pro-jects an "original totality" (186) that is a "be-all and end-all in the structure of Joyce's argument" (186).

As a form of literary production, the novel has a shape that reflects economic forces and ideologies as well as psychological ones. In discussing *Sons and Lovers,* I claimed that the notion of Family Romance transfers to the familial sphere the capitalist drive to continually maximize profits. The child's fantasy of a nobler family is a version of the young adult's pressure to marry upward and to improve his economic position through hard work.

Lawrence's novels redirect interest from class conflict to sexual conflict, but they preserve an implicit ambivalence to capitalism. On the one hand, the values of capitalism alienate individuals from each other, from their creative labor, and from the natural landscape (as seen in the alienation and bourgeois striving of Mrs. Morel, for example). The forces of mass production and mass labor turn people into machines (Uncle Tom and Winifred). Lawrence despairs over the decadence that emerges from capitalism's free-floating values cut off from their roots in a legitimate, living community (as the decadent artist Loerke represents). Yet Lawrence's interest in reforming consciousness and changing values also coincides with capitalism's drive to break up the old in a constant effort to create new products and new markets. Oddly, the destructive, disintegrative drive of capitalism may be an unacknowledged element of its progressive capability. Lawrence is caught up in this contradictory web of advanced capitalism, both celebrating the creative possibility that comes out of destruction and dissolution (as at the end of *The Rainbow*) and lamenting the lost connections that once bound people to their culture.

Certainly, Lawrence's *Women in Love* shares many of the same "feminine" traits as *Ulysses,* just as its plot explicitly rejects patriarchal values. *Sons and Lovers,* too, is an antiromantic text. Lawrence's fiction after *Women in Love* may suggest that Lawrence gives up his progressive search for new forms of relationship and returns to the forms of the past. In any case, he sticks with the novel and returns to its purest romance mode in his late writing. In *Lady Chatterley's Lover* he retreats to a simple version of the Family Romance dream and to traditional gender stereotypes, whose sufficiency and complexity his earlier work had challenged.[9]

Ulysses also renders the destabilizing force of advanced capitalism, but Joyce's attitude is entirely different from Lawrence's. Joyce celebrates the laughter and the brief moments of freedom that emerge from the gap that opens up in the wake of the destruction of old systems. He applauds change, his formal technique itself becoming the circulation of a nexus of images. *Metem-*

psychosis is both theme and style—recirculation—from Vico Road, Dalkey, to the windy newspaper rooms where the text mockishly replies to Bloom's talk of the Savior, "But, will he save the circulation?" (*U* 7.71).

Lukács argued that the lack of a critical perspective in modernism arose from disbelief in the possibility of socialism. Readers may disagree with the political slant of Lukács's analysis but agree with his appraisal. Form and style in *Ulysses* do match the situation of advanced capitalism—the constant disruption and displacement of the old with the new, the consequent unmaking (and remaking) of the individual, and the freeing of desire from any fixed object. But whereas Lukács would say the novel is a reflection or symptom of these economic forces, I would argue that Joyce employs them consciously for his own ends—for the freeing of desire from restraints.

Joyce mimics the disruptive forces of capitalism, to deconstruct belief in monolithic institutions (for instance, the church) and to mock social conventions (the Victorian paterfamilias, for example). He parodies consumer society, yet enjoys its liberating potential—for instance, in the way advertising brings together disjunct words and images. Lukács's goal is to understand historical forces in order to shape them to "improved" social ends. But Joyce's is to be freed from the nightmare of history by demonstrating that what seems the solid, determined world is actually an overdetermined stream of natural phenomena (sometimes antithetical to humans) and human-made fragments of culture that can be deconstructed and reconstructed in whatever ways humans desire. Joyce thereby celebrates the unleashing of excess desire, for its own sake, and the force of desire is directly opposite to the privileging of social utility.

If readers such as van Boheemen are right, and Molly's monologue enshrines female desire as a new totality that provides the kind of "hierarchy of significance" Lukács seeks, then the book would indeed be a romance. And while romance as a form developed from the same historical forces out of which capitalism arose, the romance form has also served social realists well, with the drive for social improvement replacing the quest for love. *Ulysses*, however, enshrines neither a quest for improvement, nor a quest for love. Bloom and Stephen just try to make it home to bed.

Ulysses shuns utility. It so thoroughly employs forces like those in advanced consumer societies (continual exchange and displacement of sign and value systems) that it enshrines no totality other than circulation and desire themselves. Circulation and desire are forces that drive advanced capitalism, but they also are forces that create all change.

Advanced consumer capitalism retains the family unit, but the function and significance of family has changed. More "families" than ever before include no children, so reproduction is less important as its function. Today two or more family members often work. So if there are children and two parents working, there may be little or no communal life that all family members share. During the workday houses are empty of people, though full of consumer items. Unlike early capitalism, which required exhausting physical labor, modern consumer capitalism is not so dependent on the family as a location for the support and reproduction of the laborer. For many, religion no longer defines the family unit as, for instance, an imitation of the Holy Family. No longer held together by work or worship, the "family" becomes merely the location for, and sentimental stimulus to, consumption. Sexual roles and sexual differences reproduced in modern capitalism reinforce buying habits and thus are flexible attributes created and manipulated to gain markets. In contrast, in a culture dominated by religion, gender difference is viewed as essential, fixed, and prescribed by God.

Ulysses gives us many families, and each is different. Despite the differences among families, all the familial conflicts played out in the book arise from the economic and social reality of an historical era preceding advanced capitalism. So to be more precise, the form of the novel does not *reflect* the economic forces of its setting (Ireland 1904), nor of its composition (Europe 1914–21), but the form *anticipates* the forces of advanced capitalism that were to emerge after World War I. Its formal style anticipates the future, while its content re-creates realistically a day in the past.

Stephen's family is Dickensian, suffering poverty and rootlessness because of the father's profligacy, combined with a tradition of male domination, female submission, and the church directive to reproduce. The Protestant Purefoys seem to have more money, and their constant reproduction does not lead to homelessness but to an imperial line of Purefoys: "Young hopeful will be christened Mortimer Edward after the influential third cousin of Mr Purefoy in the Treasury Remembrancer's office, Dublin Castle" (*U* 14.1333–36). However, in both families sexuality is sublimated to procreation, and women must face constant childbirth.

The Blooms are more modern. Religion no longer directs their family life. They have only one child, though little Rudy would have been very important had he lived. Apparently of the middle class, Bloom supports the family, in a simple frugal style. While there is no conspicuous consumption on Eccles Street, their home does have decorative touches such as the "Bath of Nymphs" above the bed. Their life is perhaps a bit bohemian. Molly's "work" is artistic, with a touch of the music hall world, and irregular. She has not gone on a concert tour for some years before the proposed trip Boylan is organizing. Women were by then well established in the popular theatre, so her occupation does not necessarily represent that of an emancipated woman. Still, Molly's singing career suggests something of the liberated Irish woman of the time. A number of Irish women of higher social standing than Molly were active in the public life of the arts. Lady Gregory, playwright and sustainer of the Abbey Theatre, and Speranza (Oscar Wilde's mother) are two examples, and the Celtic Twilight poet William Sharp even wrote under a woman's name as Fiona Macleod. The outlook for Milly is more mundane, however. Apprenticed to a photographer in Mullingar, she will apparently work and then marry. There is no evidence she will seek education, career, or an autonomous identity apart from eventual marriage.

On the one hand, the book touts change, movement, circulation, exchange of sign systems and values, and the freeing of desire—all attributes of a modern society. And its form embodies those forces. It deconstructs myths of hegemony: the central authority of church and state, English power, male domination. Molly's afternoon liaison with Blazes, and Bloom's acceptance of it, suggest too that the book endorses free sexual circulation "as natural as any and every natural act" (*U* 17.2178), as Bloom thinks in "Ithaca" just before falling asleep.

On the other hand, the families are caught up in varying, earlier historical stages. They reflect the Ireland of 1904, whereas the broader subject and style of the book look ahead to the later twentieth century. Lagging behind the rest of Europe, Joyce's Ireland was still involved in eighteenth- and nineteenth-century historical conflicts resulting from the transition from a religious to a civil society, the migration from the country to the city, the rise of nationalism, and the creation of a large middle class.[10] Joyce was acutely aware of Ireland's parochialism and voiced his intent in a letter to Grant Richards to present "Dublin to the world" (*Letters* II: 122). By his art Joyce wanted to put Ireland on the literary map of the world; he also wanted to show it as it was.

The book's stylistic modernism might seem to conflict with the apparently conventional portrayal of sex roles. Joyce's experimental form reflects the forces of capitalism, but even more anticipates those forces of the future that we now live. The sex roles, on the other hand, are rooted in real historical forces in Ireland at the time and arise from Joyce's realism.

The contradiction between an avant-garde experimental form and the conservative sex role stereotyping can also be explained as the effect of Joyce's private psychology. Molly as totalizing earth mother, for instance, may reflect an earlier cultural moment (the 1904 Irish Catholic secularized), or it may privilege the female as an absolute, above historical conflict, turned into myth. Heath and van Boheemen argue that by raising the female to mythic status Joyce reveals the same old patriarchy, only inverted, that *Ulysses* appears to mock.

A "mythic female" reading, however, underestimates how seriously the book portrays male hegemony (it is ubiquitous) and how powerfully it attacks phallic supremacy. Episode 7, "Aeolus," and episode 12, "Cyclops," especially mock the inflated icon of the phallus. The two episodes are closely related in theme, just as the characters from "Aeolus" wander into Barney Kiernan's tavern in "Cyclops." Admiral Nelson monumentalized by a stone pillar, shrieking newspaper headlines, the drunken attack of the Citizen in the "Cyclops" episode, or the myopic views of its narrator—each of these elements can function as synecdoche for the condition of being "one-eyed," a literal image of the phallus.

The monument to Nelson rises up in "Aeolus," at the center of the city, presiding over the circulation of the Dublin United Tramway Company, of the mail at the general post office, of the brewery, and of the newspaper, *Freeman's Journal*—all circulatory systems that drive the city. At the end of this episode, the tramcars clang to a halt, temporarily paralyzed by a "short circuit" (*U* 7.1047), underscoring the reversal implicit in themes of the chapter. Rhetoric is empty, mere wind; apparent movement is paralysis. Irish institutions, appearing to be engaged in a whirlwind of business, are empty, unchanging, and immovable symbolic structures.

The double entendre headlines emphasize male domination: "HOW A GREAT DAILY ORGAN IS TURNED OUT," "A DAYFATHER," "A MAN OF HIGH MORALE," "FROM THE FATHERS," "SOME COLUMN! THAT'S WHAT WADDLER ONE SAID," "ITHACANS VOW PEN IS CHAMP." But in Stephen's humorous "Parable of the Plums," the Dublin dames, not men, actually fertilize the city, overseeing it from on high. The exaggerated fashion in which they marvel at the height of the pillar while they climb it satirizes phallic pride. The parable mocks phallic iconography, which the chapter associates with the entire dominant Western Judeo-Christian tradition from Moses to Rome, from the kingdoms of Europe to the crowned heads of contemporary journalism and politics. And the "Aeolus" episode closes with a headline that subversively suggests the autoeroticism of female sexual organs: "DIMINISHED DIGITS PROVE TOO TITILLATING FOR FRISKY FRUMPS. ANNE WIMBLES, FLO WANGLES—YET CAN YOU BLAME THEM?" (*U* 7.1069–71).

The Citizen's narrowly patriotic and prejudiced tirades in Barney Kiernan's tavern along with the narrator's myopia repeat and expand the themes of the headlines of "Aeolus." Aggressively virile in his physical demeanor (*U* 12.151–67), the Citizen attacks women and foreigners for betraying Ireland. He is a misogynist and anti-Semite, as well as a xenophobic Irish patriot. He mocks Bloom because he's a Jew. The Citizen believes, wrongly, that Bloom won money at a horse race. He resents Bloom for not sharing his winnings by buying a round for all. The Citizen questions Bloom's manhood too, accusing him of not having fathered his own children.

The episode opens with the narrator, whom we know only as I (eye and ego both) telling how he was almost blinded in one eye by a chimney sweep.[11] Eyes abound in the episode: "flash toffs with a swank glass in their eye" (*U* 12.1024), "*Compos* your eye! says Alf, laughing" (*U* 12.1045), "Corny Kelleher with his wall eye looking in" (*U* 12.1081–82), "Do you see any green in the white of my eye?" (*U* 12.1088–89), "you can cod him up to the two eyes" (*U* 12.1096).

Admiral Horatio Nelson was in fact blind in one eye, having lost both a hand and vision in one eye in a naval battle. In "Aeolus" Stephen calls Nelson the "onehandled adulterer" (*U* 7.1072). Nelson had conducted a notorious extramarital affair with Lady Hamilton that, according to many historians, led to his misjudgment in the Blockade of Naples. Nelson's tag name refers to both his infidelity and physical maiming, and "the handle" manages to parody his military and sexual exploits while retaining a note of male admiration for his prowess. With the men of the newsroom, Stephen adopts the prevailing stance of male camaraderie, even as he creates a gnomic story that is not "onehandled" but symbolically suggestive of multiple meanings.

The narrator of "Cyclops" carries camaraderie to a duplicitous extreme. He hides his slavish self-interest beneath a mocking tone, adapting to every narrow-minded idea that circulates through the tavern. He mimics the bullying aggressiveness that grows out of male camaraderie, while steering clear of any threat to himself. This point of view is dangerously unstable, and it is a point of view that we first encounter in "Aeolus," Joyce's first really experimental chapter. There this point of view is a characteristic more of the *text* itself (for instance, in the headlines) than of any single character.[12]

The Citizen of "Cyclops" ironically embodies the literal one-eyed, narrow vision of Admiral Nelson, just as the narrator of "Cyclops" embodies and extends the unstable point of view born of duplicity we first see in "Aeolus." Nelson was perhaps the greatest English naval hero. He is a monument to patriotism and Victory, which was actually the name of his ship in the Battle of Trafalgar, where he defeated the French and uttered the famous line, "England expects that every man will do her duty."[13] Ironically, the Citizen (who hates the English) is like Nelson in his extreme patriotism. Another irony follows from the implied equation of Nelson and the Citizen. The Citizen believes women betray the cause of the nation, and Nelson's bungling in Naples stands as an actual example of failure attributable to a relationship with a woman.

The perhaps apocryphal story of Nelson putting his blind eye to a telescope in order to "not see" a signal to retreat is obliquely alluded to in "Cyclops" (*U* 12.1192–95). Siding with the Citizen's aggressive stubbornness, the narrator mocks the reasonable tone of J. J. O'Molloy and Bloom:

So J.J. puts in a word, doing the toff about one story was good till you heard another and blinking facts and the Nelson policy, putting your blind eye to the telescope and drawing up a bill of attainder to impeach a nation, and Bloom trying to back him up moderation and botheration and their colonies and their civilisation. (*U* 12.1192–95)

The narrator is a sycophant and a failure; he resents others but does not risk their displeasure. He is a bill collector, a trade that makes him follow people around to squeeze them for what he can get. His free circulation, guided only by self-interest, is similar to the movement of capital in advanced consumer societies and to the movement of the text itself in its continual displacement of narrative points of view. The narrator of "Cyclops" is willing to follow any view and mock it and profit from it if he can, as long as he stays at a safe distance from physical harm.

We might say that the narrator of "Cyclops" is an instance of pure circulating system, without any fixed referent or value. His appearance triggers two movements. On the one hand, Bloom proposes a countersign. On the other hand, the narrator only initiates what will become extreme textual instability, the running through of sign systems for their own sake. For two-thirds of the way through "Cyclops" there also begins to be heard the highly inflated textual voice that will modulate into the dramatizing of the stages of English literature in "Oxen of the Sun." In "Cyclops" this voice is not the narrator's nor the citizen's nor any character's: "The milkwhite dolphin tossed his mane and, rising in the golden poop, the helmsman spread the bellying sail upon the wind and stood off forward with all sail set, the spinnaker to larboard" (*U* 12.1772–74). This voice is heroic and Homeric, extremely out of place and out of touch with the reality in the bar, yet neither foolish nor satiric in its effect. This voice eludes the coding of the situation out of which it arises (a bar). What are we to make of it?

Let's suppose for the moment that we consider the narrator of "Cyclops" as the epitome of pure economic free trade. He produces nothing of his own, but circulates everywhere. He keeps moving, following only his self-interest. His trade as dunner is often associated with the Jew in literary conventions (Shylock, for instance). Nearly everyone in the tavern "sees" Bloom through the stereotyped "monoculars" of prejudice as an avaricious Jew. They all think he is concerned only with his self-interest, and they believe he secretly hoards money he made in a horse race. To the Dubliners, Bloom appears from the outside to be what the narrator actually is, a man guided solely by self-interested profit motive. Paradoxically, Bloom has come to the tavern to meet Martin Cunningham so that together they can plan how best to help the recently widowed Mrs. Dignam.

By this, the twelfth episode, the reader already knows that, inside, Bloom is generous and loving, faithful to Molly even if he is passive and neglectful of her. As Robert Kiely puts it, "he has a preoccupation, amounting to fidelity, with Molly" (197). He is not meanspirited but tries to think the best of people. He certainly has little money, and he does not seem much interested in it. A moderate man, Bloom defends the Christian principles of love and the Western values of consistent reasoning, not to promote his own self-interest (he actually endangers himself by instigating a brawl) but to defend Jews and the principles themselves (U 12.1360–1425). The narrator's values, by contrast, are unfixed and follow the trail of money. This chapter seems to set up a neat dichotomy: on the one hand, absolutely free circulation (unfettered capitalism or pure sign system or complete narrative and moral instability) leading to hatred, prejudice, and violent conflict, and on the other, Bloom, proposing "love." "But it's no use, says he. Force, hatred, history, all that. That's not life for men and women, insult and hatred. And everybody knows that it's the very opposite of that that is really life" (U 12.1481–83).

But if Bloom's declaration of "love" and insistence on moderation and reasoning are to be taken as the values the book endorses, how do we distinguish Bloom's position from that of the Catholic church, which also upholds those same values? From the outside, both his and the Church's position "look" the same.

Charity is the greatest virtue, according to Christian doctrine. The word comes from the Latin cāritās, signifying a high price or dearness. The term is not related to alms giving, but to the obligation—beyond any price—of the individual to members of the community outside the family. Closely related to charity is the theological concept of grace. Deriving from the Greek *charis*, grace refers to the absolutely free and gratuitous love given to humans by God. Opposite to charity and grace is the deadly sin of simony, the selling of the spiritual for a price.

Joyce's interest in the ironic possibilities of these theological terms goes back to *Dubliners*, where the terms *simony* and *grace* originally framed the collection. The very first story of *Dubliners*, "The Sisters," is a meditation on simony. The young boy narrator thinks: "Every night as I gazed up at the window I said softly to myself the word *paralysis*. It had always sounded strangely in my ears, like the word *gnomon* in the Euclid and the word *simony* in the Catechism" (*Dubliners* 9). "Grace" stood as the last story in the manuscript for two years before Joyce wrote "The Dead." Martin Cunningham of "Grace" pops up in *Ulysses* and so does M'Coy, who in "Grace" may be a prototype for Bloom. Like Molly, M'Coy's wife is a singer. The parallels go further. That short story touches on the stereotyping of Jews as avaricious moneylenders but turns its satire back upon the Catholic men with their distorted concept of grace and their "pious" account-book notions of morality.

The single and unified scope of uncompromising realism of *Dubliners* leaves a reader satisfied that there Joyce seizes the basic values of Irish society and scrupulously uses them in judging that society. By the "Cyclops" episode, though, the unity of *Ulysses* has already given way to plurality, realism has been fractured by textual exuberance, and the neat categories fall apart.

One complication is pinning down the textual attitude toward the narrator of "Cyclops." The exuberance with which the character is depicted may somewhat compromise the criticism implicit in parody. Ellmann identifies Joyce's own father, John Joyce, as the model for both Simon Dedalus and the narrator of the "Cyclops" episode *and* for elements of Bloom as well in that episode (Ellmann 19, 22). In the character of John Joyce, simony and grace were not neatly divided. If Bloom is for charity and the narrator for simony, fine. But the boundaries of this distinction start to erode.

Joyce's attitude toward his own father is well documented. He was irritated by his father's boasting and drinking, but Joyce forgave him his failures more than did any other of the children. Furthermore, Joyce always claimed he inherited from his father an excessiveness out of which came his creative impulse. Indeed, the "Cyclops" episode revels in textual excessiveness, both in the characters of the Citizen and the narrator, as well as in the text itself. The rhetorical excess, I think, challenges and perhaps even undermines, the categorizing capability of any moral terms.

There's another complication, too, in the moral division between charity and simony. Bloom makes his living by selling space for ads in the *Freeman's Journal*. Most recently, he sold an ad that uses an image of crossed keys to evoke an association between Home Rule and Alexander Keyes, merchant of spirits. Crossed keys also stand for the Catholic church, and Joyce frequently satirizes the church's own sin of simony. In a literal, humorous way, Bloom too is implicated in the selling of the spirit, since the ad depends on the sliding of patriotism onto a commodity that is ironically a "spirit" (another Joycean joke on the Irish whose patriotism, it implies, is aroused by the bottle). Moreover, like the narrator of "Cyclops," Bloom himself was once a bill collector, although not a very successful one (*U* 8.143). Again, does Bloom differ from the narrator, who follows the money wherever it leads? I think most readers believe Bloom is a more moral man, but the book raises the problem of how this difference can be known outwardly by the specular eye and the ego. From the monocular, Cyclopean view, Bloom literally is simoniacal, although we know he is actually generous to a fault.

Ulysses does not merely use the values of Western civilization, perhaps inverted, secularized, and carried to an extreme, to satirize the failure of those values in Irish society, as conventional satire would. It refuses neat oppositions, showing them insufficient in accounting for plurality and circulation. We cannot use

Bloom's declaration of "love" to pin down a "hierarchy of significance" in the book, just as we cannot cite Molly's monologue as a mythologizing of the female that either implies or upsets the same old patriarchal standards. Wherever we look, there is excess, a spilling over from one category to another, a circulatory system set in motion and never still enough to keep fixed values in their assigned places. The constant displacement of one value system into another, seen in *A Portrait,* increases in frequency and extremity here.

The effect cancels the text's ability to authorize any moral hierarchy. Bloom's love spills over onto the inflated language of textual excess, and so does the Citizen's harangue, and both dissolve into celebration of textual inflation and deflation itself: "And they beheld Him even Him, ben Bloom Elijah, amid clouds of angels ascend to the glory of the brightness at an angle of fortyfive degrees over Donohoe's in Little Green Street like a shot off a shovel" (*U* 12.1915–18). Rather than by neat divisions and orderly categories, *Ulysses* proceeds by a contamination of the contiguous through a spilling over of the excessive.

Lawrence is interested in representing in his novels forces of evil and destruction, and he puts his characters into situations of conflict to render dramatically the clash of opposing forces. For example, in *Women in Love,* Hermoine actually assaults Birkin, gashing him on the head, literally dramatizing the violence of a dominating will. Such scenes in Lawrence derive their power from the clear-cut opposition of "good" and "bad" forces, however unconventionally Lawrence defines them. In *Ulysses,* strangely, there really is no pure evil that does not become diluted by the sliding over of constant displacement, just as I believe there is no fixed or mythical good.

Joyce plays with, but ultimately moves beyond, the old categories of good and evil and of original sin, just as he rejects the duality of mind and body and the Western tradition of binary logic. We might say that in redirecting focus from a moral to a psychological universe, he shifts from sin to secrets. Rather than the duality of the old *cogito* and the fallen flesh, *Ulysses* renders the "seemingly" unified perceptual moment of the present in which the mind and body together register human experience. And it suggests the shadow of the one moment, repression, which is hidden but whose existence and constant implication in the present moment the text evokes.

Bloom's slips of the tongue are well known:

—Holy Wars, says Joe, laughing, that's a good one if old Shylock is landed. So the wife comes out top dog, what?
—Well, that's a point, says Bloom, for the wife's admirers.
—Whose admirers? says Joe.
—The wife's advisers, I mean, says Bloom. (*U* 12.765–69)

Here Bloom betrays his secret fears by a short circuit of practical, everyday language, commonly called a "Freudian slip." Sometimes repression makes its appearance this way through a knowing subject, such as Bloom. More and more frequently as the book develops, however, the repressed is expressed through a system of signs independent of an understanding subject. Linguistic voices unattached to any character become embodiments of pure writing conventions or speaking objects or dramatized phantasms—as in "Circe." Instead of a character, the text itself discloses its own shadowy unconscious side (in its slips, for example, or overexuberance), suggesting that repression is not merely a personal attribute of an individual but an effect of all human system making, and that it can take on a life of its own.

Margery Sabin in *The Dialect of the Tribe* offers a useful reminder, though, that language does not only betray Bloom. He also finds great solace and security in it. Sabin says language is both "powerful usurper" and "powerful preserver of life" (202) for Bloom.

Usurper and preserver might describe the two different directions that the psychic forces of the conscious and unconscious seem to take in *Ulysses*. Joyce does not privilege consciousness, however. In *Ulysses*, the mastery of the ego is not a necessary or unqualified "good" for civilization, nor are the forces of the id necessarily bad (nor, for that matter, necessarily good, either). Rather the book renders conscious and unconscious forces in dynamic relationship. The story of *Ulysses,* as well as its stylistic experimentation and excess, suggests that those psychic forces can shift roles as usurper and preserver, much like Bello/Bella who, in "Circe," can shift relational position at any time—as either master or slave, man or woman.

Freud declared that the material that arises from the unconscious is directly unknowable but can be interpreted in dream analysis. "Dreams go by contraries" says Florry in "Circe" (*U* 15.3928), the episode that dramatically renders the processes of the dreamwork that Freud described—compression and reversibility of opposites. "Among the most surprising findings is the way in which the dream-work treats contraries that occur in the latent dream," writes Freud (*Introductory Lectures* 178). In a passage that has the utmost pertinence to all Joyce's later work, Freud describes how in dream interpretation "contraries are treated in the same way as conformities" (178):

Thus an element in the manifest dream which is capable of having a contrary may equally well be expressing either itself or its contrary or both together: only the sense can decide which translation is to be chosen. This connects with the further fact that a representation of "no"—or at any rate an unambiguous one—is not to be found in dreams. (178)

Freud immediately goes on to surmise a connection between the processes of the unconscious in dreamwork and the historical development of language. "Some philologists have maintained that in the most ancient languages contraries such as 'strong—weak,' 'light—dark,' 'big—small' are expressed by the same verbal roots" (178–79). Compression, reversibility and the negation of the law of noncontradiction, along with an evolutionary/psychic theory of etymology—all these are the building blocks of *Finnegans Wake*.

Whereas Lawrence criticizes Freud's system and constructs his own *Fantasia of the Unconscious,* Joyce's interest seems to be in translating his own tradition of romantic aestheticism into the psychic processes Freud describes. But Joyce undoes the ethical direction of Freud's system as he embodies the psychic forces in the flesh and blood of character, language, and literary convention, and he pushes Freud's theories to extreme limits.

In *Ulysses,* the reversibility and compression of opposites and the negation of the law of noncontradiction can be seen in the lack of pure good and evil types, in the unstable shifting of the text itself and in the representation of Bloom's and Molly's sexuality. Both Molly and Poldy shatter as well as embody sex role stereotypes in literature. They are excessively sexual; they are androgynous. Bloom is the womanly man, the Jew who espouses Christian virtues and tolerance, the ad man who secretly harbors a Utopian socialist vision of the "New Bloomusalem" (*U* 15.1544). He is so far from phallic dominance of his wife that they have not had complete sexual intercourse for over ten years, although until a few weeks earlier they did have a shared sexual life.

Molly is a phallic woman, as so many readers have noted. She frankly assesses her physical needs and desires and manipulates her relationship with her husband and with Boylan to fulfill herself as far as possible. She has frustrations and regrets; she harbors resentments. But she loves Bloom and appreciates his abilities to write letters, understand the human body, and talk well. She enjoys being seductive, yet she rails against many injustices of being a woman. She desires men, yet resents them too. She does not glorify her own reproductive ability. She does not need to have a lot of children to reaffirm her identity as a woman. In fact, she resents men who "have us swollen out like elephants" (*U* 18.165–66). She thinks about the possibility of having another child: "yes thatd be awfully jolly" (*U* 18.168). However, she does not dwell on reproduction nor indicate in any way a lack in her life from not having more children. Commentators who try to pin moral values on fertility ignore Molly's and the entire book's critique (as in "Oxen of the Sun") of endless childbearing.[14] Indeed, Mrs. Dedalus, the other important female character, embodied the old ethic of patient female submission to fertility, and it killed her. In *Ulysses* woman participates in life *and* death, as van Boheemen notes, but she does not represent either exclusively.

In this fusing of contrary qualities, characteristics are reversible; however, the extremes do not dilute each other. Since there is no "no," they do not cancel each other out either. Thus in "Circe" Bloom experiences what it is to be a woman at the mercy of the power of the phallus in a sadomasochistic relationship with Bello, who herself dynamically shifts roles from female to male (*U* 15.2830ff.). Bloom must submit to brutal sexuality; he experiences imprisonment in dress, servitude in domestic chores, and degradation in prostitution. In acting out his own (repressed) sadomasochistic potential, Bloom demonstrates (does he come to understand this?) the reciprocal exchange between master and slave, in short, the reversibility of contraries. The feminist in "Circe" cries out "masculinely." These sex reversals suggest that gender division is not a deep or fixed difference, but flexible. "Circe" further suggests that lurking quite near the surface of conscious sex role behavior are darker, chaotic, multiply perverse, sometimes aggressive, sexual drives in women and men.

Many feminist critics deride Joyce's use of the sadomasochistic stereotype. For example, Elaine Unkeless argues that the way Bloom is depicted as a womanly man calls upon the worst sex role stereotypes of female submissiveness.[15] However, from a psychological point of view, denying the reality of sadomasochism is a defense against accepting woman's, as well as man's, capacity for—and complicity in—cruel and aggressive sexuality.[16]

However, it is true that *Ulysses* also preserves conventional notions of gender. Kimberly Devlin explores how *Ulysses* presents gender as masquerade, as a culturally constructed and commodified look ("Castration" 131). In "'Cyclops,' 'Nausicaa,' and Joyce's Imaginary Irish Couple," Tony Jackson argues that adjoining episodes 12 and 13 create "an especially heavy play upon stereotypically Irish maleness and Irish femaleness" (63) by juxtaposing the super masculine satirized figure of the Citizen against the gushingly sweet satirized figure of Gerty MacDowell. As I do, Jackson concludes that Joyce gives us "a psychocultural depiction of the generic male and female of the Ireland of 1904" (80). *Ulysses* may appear to endorse sex role stereotypes because Joyce does not underrate their pervasiveness.

Gender stereotypes are neither canceled nor transcended but ruthlessly used. When "Circe" pushes stereotypes to their extreme limits (as in Bella/Bello) and the players in the sexual drama switch sides at will, the text does not contradict the order of the quotidian world that Bloom and Molly inhabit. It just repeats in a heightened, theatrical form what Molly and Bloom, Gerty and the Citizen, play out in their daily lives—the paradox of excessive, masquerading sexuality and androgyny.

On the one hand, readers and characters experiencing role reversal discover phallic domination, feminine victimization. On the other hand, reversal itself discloses the reciprocity of gender locations and complicity in pleasures. Just as the masochist constructs the sadist and gains pleasure as victim, the reader (and author?) also participate in and enjoy the power that comes with flaunting taboos. Hence, while uncovering sadism and masochism, the text also implicates us in aggressivity and submission, *using* these drives for our pleasure and leading us to recognize the drives within ourselves and our complicity in articulating our desires through the masquerade of gender.

The ruthless way the book uses sex/gender stereotypes explodes the illusion of fixed, innate gender differences. I believe the result is that *Ulysses* depicts psychic drives as sexual but not fixed by gender. Very close to the surface, but underneath the mask of a masculine or feminine economy, the text reveals a chaotic libidinal economy, where multiform desires continually circulate and seek any opportunity for pleasure. While the book satirizes the sexual politics of phallic supremacy (husbands dominating wives, war heroes dominating nations, priests dominating women, and so on), it does not easily dismiss the psychic drive to domination and submission—as a local effect of a particular history and culture or as just the problem of men. As it does with the problems of racism and anti-Semitism, the text inscribes the problems of gender (aggression, conflicts, restrictions, inadequacies, masks), but it displaces any totalizing answer. Anti-Semitism gets hurled at Bloom, and its power is not overcome. Bloom just flees for the moment. Sex/gender stereotypes and phallic dominance are not overcome, but their hegemony may be somewhat broken up by the text's multiple voicings of desires.

Like Lawrence, Joyce is also interested in triangular relationships of two men and a woman. When I discussed *Sons and Lovers,* I noted the triangular and bisexual aspects that grow out of Paul's relationship with Clara Dawes and her husband. The primary triangle in *Sons and Lovers* is that of Mr. and Mrs. Morel and Paul. This triangle produces conflict because of the intrusion of the third party, as dramatized by the father's flinging a drawer at the mother and the infant Paul. In *Sons and Lovers,* the primary conflict of the family triangle resolves itself by the defeat of one person (first, Morel), followed by a short period of balance and reciprocity between the remaining two (Mrs. Morel and the adolescent Paul). Out of this phase, which encourages growth, comes the addition of a new third person, in a new triangular relationship, renewing conflict. Mrs. Morel, Paul, and one of his girlfriends act out this phase. Sexual conflict is at the root of these triangles. In some cases the triangles in Lawrence suggest bisexual interest through two men who share a woman (Paul and Baxter Dawes) or through two men who share sisters (Gerald Crich and Rupert Birkin in *Women in Love*). In the case of father, mother, son, and lovers, the conflict stems from the sharing of a woman (the mother) and from the sharing of a man (the son) as well as from incestuous desires.

Ulysses has a primary triangle too in Milly, Molly, and Poldy. Apparently along with Milly's maturing has come conflict from Molly's jealousy and Bloom's incestuous desires. The tensions caused by the primary family triangle have been more or less defused, however, and the triangle broken up by Milly's apprenticeship in Mullingar.

The immediate triangular relationships are not primary

family triangles but those of two men sharing a woman—in one, Stephen, Bloom, and Molly; in the other Boylan, Bloom, and Molly. The first of these is a type of the primary family triangle, re-created much like a Family Romance mostly through Bloom's imagination. He takes a fatherly interest in Stephen, as under the influence of exhaustion and sorrow he remembers his own dead son Rudy. Bloom invites Stephen home, invites Stephen to appreciate and nearly to share Molly's favors. However, Stephen will not take him up on this offer by returning the next day. Bloom first plants Stephen in Molly's imagination, and then she imagines Stephen as a potential lover and as a son figure. The triangular relationship between the three is dynamic and destabilized, however. It is imaginary, secondary—not a real but a replacement family, and Stephen does not accede to its shape. We might say his side of the triangle wobbles and recedes from view.

Although most readers focus on the Stephen, Molly, and Poldy triangle, the Boylan, Bloom, and Molly triangle has an established Joycean history. It falls under the same category of relationships that Joyce explores in his play *Exiles,* written in 1914–15 while Joyce was working on *Ulysses.* The play explores the relationship between Richard Rowan, Bertha, and Robert Hand. Bertha and Richard are not married, but have lived together for many years (like Joyce and Nora). Richard offers his "wife" to his best friend, Robert, from a kind of psychosexual need to be freely desired and chosen by her. Ellmann compares the relation of Bloom and Boylan with that of Richard and Robert, concluding: "Joyce has Bloom defeat his rival, Blazes Boylan, in Molly Bloom's mind by being the first and the last in her thoughts as she falls off to sleep. In the same way Joyce enabled Richard Rowan in *Exiles* to defeat Robert Hand in Bertha's mind" (361). "The Dead" also explores a variant of this kind of triangle, although destabilized and imaginary, since Michael Furey had died many years earlier and Gabriel replays a triangular relationship between himself, Gretta, and Michael Furey solely in his mind. There are also elements of this kind of triangle in the imaginary one of Bloom, Stephen and Molly, and in the relations of Shem, Shaun, and Issy in *Finnegans Wake*.

The triangle of two men and a woman expresses this core Joyce theme: the male's desire to be freely chosen by a woman in a passive, sexual competition with another man. This kind of triangle is sexual, but unlike Lawrence's sexual triangles, Joyce's repress or swerve from conflict and violence. Gabriel weeps "generous tears" when he thinks of the dying young man, and he feels his love for Gretta increase and his own identity dissolve into those of all the living and the dead (*D* 223). In these triangular relations, the males like Richard Rowan or Bloom refuse the conventional male position in patriarchy of the ownership and exchange of women by men, desiring instead to be freely chosen by their women—even if, as in the case of Bloom, they are chosen despite their flaws and without the allure of the phallus. Gabriel, Richard, Bloom—all are passive. They refuse the demands of the ego, the possessiveness, conflict, and violence caused by sexual jealousy (or pretend to refuse them).

But can the demands of the ego be refused, or are they merely repressed? Most readers of "The Dead" agree that Gabriel's "generous tears" contain a generous portion of self-deception. Reversibility and repetition in *Ulysses* also admit the possibility that passive Bloom, like Bello/Bella, secretly acts out the opposite quality—phallic dominance. In that case, Bloom would be a double of his triangular partner, Blazes Boylan.

This peculiar Joyce triangle suggests a psychological and a theological/economic aspect. Psychologically it may describe intrapsychic relations rather than the psychic conflicts of family members, as is often the case in Lawrence. The women in the triangles—Gretta, Bertha, Molly—are the objects desired by the male, who is split into giver and receiver, winner and loser, in a passive/aggressive, sexual competition with his own alter ego (which literally happens in the *Wake*). The split in the male role, however, transforms the relations so that the usual object, the woman, becomes the active desirer, and the male the object of desire. If we consider designations such as "male" and "female" as indicating active and passive forces within an individual, then this peculiar Joycean triangle could be read as an intrapsychic drama—acting out the relations between desire and the ego and releasing the forces of desire by splitting and hence pacifying the ego.

If we do not dismiss gender so quickly, then these triangular relations seem to suggest that female desire is activated and released by pacifying (castrating?) the male. And I wonder, then, whether this peculiar relationship is not a male defense fantasy against castration: the male assigns active desire to the female and voluntarily assumes passivity in order to protect himself by his feigned castration from actual castration. By making the female the desirer, he also preserves the power of the phallus, even if appearing to cancel it by his passivity, since the direction of desire is toward the male. Thus his phallus remains the object desired or an icon. Female desire drives the system, and thus Woman (raised to mythic level) and sexual desire (turned into thing, phallic icon) replace the old God and divine grace in our secular era.

In fact, Stephen draws attention to the substitution of the sexual for the theological in his parody of Christ's sacrifice: "Greater love than this, he said, no man hath that a man lay down his wife for his friend" (U 14.360–62). On a secular level, the theological notion of grace could be absolutely unearned sexual love bestowed freely. Richard Rowan does not marry Bertha, so their union does not involve legal, conventional, or monetary exchange. He is so obsessed with the need to be freely desired by her that he throws his friend in her way repeatedly to lure her away. Bloom's relation with Molly seems similar, although these two are legally married. Bloom knows exactly when Boylan will visit Molly, and he stays away all day allowing their affair to proceed.

In economic terms, Bloom and all these Joycean males want a love that is not a token exchanged for goods, a love that stands outside of an exchange system. Marital traditions and relations, and sexual relations, grow out of economic systems as well as from religious roots. Marriage as a legal contract, involving an exchange of property, rights, and name, can be seen as an outgrowth of the rise of capitalism. Ian Watt tells us that by the eighteenth century, marriage had become a "commercial matter" in England (142). The desire of Joyce's male characters for "free" love might seem a longing for a precapitalist notion of marriage as religious sacrament or mystic ritual. This would be a notion of love as absolute value, "whose worth's unknown, although his height be taken."

Lawrence moves in this direction, I think, although his ideal is a marriage of true bodies, not true minds. In *Sons and Lovers* Lawrence uncovers the grim economic brutality of late nineteenth-century marriage. I believe he evolved a concept of marriage as spiritual quest to replace the worn-out religion of the past and the distortion of relations as he saw it, caused by industrialism. Lawrence's marriage quest in part seems to suggest a nostalgia for a primitive culture in his return to fixed heterosexual relations, and in his emphasis on the impersonal, physical forces between men and women in rhythm with the earth. Lawrence's characters do not desire freedom *from* exchange, but instead some "authentic" exchange with an Other who is different.

Ulysses, on the other hand, mocks nostalgia and sets in motion a circulating system of signs, where nearly every sign can be exchanged for another (for example, a reader can follow "keys" to crossed keys, lost keys, and home rule, or disrule; or "plums" to "plumstones" and "Plumtree's Potted Meat" through a plethora of transmigrations to seedcakes). This series of repetitions and parodies not only mocks but wistfully dismisses any notion of "authentic" exchange by taking circulation literally and to its extreme.

What is the signature of the seashells that Stephen regards on the beach in "Proteus"? "Wild sea money" (*U* 3.19), empty shells, cockleshells—little cocks in the female flow of the sea, sign of the transmigration of souls, of the evolution of life from its watery origin, reminders of the watery grave, or shells of his own rotten teeth? Each is offered, all flow by "to no end gathered" (*U* 3.4466–67), just as Stephen's fertilizing urination vainly flows back and forth on the strand with the ebb and flow of the tide.

Earlier, I said that *Ulysses* anticipated the destabilizing forces of advanced capitalism—perpetual circulation and desire. Now I must move beyond this claim to differentiate between advanced capitalism, anarchy, and overdetermination.

The psychological desire of Joyce's male characters for a "free" love, if not nostalgia for a transcendent absolute—and Joyce always mocks nostalgia—might be their desire for love free of determining systems. They desire a "creation from nothing" (*U* 3.35), love literally "free" (here I mean the formal notion of "indeterminacy" such as "uncaused" or outside the chain of causality). But the more the males try to create a situation of freedom (Bloom staying away from his house, for example), the more it seems as though they set up a determined situation. Conversely, the more Stephen attempts to read a "signature of all things,"[17] the more he moves toward a perpetually endless sequence of potentially empty signs.

In seeking a situation of indeterminacy, to test his love, Bloom helps determine that Molly will have an affair with Boylan. Stephen tries to determine the significance of the universe, first through his senses, then through his knowledge and speculative mental powers, but ends contemplating the darkness beyond the stars, the endless universe, and the mystery—perhaps the illusion—of personal identity in an infinite, evolving universe: "I throw this ended shadow from me, manshape ineluctable, call it back. Endless, would it be mine, form of my form?" (*U* 3.412–14).

What Stephen and Bloom come up against in their efforts is the overdetermined nature of reality, its superabundance of effects and overlapping of causes—in short, the limits of causal thinking itself. As Freud said in his essay on Leonardo, there are more causes in nature than humans will ever know about. A practitioner of determinacy, Bloom loves to speculate on causes and effects and has a penchant for providing tidy solutions to the odd questions he thinks up. (He is quite often wrong.) Stephen, the literary philosopher who wants to be the uncreated creator, usually free-associates through a highly personal and peculiar chain of signs, so that following his thoughts involves the reader in a process of interpretation like the archeological uncovering of psychoanalysis. That is, as a backward chain Stephen's thoughts preserve the notion of causality as we retrospectively come to understand his associations, but these associations could never be predicted as a future sequence, so they also manifest indeterminacy.

From the perspective of modern physics, determinism and indeterminism can be seen to be two sides of the same notion, both not logically refuted, but emptied of meaning by theories of the twentieth century. In quantum mechanics "the unascertainability of exact initial values obstructs predictability and hence deprives causality of any operational meaning."[18] Unknowability or meaninglessness does not really take the place of the old concept of causal relations. Rather quantum mechanics asserts that there is an ensemble of relations among position, energy, and momentum. We can know those relations, but when we intrude into the ensemble to isolate and measure one, the others become distorted. Applied to human relations, this model suggests the multiplicity of the present moment of everyday reality that *Ulysses* celebrates.

Classic theories of capitalism use simple Enlightenment concepts of cause and effect (supply and demand, for example) and of measurement and equivalence, with money at the center of the system. Monetary theories rely on the notion that in a sign—such as money—there can be a single unified exchange system that reflects a precise equilibrium of value and relation between objects. Beneath capitalism lie assumptions (even if the belief in them seems to be discarded as old-fashioned) of a universe of simple, empirically calculable order, unified and guaranteed by some single overarching mechanism like Adam Smith's notion of an Invisible Hand.

Marxist and other socialist critiques of capitalism break up this "seemingly" unified view by pointing out that a hidden ensemble of relations—the forces and relations of production—actually produce social relations and ideology. In place of a simple concept of singleness, Marxism offers a theory of relations; in place of an external sign of value Marxism points to hidden relations. Whereas money is the icon of capitalism, in Marxism production and utility are worshiped.

Stephen's fondness for sign systems, his flight from history, his refusal to bow to utility, and his desire to perceive "the signature of all things" while remaining aloof from a commitment to change the forces and relations of production—all these traits are incompatible with classical Marxism. So Stephen (and Joyce by extension) may appear to affirm the values of capitalism, as Lukács argues. However, Joyce's values of constant transformation and freedom from restraints (even the limit implicit in arguments of utility) might also evoke another political/economic form not yet realized in history—anarchy.

For most of the twentieth century, anarchy has not been taken seriously as an alternative political/economic model to capitalism and communism. Commonly, in fact, anarchy is equated with chaos. Dominic Manganiello's study of *Joyce's Politics*, however, reminds us that syndical anarchism was a vigorous and viable political movement (especially in Italy) during Joyce's years there. Manganiello points out that Bloom's schemes incorporate many of the specific programs of that movement (see particularly chapter 3, "Perspectives: Socialism and Anarchism"). Manganiello also argues that throughout Joyce's work there is an explicit connection between forms of love and government. He attributes this idea to the influence of the work of Guglielmo Ferrero (50–52), a journalist, sociologist, and historian whom Joyce read and recommended to others. "For Joyce," says Manganiello, "the brutalism of love and politics were interconnected" (52). The syndical anarchists Joyce read and wrote to Stanislaus about in his years in Trieste advocated nonviolent socialist principles, with the emphasis on social reform and a decentralized power struc-

ture. In the United States, the IWW, the Wobblies, came closest
to the European anarchists.

Earlier I cited some characteristics of *Ulysses*, such as its
constant displacement of old for new, its freeing of desire from
an object, and its fragmentation of texts, and I claimed these
anticipate but do not contest the forces that drive advanced capitalism. Maybe these traits suggest the forces of capitalism only
because we have no historical model for a society developed upon
the ideas of syndical anarchism.

The classic complaint against anarchic theories has always
been that humans cannot live peacefully together without the
restraint of central authority and the force of law. This view
rests on a Hobbesian notion of the brutish nature of humans
and the necessity for contractual restraint and enforced obligation. On the other side would be a view of human relations very
similar to the nonjudgmental acceptance of human psychology
I have argued is present in *Ulysses*. Under this more optimistic
view, secrets would replace sin, free love would replace contractual obligation, peace would overcome violence (sometimes, by
fleeing, as Bloom flees the tavern). Multiple fragments would
replace an overarching central power, and comedy's rise and
fall and rise again would replace tragedy's downward trajectory.
Since this is not a naive Utopian social theory, during the falling
phase, there would be voices in argument, and political, social,
and familial conflict. Yet there is no necessary doom, for there
is no overarching necessary direction but an ensemble of forces
and relations. Different from the Marxist view, history's outcome
would not be inevitable; hence history is not reified. But this
decentralized, idealistic socialism is predicated on change and
flow, so it assumes an historical principle.

In *Ulysses* I believe this essentially romantic idealism is cou-
pled with a twentieth-century commitment to a scientific view
of the world, to evolution, to "hard" scientific fact, and to the
postcausal world view of modern physics. In "Ithaca," that episode parodying a scientific text, we are reminded of the obdurate-

ness of hard facts—"the irreparability of the past" (*U* 17.975), the "imprevidibility of the future" (*U* 17.980), and the "cold of interstellar space" (*U* 17.1246). Once in the summer of 1898 Bloom had marked a coin to test whether in "its circulation of the waters of civic finance" (*U* 17.983–84) it would ever return to him, and it never did. Here, the circulation of money (and with it economic philosophies) meets the reality of the modern world: "to no end gathered," as Stephen said in "Proteus."

The scientific view is not enshrined, however. In "Ithaca" we also see factual discourse used to evade the truth. Bloom does not tell Molly about Nighttown, for example, and in his precise account of the day (*U* 17.1455ff.) there are all kinds of secrets hidden beneath the orderly list. The text does not privilege factual discourse, then, but enfolds it within its ensemble of texts. Each romantic rise is followed by realistic deflation. Neither Bloom, Stephen, nor Molly is a mouthpiece of a textual center, either. Rather they constitute an ensemble of relations like position, energy, and momentum in the subatomic world of physics. When readers isolate one element, they interfere with the relations, causing distortion such as the reification of the female, or the valorizing of love and order into old Judeo-Christian platitudes.

Money circulates, but there is no invisible hand guiding it, and it does not return. Sexuality—especially Molly's, but Stephen's urine and Bloom's seed, too—circulates but comes to no apparent fruition ascertainable in the present or predictable for the future. Gender fluctuates as flexibly as Bloom's characteristic "firm full masculine feminine passive active hand" (*U* 17.289–90). From the ethic of Freudian theory, flexible sexuality is narcissistic and regressive. Without the restraint of culture and the harsh needs of reality, Freud believed humans would pursue pleasure to the point of death. There is a good deal of the Hobbesian view in this particular aspect of Freud.

In advanced capitalism, I maintained earlier, flexible models of gender suit the needs of markets, and gender roles are manipulated to expand markets. For example, in the mid-1970s a market-driven unisex fad swept Western nations, creating demand for men's earrings, women's leather clothes, and so on. Market-driven changes alter attitudes and expectations, just as concrete economic forces produce social changes too. For example, the cycles of inflation and recession in the United States in the 1970s and 1980s more effectively changed the traditional patterns of female labor and hence sex roles and expectations than the last one hundred years of the woman's movement.

Early in this century, Lawrence foresaw these effects of capitalism on gender and sexuality. When he railed against the flapper, for example, Lawrence attacked the distortion caused by the modern world of what he considered was genuine sexual Otherness. In a turn away from his bisexual impulse, Lawrence decried the fashion of the nervous, slim, boylike flapper because she denied her living female sexuality, as he saw it.

Ulysses, on the other hand, preserves both the traditional gender stereotypes of men and women (what Lawrence seems to advocate after 1922 or so), luxuriates in sexual extremes such as S and M fantasies (I imagine the prudish Lawrence would find this distasteful) and promotes androgyny as well (what Lawrence attacks when he attacks the flapper). In *Ulysses* sexuality is unrestrained and diverse. Sexuality is rendered through the conventional institutions—marriage, prostitution, the church—and history. However, the book presents these institutions from inside human imagination, revealing under the fixed forms the ceaseless movement of sexual energy.

Despite all the varied sexuality the book depicts (and hence may be argued to endorse), the one I claim it does *not* underwrite is an ethic of reproduction. Neither does the book reject reproduction. And this is an important point. For all the physical motion, the wandering, the inflation and deflation of texts and sex organs, and the free sexual circulation, the sexuality does not serve markets (as in capitalism) nor social utility (as in communism or for some evolutionary ideal). It does not look back to a religious ideal. It is anarchic and creative as well as potentially destructive.

Freud put the anarchic drives and impulses of the human in their place, so to speak, by locating them in the id. The id is archaic, narcissistic, and regressive, according to Freud, precisely because its drives are not easily sublimated to the higher goals of facing reality and submitting to the ethic of procreative sex. The circulating energy of *Ulysses,* which I claim is sexual/political/economic, avoids or subverts (passive aggressively) sublimation to overarching principles. The Freudian concept of the id may also be suggested in the way that the text itself becomes a "thing" driven by desire and excessiveness to generate many discourses. Yet if the textual components and psychic human drives portrayed in *Ulysses* resemble Freud's portrait of the anarchic id, there is one important difference. The book refuses the moral judgments of Freud just as it refuses all categorizing of good/bad.

This ensemble of relations I have gathered under the term *anarchy* has been cited, especially by French critics, as evidence that *Ulysses* is an antipatriarchal, feminine text. According to such a reading, the book deconstructs the hegemony of Western, male-dominated thinking, replacing it with a reality that is a matrix (literally) celebrating the alternative flow of the female, the spilling over of boundaries, and overcoming of force by love. This kind of reading grows directly out of the sexual themes of psycho-analysis as it occurs in the work of Jacques Lacan.

The reasoning goes like this. Anarchy is female, the rule of law is male, since Lacan's Name-of-the-Father means submission to the rule of law. To some extent, the details of *Ulysses* certainly support such a reading. The text connects the many stone statues of political men, the advertising and political testimonials, the testament of Moses carved in rock, and Bloom's testicles in a satire on the relation between the rule of law and the law of the phallus (as in "Circe," where Bloom, made "Leopold the First," swears on his testicles [15.1484]). But I have tried to map out how *Ulysses* does not respect the boundary of categories, and so itself subverts the boundaries of gender.

The text mocks the dominant phallus but also exuberantly

portrays the male excess and aggression in Barney Kiernan's tavern. Women write and dream and make plans, as well as men. Martha Clifford writes a love note to Bloom, Gerty MacDowell fantasizes on the beach, Molly lying in bed at night plans her affair with Boylan and a possible conquest of Stephen. In contrast, Lacan argues that the female is absence and is outside of the Symbolic order; she cannot write but is written. Finally, as van Boheemen argues (although from a Lacanian point of view), if the book did in fact reinsert the female at the center, valorizing the female over the male would just indicate another male act of hegemony, another instance of male control of the symbolic system. This is often a criticism of Joyce—that he writes the male's imaginary construction of the female.

The multiplicity celebrated in *Ulysses* is not tied to gender, as I see it, since I claim the book deconstructs gender. Rather the book connects multiplicity to sexuality itself. And, as I have argued throughout, in this Joyce stays remarkably close to Freud. Rather than revising Freudian theories as Lawrence did or as Lacan does, Joyce pushes Freudian ideas to extremes while stripping away their veneer of late nineteenth-century ethics. Freud claimed that neuroses had a sexual origin and that they were overdetermined, that they had multiple causes. Under every facet of civilization *Ulysses* presents polymorphic sexuality bubbling up, but the text rejects any negative judgment. Likewise, *Ulysses* presents the fabric of reality woven from multiple causes. An overdetermined universe inscribes an open-ended freedom, even as the present moment becomes laid down in a causal chain of the past, whose archeology the reader retroactively uncovers.

Ulysses continues and even increases the breakup of the too solid forms of the external world, which Stephen began as a mental exercise in *A Portrait*. Whereas *A Portrait* focused on a single character, *Ulysses* gives us many voices—from many characters as well from objects and even from disembodied text. Each is discontinuous, like Stephen at the end of *A Portrait,* who "was not myself as I am now" (*P* 240). When we follow the psychic archeology of each character backward, we discover the personal sign and signature of each—Bloom's potato, Molly's plum seed. We recognize the signature of each, once read, as a determined formation, as "I had to become," as Stephen says (*P* 240). But their futures are not predictable, because of the complex, overdetermined nature of the present.

Along with the increasing discontinuity of personality, *Ulysses* renders a more multiform reality. There are more fragments than in *A Portrait*. We never find out who M'Intosh is, or even whether the text authorizes us to refer to him by the convention of names or by reference to his coat (mackintosh). There are overlapping causes and arbitrary connections such as the blind piano tuner and the one-legged sailor, who wind through the lives of all.

A Portrait renders Stephen's mental development as he perceives the symmetry in underlying relations in the structures around him—in politics, history, religion, family structure. His progressive development assumes an orderly world and a faith in the power of ego to master it that mark a child's hope and belief in the Family Romance.

While *Ulysses* preserves the external conventional structure of family, it does not render the perception of unified whole objects, but moments and streams of perception. I claimed that *A Portrait* depicts the growth of perception in a way similar to Gestalt theory, but the stream-of-consciousness rendering of perception in *Ulysses* marks a turn away from emphasis on formal relations as in the earlier work. *Ulysses* also turns from romance to antiromance. Even though it retains conventional family structure, it refuses to authorize a "better" version of relations.

A Portrait ends with Stephen declaring his spiritual quest, which can be seen as a flight from materiality, from the female, and ultimately from accepting death. Still caught up in the web of patriarchal thought structure, Stephen uses patriarchy's metaphors to his own ends. Women represent matter, the body, and life and death, according to the symbolic significance he attaches to the figure of the old woman he conjures up to stand for

Ireland. Stephen exhibits a male psychological defense against accepting castration and death.

In *Ulysses* Stephen has not reconciled himself to death. He muses on his mother's death throughout, and her ghost comes to haunt him. I am not sure that his attack on her specter in Bella Cohen's brothel constitutes an acceptance of death (although he does seem to shut her up for the night at least). On the other hand, Bloom and Molly know death and have incorporated its reality into their respective philosophies. Molly regards death in concrete terms—her lost baby Rudy, the little clothes she knit him and buried him in. She understands how profoundly his death changed their marriage, but she has a practical, get-on-with-life attitude: "I suppose I oughtnt to have buried him in that little woolly jacket I knitted crying as I was but give it to some poor child but I knew well Id never have another our 1st death too it was we were never the same since O Im not going to think myself into the glooms about that any more" (*U* 18.1448–51).

The catechizing text of "Ithaca" questions Bloom on his meditations as he points out the constellations to Stephen. During Bloom's response, Stephen is silent, but Bloom declares a belief in the vastness of evolutionary, cosmic space and the smallness of the human. Bloom's accepting tone and his vision of human smallness are similar to Paul's vision of the universe and the tone of the text at the end of *Sons and Lovers*. Bloom professes "Meditation of evolution increasingly vaster" (*U* 17.1042) as he visualizes the astronomical dimensions and movements of stars that appear fixed but are "in reality evermoving wanderers from immeasurably remote eons to infinitely remote futures in comparison with which the years, threescore and ten, of allotted human life formed a parenthesis of infinitesimal brevity" (*U* 17.1053–56).

Accommodating death in life's affairs, Molly and Bloom readjust their relations to each other after Rudy's death. Bloom acknowledges the smallness of human proportion in the vast universe. Although Stephen's attitude to death may not have changed between *A Portrait* and *Ulysses*, Joyce's focus does change—from an interest in the mind and the force of the ego to interest in the body and the forces of desire. The adolescent point of view of a male Family Romance gives way to an antiromantic text of multiple voices. History still operates in *Ulysses*, but it is overdetermined. What we come to know retrospectively is psychic history.

Leaving behind the external world, *Finnegans Wake* plunges into the landscape of the psyche, continuing the break up of the personality and of the solid world begun in *Ulysses*. In the next chapter, I read *Finnegans Wake* in counterpoint with three other texts: Lawrence's last novella, *The Man Who Died*, and Freud's early essays, "Leonardo da Vinci and a Memory of Childhood," and "A Special Type of Object Choice." Lawrence, Joyce, and Freud all return to Egyptian mythology to find figures and narratives for describing the psyche and family relations. While both Lawrence and Joyce may seem to turn away from the Western, Judeo-Christian concept of a linear history and of gender division, I believe Lawrence grafts the Egyptian myth onto an essentially Judeo-Christian view of personality. Lawrence returns to the mode of Family Romance and to the gender roles of the Oedipal narrative. Joyce, in contrast, takes Freudian ideas—and particularly those of Freud's Leonardo essay—and uses them to his own ends, even moving further beyond Freudianism. *Finnegans Wake*, I believe, dismembers Western notions of gender, personality, and family relations and challenges us to invent or rediscover a mythology to read it by.

4

"Retourneys Postexilic": Overthrowing the Christian Holy Family and Returning to Egypt

Now this vulture-headed mother goddess was usually represented by the Egyptians with a phallus; her body was female, as the breasts indicated, but it also had a male organ in a state of erection.

—Sigmund Freud, "Leonardo da Vinci and a Memory of Childhood," *SE*

Lawrence and Joyce both turned in their last work to the myths of Egypt. Lawrence used the Isis and Osiris story in his last novella, *The Escaped Cock*, also titled *The Man Who Died* (1929, 1931),[1] and drew upon the Egyptian journey of the dead in his last cycle of death poems. Joyce wove into *Finnegans Wake* (1939) complex themes, names, rituals, and myths from the Egyptian *Book of the Dead*.[2] As William York Tindall comments, both writers often identified themselves with Jesus (*The Later D. H. Lawrence* 397). Yet—or maybe because they identified with Jesus—each felt compelled to revise the Christian narrative of death and resurrection, incorporating Egyptian figures and motifs drawn from the myths of Osiris and Isis and from the Egyptian *Book of the Dead*.

The return to pre-Christian, cyclic Egyptian mythology could be judged a retreat from the modern world, an escape from linear time and the "nightmare of history," to use Stephen Dedalus's term. In fact, psychoanalysis seems to encourage that kind of judgment. From a psychoanalytic point of view, these "retourneys" (*FW* 472.34) might indicate a surrender to the archaic, infantile, and primitive. Hence, while reimagining old myths for a new age, it might be said that these texts also exhibit "the return of the repressed."

And yet Freud himself turned to Egyptian mythology to explain and to find models for his "new" science. Neither a believer in God, nor an overardent admirer of Christianity, Freud found the ancient world conducive to his theories. A comparison of the Egyptian material in these three writers suggests that their going back to ancient myth does not necessarily signal a uniform "return of the repressed." Instead, I believe each writer's use of Egyptian myth reveals a different attitude to patriarchy.

In his 1910 essay "Leonardo da Vinci and a Memory of Childhood," Freud uses Egyptology—and particularly the androgynous Mut quoted above—as a primitive figure to stand for the sexual confusion of infantile thinking. Freud speculates on the origins of homosexuality, weaving an intricate analysis of the effects of family relations on the psychic formation of the young Leonardo. Reading Freud as he works on his emerging theory of narcissism, one is dazzled by his brilliant and complex analysis. Yet I think many readers might also feel, as I do, that Freud is particularly blind to cultural issues of gender. While Freud illustrates with Egyptian myth, his concern is to articulate the Oedipal narrative of Western, patriarchal culture, and his standpoint and norms are situated in patriarchy.

It is interesting to speculate that Lawrence may have been familiar with Freud's "Leonardo" essay, although there is no evidence he was.[3] Nevertheless, in this Freud essay there is a remarkable coincidence of phrasing and thought recalling Lawrence's remarks about *Sons and Lovers*. Freud writes of Leonardo's mother, "So, like all unsatisfied mothers, she took her little son in place of her husband, and by the too early maturing of his erotism [*sic*] robbed him of a part of his masculinity" (*SE* 11: 117). Whether or not Lawrence knew this essay or another, "A Special Type of Object Choice," these Freud essays elucidate how Lawrence's late romance plots retain as well as rebel against the Oedipal narrative.

In *The Man Who Died* Lawrence wraps Egyptian myth around the psychosexual relations of patriarchy. Lawrence's revised Jesus myth minimizes the role of the father (both divine and human) and focuses on the individual man and woman relationship. The plot rebels against authority and the father function, but in the relationship of the man and woman preserves the symbolic patterns of psychic development and gender roles under patriarchy. This romance plot thus inscribes an ambivalence to patriarchy, accepting its sex/gender roles and yet desiring to change them too—in the rebellion against the father and the romantic quest for the ideal mate, a doubled female figure and therefore a "phallic" woman.

I believe Freud's "Leonardo" essay influenced Joyce more than has been appreciated, but that its influence on Joyce accrued slowly over time.[4] Joyce owned a copy of this 1910 essay in the original German. Joyce incorporates Egyptian mythology into *Finnegans Wake* in a way that shows how thoroughly Joyce has understood Freud's thinking in the "Leonardo" essay and how radically Joyce pushes Freud's ideas. Joyce takes Freud's ideas and adapts them to his own ends to connect the mythology of Egypt with a view of human creativity that is infantile, sexual, and polymorphically perverse. Joyce makes use of the Oedipal narrative but portrays the anarchic world underneath its repression (necessary in Freudianism to establish the reality principle). Joyce does not merely recast Freud's material; he remakes it entirely because he mocks and reverses Freud's aim. In place of the lens of Western, patriarchal culture, Joyce fashions a kaleidoscope, a reimagined Joycean mythology that fuses psychology, Egyptology, and a twentieth-century evolutionary view with bits and pieces from the midden heap of human history. Joyce quite consciously enveloped and devoured his predecessors, so Freud, I believe, and perhaps even Lawrence[5] become parodied fragments of *Finnegans Wake*.

Both Lawrence and Joyce read the researches into ancient

religions and comparative cultures of Sir James G. Frazer. In "A Checklist of Lawrence's Reading," Burwell notes that in 1916 Lawrence was reading ancient history and Hesiod and Petrie's *History of Egypt* (84), Maspero's *Egypt: Ancient Sights and Modern Scenes, New Light on Ancient Egypt* (86), and another "Egyptian" book (86). Lawrence spent the 1920s in pursuit of alternative cultures in Australia, America and Europe, and he continued reading about ancient Egypt. In 1922 Lawrence reread Frazer's *Golden Bough.* In 1928, at the time he was writing *The Man Who Died,* Lawrence read Frazer's *Adonis, Attis, Osiris* (Burwell 106), an unnamed French book about Egypt (Burwell 108), and in 1929 Petrie's *Egyptian Tales Translated from the Papyri* (Burwell 110).

Joyce's research may have begun earlier than Lawrence's in the 1909–12 period in Trieste. His Trieste library contained at least two books about the Osiris and Isis myths, and the Leonardo essay by Freud (Ellmann, *The Consciousness of Joyce* 109; Gillespie 9). In the 1920s Joyce also intensified his reading of Egyptology. Joyce studied the work of Sir E. A. Wallis Budge, immersing himself in Egyptology. In writing *Finnegans Wake,* according to Mark L. Troy, Joyce also drew upon words and names of gods from Sir John Gardner Wilkinson's *Manners and Customs of the Ancient Egyptians,* ideas for puns from Sir Peter LaPage Renouf's *Life Work,* and concepts of Egyptian religion from James Henry Breasted's *History of Egypt* and *Development of Religion and Thought in Ancient Egypt* (Troy 19–20).

Research into a buried past was the passion of the times. When Howard Carter discovered King Tut's tomb in November 1922, the already strong interest in Egyptian anthropology and archeology intensified. The elaborate artifacts and mortuary furniture of the youthful pharaoh caught the world's attention.

Freud's own psychoanalytic researches had started with his interest in archeology and ancient culture. Freud specifically connected the uncovering of the psyche to an archeological expedition. Further, to Freud, all "research" points back to that paradigmatic moment when the curious child wants to know from where and how he came to be, as he struggles to understand the father's role in reproduction. Both these strands merge in *Finnegans Wake.*

FREUD'S PSYCHIC ARCHEOLOGY

Freud likened the buried past to hidden, infantile psychic life, connected to the mother, before passage through the Oedipus complex. The ancient civilization of Egypt was covered over by the domination, influence, and survival of Greek culture and Christianity in the West. As a psychoanalytic parallel, the pre-Oedipal stage of the mother-child relationship lies buried under the repression of the Oedipus complex. Constructing a similar kind of analogy, Freud referred to the buried pre-Oedipal stage as the "Minoan-Mycenaean civilization behind the civilization of Greece" in his 1931 essay on female sexuality (*SE* 21: 226).

"Leonardo da Vinci and a Memory of Childhood" and "A Special Type of Object Choice," two essays Freud wrote in 1910, incorporate these three analogies—between psychoanalysis and Egyptology, psychobiography and archeology, and the buried past and the pre-Oedipal period. Freud speculates in these essays on the effects that "arise from the psychical constellation connected with the mother" ("A Special Type of Object-Choice," *SE* 11: 169).[6]

"Leonardo da Vinci and a Memory of Childhood" was Freud's first and last "large-scale excursion into the field of biography," as his editors describe it (*SE* 11: 60). In it Freud discusses the idea of androgynous mother goddesses, presents the concept of "infantile sexual researches," and describes the emergence of the Oedipus complex (which Freud here still calls the "castration" complex). Freud imaginatively reconstructs an infantile phantasy of Leonardo's in order to understand his mental life and to theorize his repressed homosexuality and thirst for knowledge. Freud moves from a small jotting in Leonardo's notebook about a brief childhood memory of a bird coming to his cradle to an elaborate analysis that discusses "the nature and workings of the mind of the creative artist, an outline of the genesis of one particular type of homosexuality, and—of special interest to the history of psycho-analytic theory—the first full emergence of the concept of narcissism" (editor's note, *SE* 11: 62).

Freud constructs his elaborate psychoanalysis by bringing together a dream fragment of Leonardo's with the facts of his family constellation. Leonardo's mother and father were never married. A rich nobleman, Leonardo's father took a "lady of good birth" (*SE* 11: 91) for his wife the very year Leonardo was born. Apparently because this woman remained childless, Leonardo was brought to live in the father's home. From the "facts" that Leonardo spent some years alone with his mother, and that he seemingly had "two" mothers, Freud constructs an analysis of Leonardo's homosexuality resulting from his early childhood confusion over male and female genitals. By repressing and thus preserving the love of his mother, Freud concludes, the homosexual boy "finds the objects of his love along the path of *narcissism*" (*SE* 11: 100).

Freud's thinking is fascinating to follow, as he works out what will become later the Oedipus complex and a theory of narcissism. However, Freud's reconstruction of Leonardo's family relations is entirely blind to cultural issues. For example, being illegitimate would not have been a minor matter in Renaissance Italy. There would have been much shame attached, and Leonardo's presence in his father's and grandfather's house must have been marked by a communal awareness of his irregular birth. Freud assumes the stepmother extends to Leonardo the same overintense love that he assumes his natural mother gave him. Freud attributes Leonardo's repression of sexuality entirely to the overstimulation of the two mother figures. He never speculates that a remote or rejecting father might have had a role, nor does Freud ever imagine that the childless stepmother might have been resentful or jealous of this intelligent, illegitimate son taken into the patriarchal home. In particular, Freud neglects to imagine how Leonardo might have felt about his own mother remaining in poverty, while he lived under the father's patronage, although Freud makes a great deal out of the fact that later when Leonardo is a successful artist he pays for an elaborate funeral for his mother. Freud is blind to any criticism of patriarchy.

Freud's "Leonardo" essay is surely a source work for *Finnegans Wake*. Both the Freud essay and the *Wake* are concerned with the erotic attachment to the mother, rebellion against the father, and the condensation of images. Inquiring into the origin of intellectual creativity, Freud locates it in the sexual curiosity of childhood. Not only does he discuss the androgynous nature of Egyptian gods and goddesses, but he analyzes a sketch of Leonardo's that portrays male and female genitals joined in intercourse, in which the male and female figures overlap in one composite portrait. Freud criticizes Leonardo for the overlapping, arguing that the great artist made a mistake in perspective (confusing male and female feet), revealing his lack of knowledge of women and psychic orientation as a homosexual. In an act very like Leonardo's, and certainly aware of the Freudian charges of narcissism and latent homosexuality, Joyce draws an androgynous, *genital* composite portrait of the two sexes in *Finnegans Wake*.

The notion of a composite portrait itself appears in the "Leonardo" essay. Freud analyzes two of Leonardo's paintings—the Mona Lisa and the Madonna and child with St. Anne. These powerfully enigmatic female images, Freud claims, derive from their deeply buried source; they are composite images of Leonardo's "two mothers." Freud also speculates on the link between the hieroglyph for Mut (a vulture figure) and etymological descent to modern German *Mutter*. The fact that Freud's entire Egyptian speculation was based on his misreading of the kind of bird mentioned in Leonardo's notebooks would hardly have mattered to Joyce, since Joyce constructed his own etymological puns on coincidental associations more than on historically accurate lines. Finally, Freud attributes Leonardo's great power of independent observation and thinking to his rebellion against his father (*SE* 11: 122). I believe Joyce, reading Freud carefully—

including Freud's blindness to patriarchal authority—incorporates all the characteristics of Leonardo into the piecemeal self of *Finnegans Wake*.

The second Freud essay of interest is "A Special Type of Choice of Object Made by Men," written and published in German in 1910 and collected under the general heading "Contributions to the Psychology of Love: A Special Type of Choice of Object made *[sic]* by Men," published in English in 1925 in the *Collected Papers*. Freud begins this essay with a bow to creative writers. They have, he says, until now been our only guide to the motives and conditions for human love. But artists "can show only slight interest in the origin and development of the mental states which they portray in their completed form," whereas science, because of its "renunciation of the pleasure principle" can probe the depths to explain more precisely why men make the object choices they do in love (*SE* 11: 165).

Freud goes on to enumerate four characteristics of a certain kind of love choice made by men. The lover always seeks women who are somehow attached to other men, thus setting up a triangular relation. The lover seeks women who are promiscuous to arouse his own feelings of jealousy because they are a stimulant to his passion. The lover has a compulsion to serial substitution, and the lover constantly desires to rescue the women he loves.

Freud takes pains to emphasize the continuity between "normal" and compulsive love. The two have "the same psychic origin," he says, "derived from the infantile fixation of tender feelings on the mother, and [they] represent one of the consequences of that fixation" (*SE* 11: 168–69). The compulsion that a woman should not be unattached repeats, Freud argues, the earliest family configuration, so that "the injured third party is none other than the father himself" (*SE* 11: 169). The lover chooses love objects, then, that are mother substitutes, as he remains faithful to the earliest family circle. Freud explains the lover's preference for a series, "which seems so flatly to contradict the condition of being faithful to one," in terms of the unconscious, whose forces break up "something irreplaceable" into "an endless series: endless for the reason that every surrogate nevertheless fails to provide the desired satisfaction" (*SE* 11: 169). Giving an example, Freud notes the child's urge to question constantly. The child's endless series masks the one, unasked question: "how did I come to exist?" In the "Leonardo" essay, Freud names this phenomenon "infantile sexual researches," the origin, he claims, of all later, adult intellectual curiosity.

"A Special Type of Object Choice" includes several Freudian ideas important to literature that are scattered in other places. Here Freud repeats the concept of the unconscious as a unity, and the Family Romance as an imaginative acting out in fantasy of the thirst for revenge and desire to rescue, ideas initially put forward in chapter 6 of Freud's book on jokes and in Otto Rank's *Myth of the Birth of the Hero*. Joyce owned the first book, and Kimball argues that Joyce read the second and knew of Freud's Family Romance (see Ellmann, Appendix, *The Consciousness of Joyce*; and Kimball, "James Joyce and Otto Rank"). "A Special Type of Object Choice" also contains Freud's first published use of the term "Oedipus complex."

The psychic structure of romance fantasy that Freud describes in the "Object Choice" essay elucidates the structure of Lawrence's last important work, *The Man Who Died*. So too, the traits Freud discusses, of triangular relationships and seriality, are characteristic of all Joyce's work, but particularly of *Finnegans Wake*. In fact, the *Wake* and *The Man Who Died* contain similar material even though at first glance they seem nothing alike.

The two works use an underlying Easter chronology. In each there is a dead (or sleeping) hero, associated with Jesus as well as overlaid with characteristics and details of Osiris. In both works, the hero is resurrected (or arises) on Easter morning. Both emphasize the literal sexual meaning of arise, although erection in the *Wake* occurs during the unconsciousness of sleep, as does everything else.

The awakening to consciousness, a theme of both, marks the first, and greatest, difference too. Physically awake, the man who died must be rescued from spiritual death in life. His passion for living must be rekindled for "desire was dead in him" (405). On the other hand, the hero of the *Wake* (whoever he is—H.C.E., Finn MacCool, Tim Finnegan, the Master Builder, Adam, Osiris, Van Hoother) sleeps or is dead, dreams or relives over and over again the same old passions that are at once irrepressible and repressed. Just to describe this last difference requires us to enter into and reproduce the elaboration that characterizes Joyce's last work. This elaborate style seems most at odds with Lawrence's *Man Who Died,* a work of extreme spareness and simplicity.

Its very simplicity, however, leads back to its similarity to Joyce's work, for Lawrence's novella is so simple that its tone echoes the forms of fable and fairy tale, two forms repeatedly mimicked in the *Wake.* Although seemingly opposite on the surface, one simple (or even simplistic), one complex, both works rely (differently) on repetition for structure and on punning to establish a field of meaning.

LAWRENCE'S RETURN TO EGYPT: RETURN OF THE REPRESSED?

The Man Who Died begins with an animal fable, two or so pages long, that serves as a parable for the man's (and the universal male) condition. The opening echoes a folktale in its simple formula: "There was a peasant." He had a young gamecock, "a shabby little thing," that soon grows "resplendent," as it arches its neck. The peasant is proud of "his young rooster," of his "fiery color" and even the "unexpected outbursts" "roused" in him. The peasant's wife thinks that the cock "is good for twenty hens" and suspects he will flee beyond their "dirty little yard with three patchy hens," so they tie the cock up by his leg. "Body, soul, and spirit were tied by that string" (399–401).

If the symbolism of the cock is not clear enough, no reader can make a mistake as Lawrence ties the man and the cock together by the thinnest of transitions: "At the same time, at the same hour before dawn, on the same morning [as the cock was crowing] a man awoke from a long sleep in which he was tied up" (401). The man turns out to be the undead Jesus, physically alive but whose desire has died. In short, he needs to be aroused; as an almost pornographic pun, his cock needs to be awakened and freed (not tied to a string in a walled yard).

Lawrence's novella is divided into two parts. The first part revises the Jesus narrative by having him arise after his crucifixion and entombment to seek an alternative salvation to the New Testament story of death and resurrection. Instead of the abstract Christian resurrection in heaven, this story will have a physical arousal of flesh on earth.[7]

The theme of part one is imprisonment and death. The cock is the protagonist's guide in his awakening from death and in the rejection of Christian transcendence as a narrative ending, associated with the ego (420). The theme of part two is the circular journey of renewal and life in the "phenomenal world" (417) associated with the inner "eye" of the phallus, as the protagonist becomes Jesus/Osiris, the Osiris of the broken, scattered body, whose pieces Isis must find in order to restore him to life.

Before continuing with the plot of *The Man Who Died*, we might compare briefly the punning on cock here and the role of the bird with such matters in *Finnegans Wake*. We may wince at Lawrence's pun because of its too obvious sexual reference, but its function is entirely conventional. The cock as barnyard fowl initiates a chain of symbolic substitutions in a closed, finite set. The cock leads us to the man and stands for his physical and spiritual potency, joining the ranks of "totem" figures in other Lawrence works, such as the fox in *The Fox* and the horse St. Mawr in *St. Mawr*.[8] The cock crowing at the light of a new day introduces the themes of the generative power of the sun, the dying sun god Osiris, his renewal by night journey, translated literally as dark sexual union, resulting in the renewal of life through the planting of seed, the release of anxiety, and the recoiling of the "gold and flowing serpent" at the root of the protagonist's tree of life (449). The cock stands for the male set and encompasses the phoenix theme in Lawrence's familiar image of the plumed serpent. Opposite to it is a female symbolic set. The two sets are entirely distinct.

Every bird in the work reasserts the male theme in stable, symbolic exchange. Thus Caesar, whom the priestess of Isis had known as a young girl, has "eagle-like rapacity" (426). A young slave girl brutally raped by another slave at the beginning of part two turns "with a sullen movement" (424) and strips four dead pigeons with a knife, as if taking her revenge upon men in the sacrifice of the birds. This last repeats the theme of the sacrificial, victimized (and castrated) male, like the cock tied by a string in part one. The raped slave girl and her revengeful attitude suggest that male castration (symbolized by the plucked pigeon) is the result of unhealthy, distorted sexuality. Of course, from a psychoanalytic point of view, this romantic notion expresses a defense against castration.

Finnegans Wake contains many birds, all punned upon: hen and biddies (garrulous old women, a character—Kate Strong, emanation of A.L.P., flock of hens, the generic name for an Irish maidservant, deriving from Gaelic *bideach*—very small), Haun (cock), and Bennu bird (phoenix). But the *Wake*'s birds are not conventional literary symbols. They are dream elements in that each is literally convertible to something else—into another person, or gender, or into an animal, object, or place. The great female figure A.L.P. appears as Biddy the hen who finds a letter in a heap of litter (I.1: 10–12). Another old biddy Kate Strong, emanation of A.L.P. and bar maid at the Earwicker tavern, tells in I.4 of how she "left down" her "filthdump near the Serpentine in Phornix Park" (80.5, 6). The hen spills over into the phoenix (literally and figuratively), letter into litter, into defecation and fornication. The puns of the *Wake* point to the unity of the unconscious, as well as to its "apparent" opposite, the endlessly diverse series of substitutions elaborated in the dream text. Overdetermined in the sense that Ernest Jones proposed, all substitutions point back to a single sexual origin in the unconscious. Punning in *Finnegans Wake* thus demonstrates Freud's comments on seriality in his "Object Choice" essay. The *Wake*'s punning recalls the seriality associated with the "psychical constellation of the mother" in the pre-Oedipal period before sexual difference. Each pun is itself, its opposite, and interconnected with all its other appearances and all other puns. In Joyce's work, the puns do not repress otherness or establish sexual difference as the punning title of Lawrence's novella does under its original title, *The Escaped Cock*.

Both works do, however, tell the reader *how* to read their punning birds. Readers do not need external authorization to engage in Freudian symbol hunting, nor do they need to feel illicit in bringing from outside the text some foreign activity such as decoding of phallic symbols. The texts decode themselves, although differently. *Finnegans Wake* refers to itself in its condensed "Wakese" as a "cock and a biddy story":

—And this pattern pootsch punnermine of concoon and proprey went on, hog and minne, a whole whake, your night after larry's night, spittinspite on Dora O'Huggins, ormonde caught butler, the artillery of the O'Hefferns answering the cavalry of the MacClouds, fortey and more fortey, a thousand and one times, according to your cock and a biddy story? (519.3–8)

In the condensed language of the unconscious, story and meaning, phallus, gender division, and sexual activity are one. The passage above describes the style of the book: "punnermine" including puns and pantomime, sexual jealousies, and drawing-room romantics become revenge fantasy with warfare that merges into sexual activity, and the endless and repetitive story-telling of the Arabian tale "A Thousand and One Nights." The *Wake* speaks the language of the Freudian unconscious. In the unconscious system, according to Freud, there is no negation, no differences and gradations, but a unity that at bottom is sexual. Hence the Freudian unconscious is overdetermined (having many causes) and is also sexually determined (all originating from sexuality). In the same way, Joyce's whole book is a cock and biddy story, as the book itself announces.[9]

Stylistically so different, Lawrence's text speaks in the traditional language of the storyteller. It explicitly tells us to read its cock as a conventional symbol, where the vehicle and tenor are separable:

And always the man who had died saw not the bird alone, but the short, sharp wave of life of which the bird was the crest. He watched the queer, beaky motion of the creature as it gobbled into itself the scraps of food; its glancing of the eye of life, ever alert and watchful, overweening and cautious, and the voice of its life, crowing triumph and assertion, yet strangled by a cord of circumstance. (408)

The Man Who Died establishes and constantly reaffirms difference in its symbols, in the two-part structure and in the differing literary style of the two parts. While the bird stands for the male symbolic set, the flower stands for the female principle. The female symbolic set includes narcissus, lotus, bud, womb, the dream, and the "penetrable rock of the living woman" (444), explicitly revising the New Testament.

Whereas the opening of part one is formulaic and passive ("There was a peasant"), part two begins as a novel does with an action that establishes the setting: "The wind came cold and strong from inland" (422). The priestess of Isis stands on a promontory of land above the sea facing the sun in a yellow robe and white linen "like a winter narcissus" (423). She attends to the goddess Isis in her "small temple of wood, painted all pink and white and blue, having at the front four wooden pillars rising like stems to the swollen lotus-bud of Egypt at the top" (424). Rooted in place, keeper of the temple, a "penetrable rock," the female represents space, as the male marks off time with his circular return, his "queer beaky motion" and "sharp wave of life."

Finnegans Wake also makes the distinction between woman as space, man as time, even though both separable abstractions (man, woman) more often appear merged in objects—for instance "tea"—that are condensed forms of genital shapes and sexual actions.[10] According to Freud, condensation and elaboration are two sides of the same coin. So both represent the overdetermined unity of the unconscious. For example, the children's mathematics lesson of II.2 presents the geometry of the mother (293), "whome sweetwhome" as it is called in another place (138. 30), "the whome of your eternal geomater" (296.31–297.1). Studying their "lessons," the children act out Freud's "infantile sexual researches" and display intellectual curiosity. They literally here want to learn where they came from and look at the genitals of the mother. (Their curiosity to know the mother supplements Freud too, though, since he always posited this research in terms of discovering the hidden *role of the father* in reproduction—here the literal hidden *place of the mother*.) Investigating the father's purported crime in the park may also be a dream substitution for discovering his role in reproduction, and it is never quite figured out. "Is dads the thing in such or are tits the that?" (528.15–16)

Father, associated with history and wars, is full of "pugnaxities," so that rulers come and go like the inflation and deflation of the phallus "during the effrays round fatherthyme's beckside" (90. 6, 7).[11] Another common pun on time, "Dime after dime" (138. 15), connects father time to money. The connection to money suggests the equation Freud discovered in his analysis of paranoia as a defense against homosexuality in his study of Schreber. "Faeces-money-gift-baby-penis are treated there [in the unconscious] as though they meant the same thing, and they are represented too by the same symbols" (*SE* 22: 98).[12]

In *The Man Who Died* the distinction between the sexes reflects the division of consciousness. As the man literally awakes to consciousness in the story, we could say he enacts the dissolution of the Oedipus complex, acceding to the laws of culture, accepting sexual difference, and taking his place as inheritor of patriarchal culture. He accepts a structure that represents woman as castrated. Consequently, he sees the woman in her symbolic position as representing difference from the male. She is guardian of the dream; she represents (for the male) the repressed unconscious realm. Before the priestess of Isis meets the man who died, she muses in her temple in order "to go away into the dreams of the goddess" (425). Aloof and cool to all men, she lives in a dream state; "the very flower of her womb was cool, was almost cold, like a bud in shadow of frost" (426). "A maid should open to the sun" (426), but she would not. Not, that is, until the man who died comes to rescue her, a "woman entangled in her own dream" (428).

If he rescues her from her own narcissism, he does so by making her a mirror to reflect his own needs. Part one has established how tired of his own ego he has been. The priestess of Isis strikes him as unutterably alone in her "female difference" (440). She is not his ego, but different, so she offers him respite from himself. And he believes "he was only a dream-object to her" (441). Thus he escapes from the obdurateness and compulsion of his own ego he complained of in part one, as he evaporates into her dream. She restores his broken, suffering body through the healing powers of desire she arouses in him. He thinks, "I have never before stretched my limbs in such sunshine as her desire for me" (439).

Notice that male and female symbolic attributes appear to make an exchange here. He becomes part of her dream state, as "dream-object," or so he imagines. He describes her desire possessing the male potency of sunshine. They make an exchange, but each remains alone and essentially unaware of the other at the level of the ego. "She would never know or understand what he was. . . . But what did it matter? She was different" (441). "Yet she knew that he would go. And even she wanted the coolness of her own air around her, and the release from anxiety" (448). Their exchange, involving the phallic "eye," not the ego's "I," occurs at the level of the unconscious. Sexual union momentarily restores the unity of the unconscious, whose loss is experienced in the division that establishes consciousness and gender.

The priestess of Isis serves that aspect of the goddess Isis Lawrence calls "Isis Bereaved, Isis in Search" (425). This Isis searches for the dead Osiris's scattered body parts. "She must find his hands and his feet, his heart, his thighs, his head, his belly, [sic] she must gather him together and fold her arms round the re-assembled body till it became warm again, and roused to life, and could embrace her, and could fecundate her womb" (425).

Whereas Lawrence portrays Isis as a whole image, a single character, Joyce renders her in various, multiple, and humorous ways in the *Wake*. In the Osiris myth, Isis searches along the Nile. The *Wake* equates watery images with the female figure. Generally A.L.P. herself is the flowing river. Issy's name is a pun on Isis, and Issy's girlish self-indulgent nature is expressed by tears (Isis bereaved—for herself), her seductive side by lilting syllables of rain. The banks of the river, *rivae*, where Isis searched for Osiris's body parts, become the competing brothers, Shaun and Shem, and rain turns into urination and ejaculation too, so that male and female join. In the "Mookse and Gripes" story, for example, the warring twosome are analogues to Shem and Shaun. Rivals, they occupy opposite banks of the river, and Issy, as Nuvoletta, rains on them: "And as it rinn it dribbled like any lively purliteasy" (153.6–7). The searching part of the Isis story becomes "infantile sexual researches," the hen's pecking the letter out of the dump—a sort of archeological search, and the investigation of the Phoenix Park crime.

What Lawrence leaves out of the Isis myth is at least as telling as what he includes. He slides over the missing phallus. According to the myth as related by Plutarch, Osiris's body had been scattered in fourteen pieces, and although Isis found thirteen of those pieces, she never found the last: "notwithstanding all her search, Isis was never able to recover the privy-member of Osiris. . . . In order, however, to make some amends for the loss, Isis consecrated the Phallus made in imitation of it" (Plutarch qtd. in Budge 192–93).

Joyce builds many of his complex puns in *Finnegans Wake* on this detail of the Isis-Osiris myth, especially on the terms "hand-made" and "hand-maid." For example, "Would one but to do apart a lilybit her virginelles and, so, to breath, so, therebetween, behold, she had instantt with her handmade as to graps the myth inmid the air" (561.24–26) (her handgrasp makes the penis erect, restoring the mythic phallus; as well as the male hand parting the female genitals; hence, the "hand-maid" of Isis restores the missing part). Margaret Solomon, following the lead of Bernard Benstock, points out that the missing letters in god words (such as "the" minus its "o" and "diu" minus its "e") represent Osiris's missing phallus and may be the "letter" the hen pecks up out of the midden heap (81–82). Joyce's book also contains the Lawrentian version of phallic restoration, reduced to literal genitality, as Anna and Humphrey, near dawn, attempt to make love: "tanks tight anne thynne for her contractations tugowards his personeel. Echo, choree chorecho! O I you O you me!" (*FW* 584.32–34).[13]

The Man Who Died slides over Osiris's sexual mutilation, although Lawrence probably alludes to it and conflates it with Jesus' wound: "She was stooping now, looking at the scar in the soft flesh of the socket of his side, a scar deep and like an eye sore with endless weeping, just in the soft socket above his hip. It was here that his blood had left him, and his essential seed" (442–43).

If Lawrence covers Osiris's lost member in some confusion and abstraction, he represses even more completely Isis's active restoration of Osiris's missing phallus. In contrast, when we peak into the bedroom of the couple in *Finnegans Wake*, we see "photoflashing it far too wide" (583.15–16) against the window shade that "old pairamere" are engaged in "a gallop, a gallop" (583.12) with the woman on top, the man below.

In Lawrence's version, the man regains his phallic potency at the moment when the woman is "crouching," "hiding her face" (444). "He crouched to her, and he felt the blaze of his manhood and his power rise up in his loins, magnificent" (444). With the woman in a weak, submissive position, the man who died regains his potency.

In psychic terms, the man who died reenacts the passage through the Oedipus complex. Before that passage, the young boy desires his mother. But he must turn away from her in the face of the threat of castration (his weeping "eye sore"). The boy defends himself from the threat of castration by accepting sexual difference and giving up the mother for the moment. In passing through the Oedipus complex, the boy accepts the promised power and position of the father he will become in the future and accepts the law of patriarchy (the female as castrated). The man who died impregnates the priestess and thus he will become a father.

Interestingly, the priestess of Isis lives with her mother, not alone: "The mother with grey head stood at the sea's edge and watched the daughter" (436). Judith Ruderman comments that the mother is cast in a "distinctly unfavorable light" (165), arguing that she is another example of the "devouring mother." Ruderman blames the mother for the man's leaving. Although the text does indicate that the mother's slaves may be a threat to the man, it also emphasizes that his leaving is destined. "I must go now soon" (447). In leaving, he is fulfilling his male role: "But I am a man, and the world is open" (447). He leaves to retain his freedom, and he goes laughing to himself (448). Further, to see his leaving as forced ignores the cyclic returning structure of the Osiris myth: "And when the nightingale calls again from your valley-bed, I shall come again, sure as Spring" (447).

The mother really plays no role in the story other than as a figure that *watches* the man and woman. I propose that her shadowy figure might be an example of what Freud calls an uncanny doubling, and her "watching" may enact the looking of the pre-Oedipal stage, when the child is curious to see sexual difference. "Before the child comes under the dominance of the castration-complex," writes Freud in "Leonardo," "at a time when he still holds women at full value—he begins to display an intense desire to look" (*SE* 11: 96).

If we view the plot of *The Man Who Died* as a reenactment of the Oedipus complex, actually a romance fantasy derived from it, the mother as double of the female figure makes sense. After all, the male in the Oedipal drama desires to sleep with the mother (in the substitution of the story, the daughter) but must leave the mother. If the narrative sounds slightly unfavorable toward her, this merely preserves acceptance of her castration necessary for the male to make the passage away from the mother. The "invention of doubling," Freud says, is a "preservation against extinction" and "has its counterpart in the language of dreams, which is fond of representing castration by a doubling or multiplication of a genital symbol." He notes, "but when this stage has been surmounted, the 'double' reverses its aspect. From having been an assurance of immortality, it becomes the uncanny harbinger of death" ("The Uncanny," *SE* 17: 234–35). What defends against castration, reminds us of it, and comes to stand for it.

Juliet Mitchell reminds us that there are actually always four terms operating in the Oedipal drama: "The Oedipus complex, then, is not the trinity it is so often envisaged as—mother, father, child—but a relationship between four terms of which the fourth and the determinate one is castration" (*Psychoanalysis and Feminism* 79). Lawrence's story contains three of those terms—the doubled mother/daughter figure, the male child/hero and castration (the man's implied crucifixion of part one and his "wound" and spiritual malaise of part two). But where is the father?

Freud's analysis of Family Romance fantasies in "A Special Type of Object Choice" suggests the answer. Freud notes that fantasies of rescuing the mother derive from the child's impulse toward independence as well as his desire to repay the parents with a gift. Thus "rescuing the mother takes on the significance of giving her a child or making a child for her—needless to say, one like himself." Freud continues, "in other words, in the rescue-phantasy he is completely identifying himself with his father. All his instincts, those of tenderness, gratitude, lustfulness, defiance and independence, find satisfaction in the single wish *to be his own father*" (172–73).

We might say, then, that the father figure is present in embryo, implanted within the body of the woman, as germinating seed. Viewed in this way, *The Man Who Died* expresses the wish for independence through immortality. To be your own father means that you are not generated but self-begotten, and as such is a defense fantasy against the ultimate castration of death.

I suggested above that the man's rescue of the priestess of Isis from her self-reflective narcissism is not convincing. She lacks substance as an independent will, independent in the way that Ursula and Gudrun were in *Women in Love*. She lacks any characterization. This is not surprising if the psychic structure of the story is a romance fantasy expressing the hero's wish to be his own father. Like a mirror she reflects back upon him the image of his own desires, just as in dreams and fantasies the drives of the unconscious create characters to represent its wishes. As I noted earlier, her mother watches the two lovers from afar, and this also suggests the "looking" involved with discovery in the mirror stage.

In psychoanalysis, the mirror stage marks the moment of recognition of difference, the institution of self and other into the baby's unity. "[T]he baby leaves himself and then finds himself in a mirror. We can see from this game that the child constitutes the other as object, constitutes himself as the other in the eyes of the other for himself" (Mitchell 384). The foundation of the subject is "dependent upon the discovery of difference" (Mitchell 386). Discovering the mirror stage in the play of his small grandson led Freud to formulate the repetition-compulsion of the death drive.

Lacan took the importance of the mirror stage even further than Freud, postulating that its *imago* is an imaginary construct that never is identical to the self because the self does not exist before it is constructed. The mirror does not reflect a one-to-one correspondence, then, according to Lacan, but reveals a relation of an imagined one (the *imago*) to zero. Thus, according to Lacan, a search for a genuine Other (as I have argued Lawrence seems interested in) indicates that the subject is stuck in the Imaginary realm of a mirror image, actually an identification process pointing back toward a self that does not exist before it has been constructed. From Lacan's point of view, then, the romantic quest exhibits the symptoms of repetition-compulsion from which Freud formulated the death drive.

The entire structure of *The Man Who Died* demonstrates a dyadic nature. The work itself is divided into two parts, each marked by opposite subject matter and style. The symbolism falls into two categories, those accruing around the male principle and those of the female. The first dyadic relationship may be the self and its mirror image, after which comes the pre-Oedipal relation of child and mother (self and other). All this "twoness" might suggest that *The Man Who Died* represents pre-Oedipal drives and fantasies, those coming after the unitary existence of the baby but before a third term has intruded between the mother and child at the Oedipal passage.

Generally, the passage through the Oedipus complex means introducing a third term between mother and child (father/castration). I have indicated how the third (or third and fourth if we follow Juliet Mitchell) term makes its appearance in the novel. And if we consider that the "action" of the plot is sexual intercourse and passage away from the mother (to be), then we can also see that *The Man Who Died* draws upon the rich psychic storehouse of the Oedipus complex.

At first, we might think that the dyadic structure and pre-Oedipal themes of close relation with an Other contradict the notion that the plot represents the Oedipal passage. But the psyche preserves and transforms pre-Oedipal material. For example, the looking of the mirror stage during which the self is discovered/constructed as a mirror image becomes the sexual looking by which sexual difference is perceived.

Lawrence's story touches on all the Oedipal themes. It affirms sexual difference, in fact, dwells on it. The plot contains a rescue fantasy and an exchange of gifts (the giving of a child in exchange for the restoration of manhood from the threat of castration). It resembles an Oedipal Family Romance, an imaginary construct that ultimately expresses, according to Freud in his "Object Choice" essay, the wish of independence, while it preserves the dyadic relation of mother and child, and mirror relation of self to image. Oddly balanced between pre- and post-Oedipal concerns, the novel includes castration but does slide over it somewhat. It folds the father figure into the man himself (he is already castrated and he himself is father, since he inseminates the woman with his child). This Family Romance does not exactly deny death but incorporates death into the life cycle. Thus the man, following the Osiris myth, becomes enfolded into the organic. The "gold and flowing serpent" that is his life energy will sleep in his form as a tree, until it is time for another awakening.

When Lawrence revises the Jesus narrative by turning to the Isis/Osiris myth, he rejects linear time and death for cyclic return. The last words of the novel are "So let the boat carry me. To-morrow is another day" (449). But since in the story the male symbolizes time and the female space, does this ending reject the male principle by rejecting time, since on his return he comes back to the same place, male joining the female?

The joining of male/female accords well with Egyptian myth. In the earliest epochs the gods and goddesses started as separate figures, but over time they became consolidated. Freud's quote at the head of this chapter describes the goddess Mut's male/female attributes. Freud goes on in his "Leonardo" essay to note, "an androgynous structure, a combination of male and female sex characters, was an attribute not only of Mut but also of other deities like Isis and Hathor" (*SE* 11: 94). But Lawrence's Isis has no phallus, as does the Mut/Isis figure Freud describes.[14] So if *The Man Who Died* preserves the concept of androgyny, it preserves it only abstractly in the general themes of the Osiris story and perhaps in the joining of male to female in cyclic return. (This is different from the litter heap of the *Wake*, where everything is abstract *and* literal at once.)

The end of Lawrence's novel refers to two aspects of the Osiris myth. Osiris was tricked by a rival into getting into a chest, whereupon it was nailed shut. Thrown into the Nile, the chest was carried to the sea. On the coast, it lodged in some branches, "which in a short time shot up into a large and beautiful tree, growing round the chest and enclosing it on every side" (Plutarch qtd. in Budge 189). The last lines of Lawrence's novel refer to the cyclic journey the Egyptians believed occurred every day when the dead sun god Osiris traveled by boat toward the west and then in a circle through the underworld of the dead to reappear the following day in the east as the risen sun.

Lawrence returns to this aspect of the Osiris myth in his death poem cycle. In "The Ship of Death" the poet/speaker *is* Osiris, with mutilated body, dying in pieces, who must build and furnish his "little ark" for the journey of death into oblivion:

> There is no port, there is nowhere to go
> only the deepening blackness darkening still
> blacker upon the soundless, ungurgling flood
> darkness at one with darkness, up and down
> and sideways utterly dark, so there is no direction any more
> and the little ship is there; yet she is gone.
> She is not seen, for there is nothing to see her by.[15]

The ark is female. The soul setting out on the journey into the unknown is female: "Piecemeal the body dies, and the timid soul/ has her footing washed away, as the dark flood rises." Since it rises, we may think of that flood as male, but again as in *The Man Who Died* the male representation may be somewhat repressed. The dark flood is a "black waste/ upon the waters of the end/ upon the sea of death." In contrast to the blackness of death and oblivion, the end of the journey is cast in the rosy pink hues of dawn, recalling Isis's temple in *The Man Who Died:*

> The flood subsides, and the body, like a worn sea-shell
> emerges strange and lovely.
> And the little ship wings home, faltering and lapsing
> on the pink flood,
> and the frail soul steps out, into the house again
> filling the heart with peace.

The body, represented in the image of the seashell, joins the female imagery, suggesting Aphrodite stepping from the sea, as the "frail soul" steps out of the little ship and begins again a domestic existence. Seashell and house, or Isis's temple, these female symbols temporarily hold back the soundless, sightless, nothingness of the male oblivion.

The poem begins in a tribute to Keats's great ode to autumn. But whereas Keats, nearing death, fills his poem with images of plenitude and contentment, Lawrence's poem expresses the stripping away and loss of the self:

Now it is autumn and the falling fruit
    and the long journey towards oblivion.

The apples falling like great drops of dew
to bruise themselves an exit from themselves.

Here the fall of mankind in the Garden of Eden, a Christian symbol of death, merges into the Egyptian myth, in the same way as the two myths merge in the novella, with the Christian myth the prologue to the Osiris myth. The bruised apple, with its "great drops of dew," recalls the image of castration in *The Man Who Died,* with his "eye sore" weeping. And death and castration meet in the male symbol of the flood:

Already the dark and endless ocean of the end
is washing in through the breaches of our wounds,
already the flood is upon us.

In *Sons and Lovers* Mr. Morel was initially aligned with sexuality, death, and the natural world, Mrs. Morel with culture and striving. I pointed out that these associations are opposite to those of patriarchal culture, where the father usually represents the rule of law and the mother the world of nature. I argued that at her death Mrs. Morel becomes identified with the nonhuman in the starry infinitude of the universe and only then finally arrives at the symbolic position of women associated with nature. The immense size of the universe made Paul feel slight and vulnerable, a frail speck upright, suggesting that through his

identification with his dead mother he feels the threat of castration and turns away from her. I argued that the novel charted
Paul's passage through the Oedipus complex. However difficult
the passage, he turns outward from home and family at the end.

In retrospect, however, we can see that the father's role as
rival/castrator/third party is underemphasized, just as in *The Man
Who Died*. Paul's perception of his mother changes more clearly
than any change in his perception of the father. She joins the
father's realm associated with death, as perceived from the pre-
Oedipal point of view. In death she completes the threat of
castration that propels Paul to complete his Oedipal passage. We
do not really see the father coming to represent the laws of
culture.

The sexual themes of color, symbol, and image in "The Ship
of Death" repeat the earliest pre-Oedipal configuration in *Sons
and Lovers*. The female clearly symbolizes culture in the images
of house and shell. But in this late poem, culture is a haven
without any conflicts. Its images are associated with the rosy dawn
and renewal of life. Its male opposite, associated with blackness,
nothingness, and death, is not strongly marked as masculine.

The female figure has undergone an interesting change,
then, since the early fiction. In *The Man Who Died* and in "The
Ship of Death" female symbols seem entirely positive. The female
figures restore loss with the promise of new life. However, no
longer an independent will, the female seems merely a mirror
reflection of the male's wishes and thus an imaginary defense
against castration.[16]

Sons and Lovers presented a more complex and interesting
situation. Mrs. Morel herself was castrator as well as castrated.
She makes her son identify with her so entirely that he takes
on her castration, thus becoming castrated by her. As Nancy
Chodorow points out in *The Reproduction of Mothering*, in socializ-
ing her children, the mother acts out the law of the father,
reproducing patriarchy. Paul's progress through the Oedipus
complex has a lot in common with the difficult path of the female,
who must identify with, and yet turn away from, her mother.

Sons and Lovers is so interesting because the novel reveals the contradictions among the actual economic conditions that make Mrs. Morel dependent on her working-class husband, her very independent striving as a believer in individualism, and the repressed laws of culture under which, as a female, she bears the mark of castration. I argued that the novel gives a voice to the woman's position, which is usually silenced in the male narrative of the Oedipus complex, as in *The Man Who Died.*

When Lawrence postpones the reproduction of family relations, as he does in *Sons and Lovers* and *The Rainbow,* or breaks up the symmetry of dyadic relations, as the end of *Women in Love* does, the resultant asymmetry of relations opens up a space for articulating the contradictions between (repressed) psychic laws and the contemporary needs of reality. In *Psychoanalysis and Feminism,* Juliet Mitchell explains:

The patriarchal law speaks to and through each person in his unconscious; the reproduction of the ideology of human society is thus assured in the acquisition of the law by each individual. The unconscious that Freud analysed could thus be described as the domain of the reproduction of culture or ideology. The contradiction that exists between this law that is now essentially redundant but that of course still continues to speak in the unconscious, and the form of the nuclear family is therefore crucial. (413)[17]

Sons and Lovers and *The Rainbow* explore the repression of male/female sexuality under patriarchy and the resulting damage to marriage relations, while *Women in Love* explores the losses resulting from repression of man-to-man relations.

All Lawrence's writing (even the overtly phallic, such as *The Man Who Died*) expresses the desire to undo the consequences of the Oedipus complex—to return to a dyadic relation with another, to restore the loss caused by castration, to restore the female to an equal position with the male, and to engage in a "genuine" exchange with an Other—male, female, or an Other culture. But the works also focus on the Oedipal passage, because that is when sexual difference is irrevocably established. Because

Lawrence's texts both accept and desire to undo patriarchy, they are often nostalgic or ambivalent.

Lawrence's interest in self and Other, in "polar" relationship, expresses the ambivalence in the dyadic relationship—the wish to be independent and the need for another, since the self is defined through relation to another. The interest in discovering the self through relation to another as well as in merging and momentarily giving up the self suggests the early "mirror" stage of psychic development. As psychoanalysts point out, however, a subject locked into mirror relations is doomed to the uncanny doubling of repetition compulsion, expressive of the death drive.

Indeed, Lawrence is fond of doubling. He uses the double female figure repeatedly in *The Rainbow* and *Women in Love* as well as in *The Man Who Died*. The double female figure restores phallic power to the castrated woman and thus can also be seen as a sign of her castration. When I discussed *The Rainbow* in chapter 2, I noted the first Brangwen wife has added substance and mystery because she is a Polish widow and aristocrat and already possesses a child. She thus possesses both the quality of otherness Lawrence sought from foreign and minority cultures and the substitute phallus that Freud says a baby represents. The promise of a baby, Freud argues, replaces the loss of the phallus the female realizes she lacks at the Oedipal passage. But according to Freud, only the birth of a *boy* baby completely satisfies her lack; the boy child becomes her phallus. Interestingly, Lydia has a girl child, the first Anna, who is herself repeated and doubled by the second Anna Brangwen, thus setting in motion a chain of doubled, substitute women.

Gudrun and Ursula Brangwen are the two most obvious examples of doubled women in Lawrence, especially when we consider that he called his first composite version of *The Rainbow* and *Women in Love* "The Sisters." However, there are also the male doubles of Rupert and Gerald. At first, we might think the two pairs of doubles make *Women in Love* structurally symmetrical like *The Man Who Died*, where the heroine has a double in the mother figure and the hero an implied double in the shadow role of father he will become. Gudrun/Ursula and Gerald/Rupert, if viewed as composites, also seem to form a dyadic structure. However, the plot of *Women in Love* relentlessly works against this apparent symmetry by eliminating Gerald. When Gerald, child of the patriarchal Crich family, is killed off in icy coldness, the configuration of characters returns to the familiar Lawrentian relation of two, but this time in uneasy alliance.

With Gudrun left over as a reminder of failed relations, the ending implies that Ursula and Rupert will maintain their "polar" relationship only with difficulty. The novel ends with the distinctive Lawrence triad—man and woman in relation, with the woman figure doubled. Psychologically, the doubled female figure makes up for, and is also a sign of, castration. The uneasy alliance of the ending, which I called its negative dialectics, gives *Women in Love* its power because it allows an asymmetrical opening in what could have been a closed dyadic structure. Lawrence's best fiction preserves open endings, usually by the asymmetry created through the death of a character.[18] The underlying dyadic structure, the wish for the ideal relation of two, usually with a doubled female figure (who in making up for female castration is a differential sign of the missing phallus), expresses the distinctive Lawrentian point of view, accepting and yet wishing to undo, the Oedipus complex, the rule of patriarchy.

OVERTHROWING THE CHRISTIAN
HOLY FAMILY IN *FINNEGANS WAKE*

Joyce's "book of Doublends Jined" (*FW* 20.15–16), needless to say, has doubles galore. Doubling is necessary to read the text up close, word by word, phrase by phrase. By their look-alike, sound-alike distortions, the words on the page evoke memories of conventional language of the everyday Dublin world. The text generates meaning from the conflict between its hovering double (what is not on the page, but what we as readers supply) and the distortions on the page. But doubling quickly leads to further multiplication in the *Wake*. The text calls up not only its double from everyday language but also its counterparts from many languages and cultures throughout history. All readers, I think, feel a lack in themselves that the text evokes.

Each character, story, phrase, or even consonant (such as P, T, L) return in disguises, multiplying and repeating themselves. The process of multiplication replaces narrative development, occurring as one moves through the book as well as through the word, phrase, and sentence. I think most readers—if they stick with the book long enough—will eventually experience the book's repetition as consoling, because it makes possible identification and comparative reading (another doubling) by which understanding of the book's richness is enlarged. Slowly advancing through the amplifications, a reader starts to make sense of bits and even to laugh at insider's jokes. So the repetition partially makes up for the reader's initial feelings of inadequacy. From a psychological viewpoint, the book's "secondmouth language" (37.15) at first provokes an experiencing of castration, which then must be worked through. In this way, doubling functions as Freud described in his essay on "The Uncanny" and as the doubled females do in Lawrence—both as sign of and way of overcoming castration.[19]

Finnegans Wake is not a romance, however, and castration cannot be ever completely overcome. The book eludes transparency and decoding, remaining ambiguous, opaque, rich in possibilities, and always beyond any reader's total grasp. Indeed, some readers are disturbed by the book's endless repetition, and they often call upon psychoanalysis to back up their response. In *The Decentered Universe of Finnegans Wake,* for example, Margot Norris argues that the Viconian plan Joyce adopted could potentially indicate both a "cyclical and evolutional" (24) view of history. However, the progression of time "is abandoned" (25) and repeated events appear to be "compulsive, that is, produced by irrational rather than logical necessity" (25). The book's "pseudostylic shamiana" (*FW* 181.36–182.1), its tortured intelligibility that requires readers to study the author so intensely, leads Colin MacCabe to declare, finally, its perverse narcissism pointing away from history and the external world back to the private peculiarities of Joyce himself (*JJ and the Revolution of the Word*).

Joyce always anticipates his critics, as the *Wake*'s self-parody and out-and-out parody of various critical "schools" (I.6) abundantly demonstrate. One could say that viewing narcissism and perversity as the unfortunate residue of the author's own excesses is a way to resist the book's message from "that other world." But that need not be said, since Joyce already declares that the text is constructed from "his wit's waste" (185.7–8). He preempts psychoanalytic excuses to dismiss his work: "I can psoakoonaloose myself any time I want (the fog follow you all!) without you interferences or any other pigeonstealer" (522.34–36). Blocking escape or denial, the text draws the reader into that other place, inside the mirror (Alice's looking-glass world) because it is made out of its own (private, yes, echoing Swift's private baby talk) language that undoes the law of noncontradiction: "in the Nichtian glossery which purveys aprioric roots for aposteriorious tongues this is nat language at any sinse of the world" (83.10–12). The text "immerges [us in] a mirage in a merror" (310.24). Undoing repression, *Finnegans Wake* explores the unconscious and the relation there between narcissism, perversity, and intellectual creativity, an exploratory project Freud began in his "Leonardo" essay.

Discussion of repetition compulsion and mirror worlds comes back to the concept of mirror stage, to early psychic development before passage through the Oedipus complex, where narcissism and perversity hold sway. The opposite of neuroses, according to Freud, perversions are "the acting out by the adult of one or other of the undirected, hence polymorphously perverse, sexual drives that the child manifests" (Mitchell 10). Remember that at the mirror stage, the infant discovers its own image and thereby constructs himself as an object in the world for others. In Lacan's terms, the mirror image never equals the self (an absence), and so by the child's own lack he propels himself forward. To Freud, seeing his little grandson repeatedly play a here/there game with a spool and thread meant that the child was mastering the mother's absence through repetition and thereby learning that he was separate from the mother by creating a game. To be locked into the mirror stage, however, is to be bound to repetition compulsion, never advancing, but always reenacting the backward connection between the self and the lost other.

The mirror stage of psychic development is at the core of Joyce's exploration because as a concept it stands for a psychological moment where two puzzling ideas converge: perpetual exchange (locked in the mirror) and change (constructing an image that propels the self to develop). In chapter 3, I traced a conundrum emerging from *A Portrait* and taking shape in *Ulysses*: "how does change come from exchange?" Wakese expresses this riddle immediately on the first page in a condensation that unknotted—as one of many readings[20]—might be put as the question: "What is the difference between a vicious circle and 'commodious vicus of recirculation'"? (3.2).

Commodius, of course, means spacious, convenient, suitable, suggesting there is room for something new. By soundalikes, it reminds the reader of Molly's commode, thus leading to ideas of urinating and defecating. (Recirculation, too, refers to the river Liffey and so includes A.L.P. and all watery analogues.) It also introduces the associated word "commodity," especially in their common etymology as "a convenience, a profit," and "a quantity of goods" from the Middle English and extending back to the Latin *commoditās*, combining both advantage and convenience. "Vicus" is a Joycean coinage incorporating Vico, sounding like "vicious," and connected semantically to "vicinity." "Vicious" descends from Latin *vitium*, vice, and "vicinity" from the Latin *vicus*, village, quarter, or district of town, which itself comes from the far older Indo-European root *weik* meaning "clan."[21] The text sets up its own Viconian dialectic between what is given and what is evoked. Beneath the euphonious surface of the text's language, sounding a lot like a real estate broker selling land (a commodity exchange of capitalism), lie scatology, vice, viciousness, and the earliest structures of culture, the clan, with hints of the exchange of women, as commodities, by men. How did humans get from clan to community, from incest and internecine warfare to "muddlecrass" (152.8) family structure?

John Bishop argues that Vico's theory of the dialectical development of human culture appealed to Joyce in deeply held ways, and that Vico's *New Science* does more in *Finnegans Wake* than just "transmit the news that the same things happened over and over again in quadrupartite cycles" (175). Bishop reminds us that Vico is taken very seriously by historiographers. Vico developed "a form of internal dialectic to which Marx would later refer in *Capital* and which the Marxist philosopher Georges Sorel would even later apply to the theory of the general strike" (179). Moreover, Vico argued that the dialectical development of culture could be traced through etymology, and he described human evolution in terms of human psychology. "Vico's peculiarly modern willingness to admit total unreason along with reason as a motivating force of history," Bishop points out, must have also endeared him to Joyce (180).

There are pronounced similarities between Freud and Vico. Freud's theories of psychic development are also dialectical, emphasizing the role of the irrational in structuring the ego. His theory of human culture is also evolutionary, and Freud even speculated on the connection between linguistic development and dream analysis, engaging in his own etymological demonstrations. Joyce always claimed that he was more influenced by Vico than by Freud. "My imagination grows when I read Vico as it doesn't when I read Freud or Jung," he reportedly told Tom Kristensen (Ellmann, *JJ* 693). However, despite Joyce's disclaimers, there is ample evidence that both thinkers find their way into the synthetic accretion of *Finnegans Wake*.

Of course, in this century filled with mass destruction, many people find it difficult to see any sign of human progress, let alone believe in it. As in the darkness of night and sleep, "we are circumveiloped by obscuritads" (244.15). We no longer easily believe that contradictions lead to change, that thesis and antithesis lead to a new synthesis. More often, to twentieth-century eyes, tyrant and victim seem merely to exchange roles and take turns oppressing one another. Foes produce their opposite mirror images, locked in perpetual warfare with no resolution in sight. One example, relevant to Joyce and still unresolved, are the troubles of Northern Ireland. Catholic and Protestant factions continue their conflict, like Shem and Shaun, stuck in perpetual battle and rivalry, each pointing to the other, in the same old vicious circle.

If we can no longer believe in dialectical progression, we might answer the initial question, "how did we get from there to here," by denying that we did and pointing out that beneath the false surface of civilization are the same old primitive impulses. Conventional satire often renders such a view, and the *Wake* incorporates the conventions of satire in the familiar Joycean satiric inflation and deflation and in its irony of double speech. I believe the *Wake* includes satire's conservative stance ("from each equinoxious points of view, the one fellow's fetch being the other follow's person" [85.28–29]). But the book does not stop there. It covers satire's "twos" with the "threes" of dialectics.[22]

A third term, even if it can barely be made out in the bad light and confusion of the dream world, admits the possibility of dialectical movement and escape from the closed, vicious circle that mirroring can represent. Simple puns talk the double language of irony. But the complex puns of the *Wake* most often act like a third force, bending the field of meaning in many directions beyond (but including) a simple contrary inversion. The result is not dialectical progression by resolution of opposites but proliferation and multiplicity, creation flowing outward from excess.

In *Negative Dialectics,* the philosopher T. W. Adorno argues that dialectics is not a standpoint but movement propelled by excess, by "the remainder" (5) for which our present concepts are inadequate. Adorno dissolves the substantiality of contradiction. "Contradiction is nonidentity under the aspect of identity," he argues, and "the dialectical primary of the principle of contradiction makes the thought of unity the measure of heterogeneity. As the heterogeneous collides with its limit it exceeds itself" (5).

Superimposed over dualities in the *Wake* are triads. Between H.C.E. and A.L.P. are their three children, crying in the night and disturbing the parental coupling. A distinctively Wakean *"tertium quid"* (*FW* 526.12), Shem, Shaun and Issy also call to mind the triangular relationships found in other Joyce texts:

—*Three in one, one and three.*
Shem and Shaun and the shame that sunders em.
Wisdom's son, folly's brother. (526.13–15)

Children of the Earwicker or Porter family, the twin brothers and their sister continue Joyce's preoccupation with triads formed by two rival men and a woman. I discussed this configuration in *Exiles* and *Ulysses,* concluding that it expresses a male wish to be chosen freely by the female. By splitting the male self into active and passive, aggression can be disowned, leaving the passive self to compete (passively/aggressively) by being chosen as a love object. I think this structure might be a psychic manuever that defends against castration by taking on certain (protective) aspects of castration. In his "Object Choice" essay, Freud describes the preference for this kind of triangular relationship and claims it arises from the "psychical constellation connected with the mother," revealing a wish to reenact the pattern of the original family configuration (in which the father possessed the mother first).

In the game of Angels, Devils, and Colors in II.1, the children play a guessing game in pantomime, *The Mime of Nick, Mick and the Maggies.* Shem, the Penman, the passive aggressive artist, plays Glugg. Shem/Glugg wishes to be chosen by Issy, but he is the "bold bad bleak boy" (219.36). Issy, appearing as "Miss Butys Pott," plays Izod, accompanied by the floras, a version of the rainbow girls, refractions of Issy, which I will discuss later. Sean is Chuff, the angel associated with light and the sun, and the phallic brother. The riddle has to do with the genitals and sexuality, but the children do not quite know enough to perceive clearly: "Up tightly in the front, down again on the loose, drim and drumming on her back and a pop from her whistle. What is that, O holytroopers? Isot givin yoe?" (223.9–11). Glugg the loser feels the tortures of hell; "For poor Glugger was dazed and late in his crave, ay he, laid in his grave" (240.3–4). Hereafter, Glugg merges into H.C.E. in a retelling of his resurrection, suggesting that in the figure of the father Shem/Glugg arises to get retribution (a mirror repetition) on his rival, Sean/Chuff. Meanwhile, Sean/Chuff gets all the praise from the rainbow girls: "And Sunny, my gander, he's coming to land her. The boy which she now adores. She dores" (249.18–19).

The answer to the riddle, "heliotrope," is associated with Shaun, who like the dying sun god Osiris sailing in his boat through the night, floats down the river in a barrel and rises on Easter morning at the end of III.2 to fall again (or maybe he never rose?) at the beginning of III.3.[23] Pragmatic, literal-minded and sermonizing, Shaun the Post delivers the letter of the law: "a letterman does be often thought reading ye between lines that do have no sense at all. I sign myself. With much leg. Inflexibly yours. Ann Posht the Shorn" (454.4–6).[24] Shaun has numerous counterparts (Burrus, Justius, Kev, Taff, Chuff—to name a few) within the *Wake*. I would like to suggest that the text at the end of III.2 may also invoke the figure of D. H. Lawrence in the inflated encomium to Shaun.[25]

Rival to Joyce, as Shaun rivals Shem, Lawrence *may* be a parodied allusion into two ways: through words associated with him or his works and through similarities between Shaun and the protagonist of *The Escaped Cock (The Man Who Died)*. I stress the equivocal "may" because of the difficulty in determining what might constitute evidence in the *Wake* notebooks, considering Joyce's accretive method of elaboration and the way additions are disseminated in scattered pieces. Volumes 57–62 of the *James Joyce Archive*, the facsimile drafts, typescripts, and proofs, contain the developing text of *FW* III.1–2. I think there is some evidence in these volumes to support my contention that Joyce parodies and makes allusions to Lawrence through additions and small changes made in the mid to late 1930s.[26]

In the space of three pages, from 470 to 473, the *Wake* text seems larded with words and themes associated with Lawrence and his work: "Frida! Freda!" (470.36) (added in a list of words for "peace" in June 1928, see *JJA* 57: 415, but also Lawrence's wife's name); "Ursulinka" (471.31) (added sometime after the 1928 *transition* text); "rommanychiel!" (472.22) (did this retroactively suggest Lawrence's *The Virgin and the Gipsy?*); "our pattern sent!" (472.25) ("Give Her a Pattern"?); not to mention the numerous general references of Christ, cock, and phoenix. To borrow the *Wake*'s words, I am suggesting these Lawrence references are "overlorded by fate and interlarded with accidence" (472.30–31). That is, they retroactively suggested a Lawrence connection, which later may have been enhanced.

The two details from Lawrence's novella that coincide with *Wake* material appear in part one of Lawrence's *Escaped Cock*, the name under which *The Man Who Died* was first published, separately, in 1928 in the *Forum*. Joyce worked on the watches of Shaun, one of which is this chapter of the *Wake*, in 1924, 1925, and 1926. In the early months of 1928 he revised it for publication, and it appeared in *transition* No. 13 in Summer 1928 (see Ellmann, *JJ* 794–95). There is a slight possibility, then, that Joyce was aware of the first part of *The Man Who Died* while he was revising this *transition* piece.

However, if indeed Joyce worked in allusions to Lawrence, it is more probable that he noticed a possible correspondence later and then increased its effect by small additions. A possible scenario might be that the similarities between Lawrence's *The Man Who Died* and *Finnegans Wake* began purely as coincidence until Joyce became aware of them and increased their effect in later revisions. Ellmann reports that Joyce was always on the lookout for works that broadly resembled the *Wake*, especially ones with similar themes (*JJ* 732). And Joyce had an opportunity to learn of Lawrence's Egyptian story firsthand.

The link between Joyce and Lawrence is Harry Crosby, and

the story of the brief relations among the three writers is surely one of the literary oddities of the twenties. Crosby published Lawrence's *Escaped Cock* for his Black Sun Press and also under the Black Sun imprint republished some fragments of *Finnegans Wake* that had previously appeared in *transition*. He visited with both Lawrence and Joyce during the Easter season of March–April 1929. Crosby was an ardent Egyptologist and follower of modern writers. He was very rich, very decadent, he wanted to promote modernism, and he had aspirations for his own writing. He got Lawrence to write a preface to his own *Chariot of the Sun*. A friend of Eugene Jolas, Crosby from time to time helped underwrite the costs of *transition*. When Crosby met Joyce in 1929, he presented him with a valuable copy of *The Book of the Dead*.

Luckily, Crosby was an excellent journal keeper and recorded his meetings with Lawrence and Joyce in 1929. On his March 29 visit with Lawrence, Crosby played a recording of Joyce reading *Ulysses* for Lawrence and Frieda (Crosby 244). Together again on Easter, March 31, Lawrence related his new story, "The Escaped Cock," to Crosby and his wife Caresse (244). Just three days later, on April 3, Crosby visited with both the Lawrences and Joyce on the same day. Visiting Joyce first, he asked Joyce if he would come round to meet the Lawrences. Crosby recorded in his diary that Joyce "didn't want to meet Lawrence—said his eye hurt him—he is very timid" (245). Crosby's biographer, Geoffrey Wolff, reports that while Lawrence and Crosby disliked each other, Joyce and Crosby got on famously. If Crosby talked to Joyce about Lawrence's novella, the conversation remains unrecorded. A year later, both Lawrence and Crosby were dead, Lawrence ravaged by the effects of tuberculosis, Crosby a suicide.[27]

Joyce made changes in the text of this section of the *Wake* between the time it was published by *transition* in the summer of 1928 and its final book form of 1939. When a line-by-line comparison is made, the changes seen suggest that Joyce is indeed increasing the Lawrence references in his final version. The 1939 text adds more than a page worth of new words, among them, these suggestive phrases: "hellyg Ursulinka" (471.31); "our pattern sent!" (472.25) (added in third set of *transition* pages, second set of additions, 1933–34? see *JJA* 62: 402–3); "ere he retourneys postexilic" (472.33) (added in third set of *transition* pages, second set of additions, 1933–34? see *JJA* 62: 402–3); "The phaynix rose a sun before Erebia sank his smother! Shoot up on that, bright Bennu bird! *Va faotre!* Eftsoon so too will our own sphoenix spark spirt his spyre and sunward stride the rampante flambe" (473.16–19) (not included as of 1936 additions, see *JJA* 62:52).

In *The Man Who Died,* the protagonist arising from the tomb described how he felt at his reawakening to consciousness. He did not wish to return to consciousness: "he had wanted to stay outside, in the place where even memory is stone dead." Life returned to him "like a returned letter, and in that return he lay overcome with a sense of nausea" (401). It is tempting to speculate that Harry Crosby may have described this plot to Joyce, and that the more obvious parallels with *Finnegans Wake* caught Joyce's attention. Both works incorporate Egyptian myth, references to Osiris and *The Book of the Dead*, include an Easter setting, and revise the Jesus myth along antiheroic lines. There are even strange similarities in small details. For example, the linked image of being stone dead and then waking to consciousness as a returned letter resembles H.C.E. and Shaun's situation in III.2 and III.3 to a startling degree. As Margaret Solomon points out, in the *Wake* the stone, *testes*, signifies the rigid law, and may be one of the two testicles, which the rival twins stand for. Together with its other mate, the elm, and the capital T— the erect penis and living tree—they form the holy trinity, the phallic hero, who is "not permanently dead—only petrified— and Joyce's resurrected 'letter' means to reanimate Him from stone to tree" (70,83).[28]

Shaun is not only a postman delivering a letter, but at the end of III.2 Shaun himself becomes the letter: "And next thing was he gummalicked the stickyback side and stamped the oval badge of belief to his agnelows brow with a genuine dash of irrepressible piety" (470.28–31).

At the end of the chapter, Shaun rises up, seemingly transcendent ("The phaynix rose"), by the words added sometime after 1936. The Bennu is a phoenix, the symbol of ascension, while Benni, Mark Troy points out, is also the Egyptian god of erection (57). Usually readers take this passage to refer to Joyce's own writing, since the next few lines refer to "Work your progress!" (*Work in Progress* or *Finnegans Wake*) and "lightbreakfastbringer" (generally taken to be a reference to Bloom in *Ulysses*) (473.21, 23). No doubt, Joyce does refer to his own work on one level, but I would like to suggest that he also works in, "postprophetical" (11.30), Lawrence references, so that Joyce/Lawrence become fused here, just as Shem and Shaun ultimately fuse as two sides of one figure. The "retourneys postexilic" of 472 fit both Lawrence and Joyce, as well as Osiris. A similar repeated cluster near the end of the *Wake* joins Glugg-sounds (Shem/Joyce) with the concept of the nausea of awakening to consciousness from *The Man Who Died,* the "breakfast" motif of the end of III.2, and the *Wake*'s rainbow theme (perhaps owing something to Lawrence's *Rainbow*):[29] "onegugulp down of the nauseaous forere brarkfarsts oboboomaround and you're as paint and spickspan as a rainbow" (613.23–24). Just above at 613.15–16, the text reads, "Lo, the laud of laurens now orielising benedictively when saint and sage have had their say." This may be a reference to Lawrence and was added to galley proofs dated 29 Nov. 1938 (See *JJA* 61: 308–9).

The rising of the sun brings a new day, and the breaking of the night's fast consecrates its promise as the rainbow marked the promise of the future to Noah after the storm and to Ursula at the end of Lawrence's *Rainbow.* The twins *are* breakfast. As the young counterpart to the father, in one guise Humpty Dumpty, the twins are a "homelette" (59.31) who will one day replace the father both because "eggs will fall" (163.27) and because cells will divide and new life will grow: "Your hegg he must break himself. See, I crack, so, he sit in the poele, umbedimbt!" (59.31–32). The egg breaker is Shem the artist (184.17–19), and the broken egg is Juan the fetus (429.20–25, 468.31–34).

Shem and Shaun, the twins, are mirror images of one another, "singlebarrelled names for doubleparalleled twixtytwins" (286.F4).[30] Hence, though they have distinct attributes, they also exchange positions as they converge and exchange places. Shem, associated with hyacinths and secret homosexual bents, is coward, boaster, forger, and artist, under one guise "Hyacinth O'Donnell, B.A., described in the calendar as a mixer and wordpainter" (87.12–13). In the passage that may parody *Lady Chatterley's Lover*, Shaun, here known as "Show'm the Posed," is fluttered, flattered, and flirted with by girls who are "stincking thyacinths through his curls" (92.13, 16–17). This example shows how the Lawrence/Joyce rivalry is subsumed under that of Shaun/Shem. (Of course, there are many other associated pairs subsumed under the Shaun/Shem rivalry; the Lawrence reference is only one very small addition.)[31] This example also shows an exchanging of attributes, since Shaun's usual heliotrope nature becomes hyacinthed.

Locked in a mirror relation, the twin rivals constantly war. Having many associations and functions, the twins also stand rhetorically as a synecdoche for warring nations, tribes, and the overthrow of the father by the son. Sly hints and slips of the tongue suggest that at the back and bottom of all these male activities is a homosexual attraction.[32] The homosexual slant of these male-upon-male activities anticipates some recent feminist critiques of patriarchy. Like Joyce, Irigaray, for example, posits a homosexual relation hidden beneath the dominant Western culture because it has expressed male univocity since Greek times.[33] The *Wake* expresses the possible homosexual relation among logic, law, and the phallus in condensations such as "your noes and paradigm maymay rererise in eren" (53.13) (may realize, rise, rerise, as well as the guilty stutter associated with the possible homosexual crime in the park), and "Who his dickhuns

now rearrexes from undernearth the memorialorum?" (610.3–
4) (rear access, rearrests, rexes—kings, resurrects—all done by
his dickuns and repressed from memory).

As all things constantly oscillate and realign themselves in
the *Wake*, Shem, Shaun, and Issy also converge in the mirror
theme. The twins are "dubbledecoys" (603.29) to their sister,
Issy, "the alter girl" (603.14), "me altar's ego in miniature"
(463.7), who herself is the mirror by which they construct themselves as the young male. The brother knows himself as a gendered individual by looking at the sister's difference:

Juan after those few prelimbs made out through his eroscope the appari-
tion of his fond sister Izzy for he knowed his love by her waves of
splabashing and she showed him proof by her way of blabushing
(431.13–17)

Issy herself is also doubled; she is a mirror (reflecting outward for the males): "Nuvoletta listened as she reflected herself"
(157.17–18). But she also leads a double life inside the mirror
where she is multiple. As mirror reflection, she reassures her
"male corrispondee" (457.28) of his masculinity by her own se-
ductiveness:

Of course, engine dear, I'm ashamed for my life (I must clear my
throttle) over this lost moment's gift of memento nosepaper which I'm
sorry, my precious, is allathome I with grief can call my own but all the
same, listen, Jaunick, accept this witwee's mite, though a jenny-teeny
witween piece torn in one place from my hands in second place of a
linenhall valentino with my fondest and much left to tutor. X.X.X.X.
(457.32–36–458.1–3)

Issy plays out the role of castrated female in order for the
male to gain his identity. Her torn "witwee's mite" she gives to
brother Juan is a valentine gift of castration, signed with the
kisses of the double X chromosome of the female, conferring
on him the allure of a Valentino."[34] As the reflection the male
needs to see for his own phallic identity, she is "eysolt of binnoculises memostinmust egotum sabcunsciously senses upers the de-

profundity of multimathematical immaterialities wherebejubers in the pancosmic urge the allimmanence of that which Itself is Itself Alone (hear, O hear, Caller Errin!) exteriorises on this ourherenow plane in disunited solod" (394.30–35). The binocular, eye, and exterior solid in this passage recall the Nelson material of *Ulysses,* which, I argued, deconstructed the false iconography of phallic supremacy at the same time as it appreciated phallic excessiveness. This attitude continues in the *Wake:* "Nielsen, rare admirable" (553.13).[35]

Remember that Nelson turned a blind eye to the telescope to "not see" a signal, in order not to retreat. He saw, therefore, what he needed to see (or not see, as the case may be) to suit the needs of his ego. His love affair with another man's wife may have led to his defeat. The Tristan and "Isolde" story connects the themes of romance and betrayal with the male ego's need to perceive the castrated female and its inverse, the female's passive/ aggressive need to be viewed as castrated. Her name indicates both "I am sold" (500.21), the woman exchanged by men and betrayed, and I sold myself, the woman as self-betrayer. Another variation, "Trustan with Usolde" (383.30), presents the male view; he trusts, while she sells him out. Further, the passage on 394–95 connects the need of the male ego for the betrayed/ betraying imaginary female with H.C.E., Ireland, and God, "the higherdimisssional selfless Allself" (395.1–2). The puns and condensations suggest that the idea of God is merely the projection of the male ego, which is just another "theemeeng Narsty meetheeng Idoless" (395.2) (scheming, seem-ing—hence an illusion, nasty, me-thing, nothing, empty and lazy idol, eye and i-doll— phallic icon or substitute penis—and idyll?).[36]

Issy has four X chromosomes, rather than two, I would suggest, because she is a double girl. She lives another life, inside her mirror, where she converses with many, among them "with nurse Madge, my linkingclass girl" (459.4). Within the mirror, she is multiple "We. We. Issy" (459.6). She and Mag in the mirror "thalk thildish" (461.28) in their own special baby language. There is the suggestion that this aspect of Issy is autoerotic and self-stimulating: "afterdoon my lickle pussiness" (461.13) and "theated with Mag at the oilthan we are doing to thay one little player before doing to deed" (461.28–30). Potentially cut off from the outside world and lost in her own dreams of herself (526.20–36), this aspect of Issy recalls the female figure of Lawrence's priestess of Isis, lost in her dreams.

Issy's condition, though, suggests a more complex aspect of the mirror stage than anything in Lawrence's work. The child's construction of the mirror *imago,* Gestalt psychologists posit, comes at the developmental stage when the child is learning its body is a whole. The image in the mirror not only constructs an idea of the self from visual image but constructs the concept of the unified body instead of separate pieces. Issy's multiple selves inside the mirror world may therefore be the piecemeal self behind the reflected unity (a mirage). Issy's companions, the floras and the rainbow girls, may represent these pieces. If this is so, then Issy is another analogue to Osiris, or very properly according to Egyptian myth, she is Isis/Osiris, both the scattered pieces and the restorer of the pieces to the whole.

But there may be one further analogue, too. Lacan derives his concept of the mirror stage from Gestalt psychology as much as from Freud. Where Gestalt posits the perception of a whole image, Lacan talks about the construction of the self through realizing a lack, that there was nothing there in the place of the self before the image in the mirror. In other words, Lacan looks at the hole instead of a whole. The *Wake* works through the idea of the mirror as a hole, too. The female's prism effect (the refracting multiplicity of the rainbow girls) combines with the concept of lack in the condensation, "a prisme O" (287.10), as A.L.P. is called. Being inside the mirror, which is a prism and a hole, is like falling down the rabbit hole and going behind the looking glass of Lewis Carroll's Alice stories.

That place of "Is, is" (570.30) is the "chapelofeases, sold for song" (571.11), the chapel of Tristan and Iseult, the vagina, and, perhaps by condensation and connection with other puns, the anus and Ireland as well. It is "our lake lemanted, that greyt lack, the citye of Is is issuant (atlanst!), urban and orbal, through seep froms umber under wasseres of Erie" (601.4–6). I claimed above that the mirror's *reflective* property constructed the romantic female for the phallic male, constructed castration, and set up betrayal: "he'd begin to jump a little bit to find out what goes on when love walks in besides the solicitous bussness by kissing and looking into a mirror" (618.17–19).

I have gathered the mirror's reflective function under the "eysolt of binnoculises" term. But the mirror theme also includes a genital/symbolic location as an interior place inside the mirror, a great lack (castration, need, the place we lack now that is to come). That interior place holds the utopian hope of the future ("is issuant"): in a physical sense, the child-to-be-born; and in a lexical/logical sense, the rainbow refractions, as complex pun analogues, offering dialectical promise in their multiplicity of meaning. As a mirror reverses an image,[37] that interior place reverses the merely reflective properties of castration and betrayal caused by repetition compulsion. Inside the mirror is plenitude and promise.

In unknotting the condensation of the "prisme O," I have organized my discussion along a psychological axis, using the mirror stage to explain the reflective and refractive properties. Because the mirror is associated with Issy, and because there is also the genital and symbolic condensation in "prisme O," it might seem that Joyce is valorizing the female over the male. But I do not believe this is the case.

Both Issy and the twin brothers exhibit negative, reflective properties (rivalry, betrayal), and sister and two brothers fold into each other in one, composite genital shape as I will describe below. Furthermore, the Egyptological analogues, traced by Mark Troy, also suggest the condensation of male and female in the nexus I call the "prisme O." Troy points out that Thoth, the god of speech, magic, and writing, was thought responsible for writing *The Book of the Dead,* that within a short space (452–54) the *Wake* makes numerous references to Egypt "with Shaun taking on the part of a prophetic Thoth" (56). Troy suggests that the sexual power to rouse and the power of words to rouse meet in a juncture of the Egyptian word "thoth" with the Gaelic word "toth-ball" (meaning "female place") and with the English word "thought" (Troy 55–57). Hence, "it is always tomorrow in toth's tother's place. Amen." (570.12–13), condenses male and female, the god Thoth with the female place, "toth-ball." "Amen," Troy notes, is Egyptian for "concealed, hidden" (57). The *Wake* asks, "Where did thots come from?" (597.25) and offers an implied answer. If I could try to articulate the multiplicities in one sentence the answer might look like this: thoughts come from the creative place—down the hole, or behind the mirror, a hidden place, female/male, that is sexual in origin. That sounds very like the Freudian unconscious.

As all characters condense into one another, Issy also folds into A.L.P., the mother. In this regard, the double girl suggests the dyad of the mother-daughter relationship that Freud noted in his late essays is so difficult to overcome. A.L.P. repeats Issy's attributes: "discinct and isoplural in its (your sow to the duble) sixuous parts" (297.25–26). And, since A.L.P. pecks up the letter from the litter heap, she too is Isis in search of the scattered pieces of Osiris.

The composite boys and their alter sister mirror each other, then, in an additional way. Each has two sides: the boys are outwardly doubled, the sister inwardly. For brother or for sister, interaction with the self's double leads to introversion, that term Freud used for homosexuality. For the male figures, introversion is expressed in two ways, either in a cluster association of rivalry/war/capitalism/homosexuality or in the self-reflexive creativity of smearing the self with feces/writing on/of the self.[38] An example of the first appears in the Burrus and Caseous story, a Shaun/Shem analogue:

for to this graded intellecktuals dime *is* cash and the cash system (you must not be allowed to forget that this is all contained, I mean the system, in the dogmarks of origen on spurios) means that I cannot now have or nothave a piece of cheeps in your pocket at the same time and with the same manners as you can now nothalf or half the cheek apiece I've in mind unless Burrus and Caseous have not or not have seemaultaneously sysentangled themselves, selldear to soldthere, once in the dairy days of buy and buy (161.6–14)

For the female, introversion leads to narcissistic submersion behind the mirror: "Sure she was near drowned in pondest coldstreams of admiration forherself, as bad as my Tarpeyan cousin, Vesta Tully, making faces at her bachspilled likeness in the brook after and cooling herself in the element, she pleasing it, she praising it" (526.28–32) (Vesta Tilley a male impersonator of the 1890s—McHugh 526).

But both male and female introversion can be creative. Shem writes with his feces and urine "all marryvoising moodmoulded cyclewheeling history" (186.1–2). "Nircississies are as the doaters of inversion" (526.35) suggests that Issy is the daughter of invention, that is, A.L.P. "Making faces at her backspilled likeness" also echoes the male writing with feces on the self and about the self. Remember, too, that the Tristan and Iseult story suggests that heterosexual romance may be no better than an imaginary construction needed by the ego. The castrated female is a reflection by which the woman-as-mirror-to-male-needs constructs the myth of the all powerful phallus.[39] Romantic heterosexuality also contains its hidden counterpart of betrayal. Like *Ulysses*, *Finnegans Wake* does not privilege heterosexuality as better or more moral than any other kind of sexuality. Rather it proclaims "the merits of early bisectualism" (524.12) (bisexuality, the division of the sexes, cell division).

According to Freud all characters in a dream are representations of the dream wish and the origin of dreams is sexual. In *Finnegans Wake* each character also is a sexual organ. But just as all the characters fuse into one sleeping dreamer, so all the various sexual parts join in one human genital shape. That shape is bisexual, perhaps because all potential humans in the fetus start out sexually similar: "as sure as my briam eggs is on cockshot under noose, all them little upandown dippies they was all of a libidous pickpuckparty and raid on a wriggolo finsky doodah in testimonials to their early bisectualism" (524.33–36). However, an androgynous genital shape also results because the two sexes are overlaid, one on another, the female three—two labia of the vagina and the clitoris—over the male three—two testicles and penis. This occurs literally in the intercourse of the parents (woman on top) and geometrically in the math lesson of II.2 where in bisecting the circle the children construct a diagram of the six parts of the male/female genitals overlaid (293).[40] "Now, as will pressantly be felt, there's tew tricklesome poinds where our twain of doubling bicirculars, mating approxemetely in their suite poi and poi, dunloop into eath the ocher" (295.32–36). Finally, each "sixuous part" functions somewhat independently or as a pair; they change places and transform themselves into their opposites, implying finally one composite shape.

Issy often is synonymous with the lips of the vagina: "Now open, pet, your lips, pepette, like I used my sweet parted lipsabuss with Dan Holohan" (147.29–30). Shem and Shaun, the twins, are testicles (like eggs and two peas in a pod).[41] In fetal development testicles evolve from the same cells as the labia, so "in the hyper-chemical economantarchy the tantum ergons irruminate the quantum urge so that eggs is to whey as whay is to zeed like your golfchild's abe boob caddy" (167.6–8). "Zeed" may combine seed with zed (zero), the hole of the vagina that both lips and testicles define. Perhaps this expresses in a condensation the a,b,c's of sexual reproduction: the zero state before sexual division, the nonself before construction by the mirror image (which Lacan describes as a "zero" state), and the hole of the vagina, down which the seed passes to fertilize the egg. Perhaps, too, "tantum ergons irruminates the quantum urge" parodies the language of quantum physics?

The female's clitoris is a little phallus, or "dickey." And female sexuality is associated with water-making capabilities of peeing, making tea, and raining: "Even the Lady Victoria Landauner will leave to loll and parasol, all giddied into gushgasps with her dickey standing" (568.6–8). By synecdoche and substitution little p's, peas, and peeing relate to the little female phallus and are linked with the Prankquean story,[42] the lilting l's of rain (via "parasol") to the seductive daughter. In the Burrus and Caseous tale, Issy's counterpart is Margareena. Shaun (Burrus) loves to eat and later in chapter III.1 gorges himself on "gorger's bulby onion (Margareter, Margaretar Margarasticandeatar)" and "in their green free state a clister of peas, suppositorily petty" (406.7–8, 19) (linking Ireland, enemas, and cunnilingus?). Peas, "in their green free state," also condense into the Tristan and Iseult story, which combines a young, seductive girl, water, tears—the little p cluster we might say—with Ireland as a "cluster of peas."

Freud described the little girl as like a little man at that stage before the little girl realizes the distinction between the sexes, and when she is very closely attached to the mother. Before she realizes her lack, she is happy in the autoerotic possession of her own little phallus (*Introductory Lectures* 318). Issy is also a "little man" with a hidden "mascular personality,"

I am closely watching Master Pules, as I have regions to suspect from my post that her "little man" is a secondary schoolteacher under the boards of education, a voted disciple of Infantulus who is being utilised thus publicly by the *seducente infanta* to conceal her own more mascular personality by flaunting frivolish finery over men's inside clothes (166.20–25)

Thus in the little p the little girl and the little boy meet, for the boy also has a little phallus, which really can pee. "Like pah, I peh. Innate little bondery. And as plane as a poke stiff" (296.33–35). Issy's "footnotes" 4 and 5 call attention to the cognate in the opposite sex. "Pah" is footnoted, and she comments below: "Hasitatense?" (296.F4) (has it a tense, and hesitance, associated with the stutter and the crime). For "poke stiff" she footnotes: "The impudence of that in girl's things!" (296.F5).

But as "Shaun replied, while he was fondling one of his cowheel cuffs," the little penis is "too soft for work proper" (410.31–32, 33). "I am always telling those pedestriasts" (410.35).

There is the suggestion that Issy knows how to make use of her own little phallus and indeed can, better than her brothers: "I'll strip straight after devotions before his fondstare—and I mean it too, (they gape to my gazing I'll bind and makeleash) and poke stiff under my isonbound with my soiedisante chineknees" (461.21–24). "Poke stiff under my isonbound" may be her own little erection inside her mirror world, as well as the result in the brothers of her sexual gaze. Clearly, she understands the power of sexual bondage ("bind," "makeleash," "isonbound") caused by the sexual gaze and wishes to make use of it. The repetition of key words in this Issy passage ("poke," "stiff," "bound") recalls the passage on 296 describing how the little boy pees ("innate little bondery," "as plain as a poke stiff"), suggesting the fusion of brothers and sister, and of their little p's.

If the sister merges with the brother in the little penis, the twin brothers mirrorwise form the lips of her vagina, as rivals and *rivae*, banks of the river. At the end of I.8, two washerwomen gossiping on the banks of the Liffey turn into tree and stone, analogues of Shem and Shaun.

Freud states that dreams suspend the law of noncontradiction. When Chuff competes with Glugg for Izod, his prize is looking at her "vied from her girders up" (247.19). He lifts the veil ("Lift the blank ve veered as heil!" [247.30–31]) but denies seeing the female wound of castration and also acknowledges seeing it.[43] (Lift the blanket, blank/zero be viewed [veered, distorted] as whole, hole, hail [I recognize you]). Behind the "Meetingless" (247.16), inside the mirror, instead of a hole or wound, he sees the flower girls, "prettymaid tints" (247.34), flower and rainbow images joined here. But as all changes and rearranges itself in the *Wake*, the flowers are also the brothers, heliotrope and hyacinth, who themselves form the lips of the vagina: "Debbling. Greanteavvents! Hyacinssies with heliotrollops! Not once fullvixen freakings and but dubbledecoys! It is a lable iction on the porte of the cuthulic church and summum most atole for it" (603.26–29). So in her mirror, he meets himself.[44]

Characters merge, and since characters are sexual organs, their organs intermingle. Characters also represent forces and values that can be catalogued individually to a certain extent. However, the punning of the *Wake* equates boundaries with sexual bondage, and indeed the characters and their values spill out of their innate little boundaries into their opposites. In chapter 3, I traced Joyce's use of charity and simony from *Dubliners* to illustrate how a progressive excessiveness in *Ulysses* breaks down the boundaries of moral terms. *Finnegans Wake* continues this trend, but in this last work the transformations between values, characters, and objects occur at dazzling speed.

The *Wake*'s two females, Issy and A.L.P., for example, represent charity and grace: "O Charis! O Charissima! A more intriguant bambolina could one not colour up out of Boccuccia's Enameron" (561.22–24). But though "she is dadad's lottiest daughterpearl" (561.15) and "to speak well her grace it would ask of Grecian language, of her goodness, that legend golden" (561.17–19), the daughter is also "a gracecup fulled of bitterness" (561.14–15). Anna (Hannah) means "graciousness" in Hebrew. But as Prankquean, A.L.P. also is "her grace o'malice" (21.20–21), condensing grace as virtue with its contrary vice. Grace O'Malley, or Grania Ui Mhaille, was a female pirate of Elizabeth I's era, whose "name came to stand for Ireland" (Glasheen, *Second Census* 192). Like the Prankquean who knocks on Jarl van Hoother's door, the legendary Grace O'Malley was refused admission to Howth Castle and in revenge captured the Earl's heir. The historical counterpart suggests that "grace" does not stand as a positive (or negative) value sign of the female, although it probably signals a powerful figure.

While grace is associated with the female characters, it also appears as a title for high and mighty men, as in "Your Grace" (25.36), referring to the fallen mythic figure of the composite male hero. Shaun is called "Shaun of grace" (424.14). And in the fable of the Ondt and the Gracehopper, the latter surely is a Joycean/Shem figure very like Simon Dedalus: "now whim the sillybilly of a Gracehoper had jingled through a jungle of love and debts and jangled through a jumble of life in doubts afterworse, wetting with the bimblebeaks, drikking with nautonects, bilking with durrydunglecks and horing after ladybirdies" (416.8–12). Even more than in *Ulysses*, the *Wake* cancels sexual difference and moral categories by suspending the law of noncontradiction.

When I discussed the concept of grace in *Ulysses*, I contrasted it with its opposite, simony. I traced Joyce's use of the two terms in *Dubliners* to their stylistic manifestations in *Ulysses*. Love and the selling of the spirit for money, I claimed, came to signify textual inflation and deflation more than opposite moral categories. *Finnegans Wake* continues this particular thread in the romanticism of the Tristan and Iseult story with its underlying themes of selling of the self and betrayal (deflation) and the romantic construction of the imaginary phallic hero (inflation). But *Finnegans Wake* may also continue the grace/simony theme in the symbols of keys and rock/tree. If we follow the transformations of these objects, we see how sexually androgynous the *Wake* universe really is.

I have already discussed how the twins appear as rock and tree, standing for the two male testicles. According to Margaret Solomon, the father is the phallic T (81ff.). All together they form the holy trinity, the phallus tree, as is fitting in an Osiris tale, since Osiris, dead in his coffin, was encased within a tree or "petrified." A petrified tree is a rock, and upon a rock Simon Peter was told to build Christ's church. All these male figures come back to the stone-cold figure of Finnegan, dead or dead drunk, who must be revived by the female.

But the firmness of this apparent sexual division gives way to a series of condensations and transformations. Male and female symbols, reviver and revived, merge. The tree of life itself, "it is scainted to Vitalba" (600.22), appears to join male/female signs and characteristics. "There an alomdree" (almond's bitterness suggesting connection with "gracecup full of bitterness" and all-man-three) "begins to green, soreen seen for loveseat, as we know that should she, for by essentience his law, so it make all" (600.20–22). The tree combines s/he. Even the capital T itself may be more of an androgynous sign than *Wake* commentators have realized. According to Egyptologist Sir E. A. Wallis Budge, the T is the feminine article in ancient Egyptian, and from it comes the word "Thebes" (Budge 3).

Another example of the androgynous sign concerns the sexual connotations of door and key. Jarl van Hoother, analogue of the hero, is "dour"—combining the characteristics of a rock with a stern demeanor. Yet he is also literally a door, which the Prankquean wets and finally gets him to open (Solomon 50–57). The Prankquean "provorted him" to become a "tristian" (*FW* 22.16, 17), a lover, a sad man who cries, and who therefore is wet like her, and also a Christian.

In *Ulysses*, the crossed keys, sign of home rule for the Isle of Man and sign of papal authority in the Roman Catholic church ("the power of the keys"), are also used for an ad, the literal/ humorous selling of the spirit to sell the spirits of Alexander Keyes, wine merchant. But in *Finnegans Wake*, the key is associated with the female figure. Key is part of O.K.—the *Wake's* equivalent of "yes": "Ohr for oral, key for crib, olchedolche and a lunge ad lib" (302.21–23). And "there's a key in my kiss," Issy declares (279.F1),[45] suggesting by parody that here the power of the keys is to open as well as to bind sexually (echoing the bondage of Issy's sexual gaze). The last lines of the entire work combine key, lips (oral/genital), and yes function: "Lps. The keys to. Given!" (628.15). Whereas Christ gave Simon Peter the power to bind and to absolve sin, in the *Wake* the female lips are keys that are already a given and that can lead to sexual bondage (both deliciously perverse and a betrayal of the male).

Traditionally the key is seen as a symbol of the male, and the door of the female. Freud, for instance, makes this point:

We are acquainted already with *rooms* as a symbol [of the female]. The representation can be carried further, for windows, and doors in and out of rooms, take over the meaning of orifices in the body. And the question of the room being *open* or *locked* fits in with this symbolism, and the *key* that opens it is a decidedly male symbol. (*Introductory Lectures* 158)

In *The Man Who Died* Lawrence calls the woman "the penetrable rock." Keeper of the temple, she represents space, a conventional psychological symbol for woman. Reversing Christian symbolism, however, Lawrence puts the woman in Simon Peter's place, the rock upon which the Lawrentian church is founded. Lawrence establishes his faith upon the rock of the woman's desire for the male, then, instead of on man's loyalty to the law of God the Father. Hence, while he reverses Christian concepts, he retains the symbolic sexual psychology of patriarchy.

In contrast, *Finnegans Wake* reverses traditional sexual and religious symbolism, but reversal usually does not end the movement. Reversals reverse again and unite: "A so united family pateramater is not more existing on papel or off of it. As keymaster fits the lock it weds so this bally builder to his streamline secret. They care for nothing except everything that is allporterous. *Porto da Brozzo!*" (560.28–32). Here the male hero is "keymaster," but he is also a s/he ("pateramater" father/mother). Wed by function and in functioning, rather than by paper or papacy, they are "allporterous"—all portals (doors both), all porters (gatekeepers), all transporting, portents, ports (from the Italian), and portions of the whole, and perhaps both drunk on porter. When we read the sentence with its additional pun, "[parameter] is not more existing," it also denies the family (and father and mother— *pater* and *mater*) as a constant that determines a specific form.

Male and female, father and mother, brother and sister exchange positions, values, functions and flow into one another "as highly charged with electrons as hophazards can effective it" (615.7–8), revealing "the sameold gamebold adomic structure of our Finnius the Old One" (615.6–7). The atomic structure of humans may be the same since days of old, but the individual, the family, and culture are changing and evolving: "Charley, you're my darwing! So sing they sequent the assent of man. Till they go round if they go roundagain before breakparts and all dismissed" (252.28–30).

Individuals, as well as the entire human race, change: "He does not know how his grandson's grandson's grandson's grandson will stammer up" (252.35–36), "since in the mouthart of the slove look at me now means I once was otherwise" (253.4–5), echoing *A Portrait*'s "I was not myself as I am now." The *Wake* asserts a modern world view, evolution toward consciousness in a random, accidental world: "reflecting from his own individual person life unlivable, transaccidentated through the slow fires of consciousness into a dividual chaos, perilous, potent, common to allflesh, human only, mortal" (186.3–6). As Freud says in his "Leonardo" essay, "we are all too ready to forget that in fact everything to do with our life is chance, from our origin out of the meeting of spermatozoon and ovum onwards—chance which nevertheless has a share in the law and necessity of nature" (*SE* 11: 137).

Multiplicity flows out of unity, by doubling, and then from the colliding of contraries spills the excess. The book grounds this assertion in an analogy of literal cell division/self-division. Fertilized eggs split into two, siblings oppose and provoke each other, begin to fight, fighting turns to lovemaking and uniting, producing more fertilized eggs—in short, "eggoarchicism" (525.10) (egg as ruler, egg as archaic, egg as anarchism).

As child replaces parent, so the polymorphic perversity of the infant's psychic universe replaces the orderly, repressive logic of the adult, daylight world. The infant brings anarchic energy before repression and stands for the promise of the future ("The child we all love to place our hope in for ever" [621.31–32]). However, I do not believe the book endorses some value of procreation, just as I argued *Ulysses* does not endorse reproduction. Rather the *Wake* celebrates the infant's perverse, multiple (the pieces before the constructed self), plastic quality, as it pokes fun at the stone, cold deadness of the old man.

The unrepressed infant does not overthrow but provokes, perverts, teases, the Old Testament Father—the Lawgiver:

"They know him, the covenanter, by rote at least, for a chameleon at last, in his true falseheaven colours from ultraviolent to subred tissues. That's his last tryon to march through the grand tryomphal arch. His reignbolt's shot. Never again!" (590.7–10). Arching across the sky, the Old Testament covenant proclaimed rule by force ("ultraviolent" "reignbolt"). In contrast, the *Wake*'s rainbow comes from sexual intercourse (trying and failing,[46] not triumphing?) (of many colors, kinds?) and refracts from within "the grand tryomphal arch," our natal/naval connection with past and future.[47] Rather than an outward sign of the covenant with the one, "true" God, the rainbow signs of *Finnegans Wake* are associated with sham, chameleon, St. Patrick the Arch Druid (611.5–7), and the diffuse pieces of the interior Issy.

Finnegans Wake claims allegiance to evolution: "though his heart, soul and spirit turn to pharaoph times, his love, faith and hope stick to futuerism" (129.35–130.1). At the same time it pushes backward to reuse shards from earlier civilizations. It pushes back past Christianity to "ennemberable Ashias" and "the Phoenican wakes" (608.31, 32).

Joyce returns to Egyptology perhaps because the hodgepodge of family relationships in Egyptian myth resembles his portrait of the unconscious creative mind. Each Egyptian figure had its own story, yet all gods and goddesses merged over time into a dying sun-god figure, usually represented as Osiris in the later dynasties. Moreover, the Egyptian deities were frequently male/female pairs, variously rendered as consorts and as twin counterparts of each other that merged into one. The stories of their escapades, like the events of the *Wake*, are fragmentary, overlapping, and obscure, though clear in parts. I believe Joyce found the flexible multiplicity of Egyptian myth congenial to his interests because Egyptian myth is naturalistic and overdetermined. Joyce replaces the Christian Holy Family with an Egyptian model because Eypgtian myth does not subordinate any one story, god or goddess, parent or child, to an overarching principle or idea. The sole plot mechanisms for Egyptian myth are the great events of life—birth, conflict, love, struggle, and death.

Insofar as birth comes first, the female forms of the deities may appear to have preeminence, but they are always counterbalanced by their male counterparts.

To give an example of the interrelatedness and overlapping of the stories and figures in Egyptian myth, of the male/female condensations, and their correlation to the *Wake*, I will relate one Egyptian story of creation taken from the accounts given by Sir E. A. Wallis Budge, whom Joyce read. This is the story of Nut and Seb, mother-sky and father-earth. Seb was the brother of Nut, as well as her consort, and the father of Osiris and Isis (94). "He and his female counterpart Nut produced the great Egg whereout sprang the Sun-god under the form of a phoenix. Because of his connexion with the Egg, Seb is sometimes called the 'Great Cackler'" (95–96). A very interesting parallel to the parricide themes in *Finnegans Wake* concerns the story of how Osiris, Seb's son, shut up Seb and Nut and caused the father to mutilate himself. According to Budge, the word used to indicate this slaughter is *shāt* (99–100). The story is confusing in that it is only told in two rare versions, and the father is called Ra sometimes, and also Seb.

The *Wake* analogue to the father's downfall is sometimes referred to as Humpty Dumpty's fall (*FW* 44.25). An obscure event, whatever it was that occurred in Phoenix Park, is in one guise a political conspiracy, has something to do with seeing the father's backside or with his defecating, urinating, or perhaps exposing himself in front of two young girls: "Ever thought of that hereticalist Marcon and the two scissymaidies and how bulkily he shat the Ructions gunorrhal?" (192.1–3). The word "shat" frequently cues a replayed version of this scene.

Hieroglyphics show Seb laying on the ground with one hand outstretched in the same position as the sleeping male hero of *FW*. Arching in a semicircle above Seb in the sky is the female goddess Nut, who was lifted up from her embrace with Seb by "Shu when he insinuated himself between their bodies and so formed the earth and the sky" (98). In the bedroom of the *Wake* couple, we see the woman on top of the man and then their intercourse interrupted by the child who awakes crying. The Egyptian source reverses the more familiar Western archetypes of the female as *gea tella,* earth goddess, and the male as ruler of the sky.

Shu, the intervening figure, may be a source for Shem/Shaun, the interrupting child. Shu was considered a creative god, "lord of the watery abyss, and the dweller in the watery mass of the sky" (98). He was also lord of the Underworld, "porter of heaven's gate" (98) (the Porter family of *FW*?), and shared attributes of Nut.

Among the many details Joyce weaves into *Finnegans Wake* are the male/female embrace with woman on top and the creation of the universe from an egg ("And let every crisscouple be so crosscomplimentary, little eggons, youlk and meelk, in a farbiger pancosmos"—*FW* 613.10–12). "Putting Allspace into a Notshall" (*FW* 455.29) describes that space between the parental embrace the intruding third party creates, and from that space comes creation. It is Nut's shell, the microcosm of a nutshell, and the contrary commandments of human desire: "not" for the repressed unconscious world, "shall" for human desire, creativity arising from the two contrary forces, and the two words inverting and substituting for the Christian "shall not."

Joyce's turn to Egyptian myth is a turn entirely away from the Christian account of the individual, sexuality, the family, time, human origin, and human destiny. Christianity preaches individual salvation, a single God, and an intact self with a "soul" that exercises "free will." *Finnegans Wake* speaks of collective human civilization, incorporates references to many gods (*FW* 80.23–28), and celebrates physical body parts. In place of the ego exercising free choices and a single God, the book babbles and gossips about the "chaosmos of Alle anyway connected with the gobblydumped turkery was moving and changing every part of the time" (118.21–23). The book replaces the patriarchal order of the Christian family with the multiplicity and disorder of Egyptian family myth.

Finnegans Wake has been called an Oedipal narrative in sev-

eral different ways. Margaret Solomon emphasizes the importance of the killing of the father in the Oedipus myth to Joyce's
"Book of Kills." She argues that in the *Wake* the phallus is "a
substitute for *Theos*" (83). While I agree with Solomon that the
book makes a genital substitution for God, I believe that the
genital shape it draws is not overwhelmingly phallic but a composite male/female portrait, very like that drawing of Leonardo's
that Freud found so revealing.

Margot Norris sees the book's structure as dependent upon
the structure of the Oedipus myth. "*Finnegans Wake* explores the
nature of the family itself, via a quest for original sin" (28). Norris
argues that Joyce sets up a "familial/linguistic homology" (126),
showing that "the social structure of the family and the linguistic
structure of the sentence is intelligible only if certain laws of
combination are observed" (127).

But with effort and creativity, readers can construct a reading of the *Wake* eventhough its language breaks linguistic laws,
because the text generates its own patterns of language, demonstrating language in the making. Just as linguistic rules may
change over time, rules of family structure change, too. My major
disagreement with Norris is that she tends to make Joyce sound
like an upholder of the laws of language, patriarchy, and family
structure, the very rules that he purposely disrupts and plays
with, exposing their constructed, contradictory, accidental evolution.

Finnegans Wake parodies the Freudian narrative of the Oedipus complex as much as it uses it. As the *Wake* says, "The twyly
velleid is thus then paridicynical" (610.14–15). Joyce satirizes
pompous pronouncements about what The Family symbolizes.
There is beneath "a triptychal religious family symbolising puri-
tas of doctrina, business per usuals" (31.22–23), a dirty, funny
business based on the body's sexual organs from which family
structure haphazardly evolves. The book's formal, linguistic experimentation likewise demonstrates how haphazardly meaning
can be produced and extracted from language fragments.[48] The
Wake family is an evolutionary one, starting with "our family

furbear" (132.32) and revealing the many permutations of "the family umbroglia" (284.4) that are possible, including "The Uses and Abuses of Insects" (306.30), for example.

From a Freudian point of view, the *Wake* draws a psychic portrait of an infantile mind before passage through the Oedipus complex, or a portrait of the unconscious beneath repression. Distinctions between the sexes are not fixed. All characters are bisexual and multiply perverse, showing the child's manifestation of narcissism, sadism, masochism, homosexuality, voyeurism and coprophilia (Freud *SE* 11: 44–45). The characters do and do not have fixed boundaries between each other.

Rivalry abounds, but rivalry is also self-division. H.C.E. appears to be guilty of something, and fathers (and eggs) fall again and again. Yet, if there is any killing of the father, it is "clearobscure" as are all events: "The unmistaken identity of the persons in the Tiberiast duplex came to light in the most devious of ways. The original document was in what is known as Hanno O'Nonhanno's unbrookable script, that is to say, it showed no signs of punctuation of any sort" (123.30–34).

Freud tells us in his "Object Choice" essay that seriality, like the dyad, is connected to the constellation of the mother. Whereas Lawrence focuses on dyadic relationships, Joyce explores seriality from his earliest work onward, using and then moving through symbolic systems at ever faster rates and in ever smaller units. Characters from *Dubliners* or *A Portrait* become symbols in *Ulysses,* and by *Finnegans Wake* are merely syllables or consonants. Emma Cleary under her parasol becomes rain as a symbol of romantic fertility and ultimately just I's.

Some readers feel Joyce privileges Molly and A.L.P., making them narcissistic and simpleminded, but life-giving, all-nurturing earth goddesses. While I have been arguing that the females merge into the males, into masculine/feminine composites, I do agree that Joyce more often criticizes male, rather than female, ideology and actions. The females of the *Wake*, for example, can be stupid, narcissistic, and cruel, and they can betray themselves and men. But the women may be more direct than the males.

The males are more devious, twisted, and secretive. Issy frankly lures her brothers; they deny their attraction. The Prankquean demands entry at van Hoother's door; H.C.E. conceals/reveals and remembers/forgets his crime. Especially in comparison to Lawrence's attack on women in his middle period (see Ruderman), Joyce does seem sympathetic to women.

The benign, or at the worst silly, female figures and serial substitutions may indeed indicate that the book replays pre-Oedipal material and concerns, manifesting the connection to the mother. However, to describe the book as "pre-Oedipal" leads to value judgments I think Joyce would disagree with. The Oedipal and pre-Oedipal distinctions privilege the adult ego over the child's piecemeal self, and conventional gender division over the polymorphous sexuality of childhood. Since the pre-Oedipal marks only a stage in the child's development, the text is then characterized as childish, reflecting a failure of development. However, *Finnegans Wake* already proclaims its childishness; in fact, insists on it, just as it insists on the polymorphously perverse bisexuality of childhood rather than the fixed gender boundaries of adulthood.

Besides expressing the psyche's lost connection back to the mother, seriality also describes modern commodity relations in mass societies. Each new consumer item replaces the next in continual, fast-paced substitution.

In a very important essay about Joyce written twenty years ago, "Seriality in Modern Literature," Fredric Jameson notes the serial nature of modern life that Joyce's style "transpose[d] into the realm of language" (78). Mass advertising and mass production make us constantly aware that we carry out our activities with a myriad of others. "Thus, in such activities," writes Jameson, "the uniqueness of my own experience is undermined by a secret anonymity, a statistical quality" (76). In mass society, we lose our originality.

Using the fragments of culture, Joyce appears to construct a new language. But reminding us it is "nat language at any sinse of the world" (83.12), *FW* insists on its unoriginality, on its "spurios" (161.09) plagiarism ("Pelagiarist!" [525.07]) (Pelagianism, a heretical doctrine of the Irish or British monk, Pelagius, denied original sin and affirmed man's ability to be good by the exercise of free will). Freud also stressed the unoriginality of the unconscious, but (unlike Joyce) he postulated a "real" original sin, the ancient killing of the father, in *Totem and Taboo*. There Freud also argued that the unconscious is a repository of all the debris of human life, not only that actually experienced by the individual but all the repressed material of our culture that each individual inherits, which he called "the collective mind." (This should not be confused with Jung's "collective unconscious," which Freud repudiated as a form of group psychology.)

The *Wake* presents such a collective mind and shows writing as rewriting old letters. Its rewritten language requires a new kind of reading, too, indeed a collective reading, requiring us to read not only the text itself but also the work of other scholars who "read" the text, and to read Joyce's reading, too. Joyce and Freud would also agree on the bliss of childhood and the importance of play in creativity, two points Freud emphasizes in his "Leonardo" essay.

The Freudian unconscious has no narrative or development, and likewise the *Wake* has no unified point of view. On the other hand, the Oedipal narrative expresses familial conflict and its resolution from the point of view of consciousness and the reality principle. Though the book presents pieces of childhood—playing, miming, games—the *Wake* also presents fragments of adult concerns (the mother going to comfort the crying child in the night, for example). The book tells us outright "the words which follow may be taken in any order desired" (121.12–13). Reading the book is like interpreting a dream; we may construct meaning in any direction or by any means we can using the fragments at hand.[49]

In the dream world, context is never clear. Without sequence and controlling context, any linear "plot" movement becomes obscure. The book's shape has been frequently described as circular and repetitious. Norris, for example, believes that the book's repetition connotes the fixated circularity of a trauma become neurotic symptom made into myth (25–26).

This kind of reading uses the values of psychoanalysis to judge the text in a way that I think misses Joyce's final joke on his Freudian source. Freud valued a straight-ahead, productive, linear, and progressive orientation to the world—a "phallic" view, we might say. His main line of investigation in his "Leonardo" essay, in fact, is to discover "the factors which have stamped [Leonardo] with the tragic mark of failure" (*SE* 11: 131)! Leonardo's tragedy, Freud believes, was his inability to complete his projects. "It is not so much a question of their being unfinished," Freud declares, "as of his declaring them to be so" (*SE* 11: 66). Freud describes Leonardo's trait in terms of "hesitation" and "withdrawal" (*SE* 11: 68).

I think the circular, unfinished shape of the *Wake* and its themes of hesitancy and withdrawal parody Freud's judgmental attitude toward Leonardo and further point to that essay as one source of *Finnegans Wake*. Joyce's book goes on and on, forever unfinished; the last word connects to the first, starting the stories over again. The book continually plays upon the terms "hesitancy" and "withdrawal." Hesitancy is associated with Parnell's acquittal and the guilty stutter of the father, in particular with his possible homosexual act in Phoenix Park.[50] The stutter also connects to Oscar Wilde's trial, and the stutter may be another form of the thunder. Withdrawal also describes how the attempted sexual intercourse ends in chapter 16, as well as describing the founding principle of the universe—which may be a bird laying an egg on the water and then withdrawing. As Issy does with her mirror writing (*FW* 262.F2), Leonardo wrote in reversed, mirror script in his famous notebooks, although no one knows why he did so. In short, Joyce's text incorporates all the psychological traits and personal characteristics of Leonardo. Thus, in a playful reversal, the text identifies itself with Leonardo rather than with Freud.

In his "Leonardo" essay, Freud says, "what an artist creates provides at the same time an outlet for his sexual desire" (*SE*

11: 132). In *Finnegans Wake,* Joyce demonstrates the reverse: how sexual desire is at the base of creation. The two points of view are critically different in one respect. Joyce celebrates the anarchic creative potential of unrepressed desire, while Freud focuses on sublimation. Whereas Freud considers androgynous Egyptian myth as primitive, revealing the child's uncertainty in knowing the role of the father in reproduction, Joyce celebrates the creative gap opened up by lack of knowledge. Joyce's universe is Pelagian plagiarism. There is no actual killing of the father, although there is plenty of guilt and fighting about what is not known. Trying to understand and see the mother's genital triangle, Dolph and Kev, analogues of Shem and Shaun, provoke each other to fight and then gloss over/retain their mutual resentment by forgiving/confirming guilt: "I'm only out for celebridging over the guilt of the gap in your hiscitendency" (305.8–9). That gap in knowledge causes the desire to know, as the child's gap in sexual knowledge leads to "infantile sexual researches." That gap also causes guilt, from which stories arise, of the killing of the father and other founding myths. That gap is like the space opened up by the intruding third figure of Shu in the Egyptian portrait of father earth, Seb, and mother sky, Nut. Joyce does not turn to Egyptian myth, then, because it is primitive, but because it is a fertile, nonauthoritarian source to reimagine culture.

The gap caused by the intruding third figure of Egyptian myth connects the sexual and genital threes to the dialectical effect of the book's puns, which bend double meaning into diverse and multiple directions. The gap is also the space that is created when an apparently closed circle, as a flattened spiral appears, opens up into a recursive spiral. History appears circular in *Finnegans Wake* when it is looked at collapsed: "it mought have been due to a collupsus of his back promises, as others looked at it" (5.27–28). There is no founding act (such as parricide) but a lack of knowledge and desire to know (at root, sexual), confusion of memory and projected desires (as in early childhood), all which set in motion ascent up the evolutionary spiral.[51] If the circle is pulled apart, its spiral shape reveals a recursive progression—a model for dialectical progression where we revisit, at a changed level, bits from the past, litter transformed to letters.

5

"Afterthoughtfully Colliberated": *Resituating Lawrence and Joyce Within Modernism and the Postmodern*

At the end of the twentieth century and viewed retrospectively through the kaleidoscope of postmodern glasses, the defining traits of modernism are shifting and rearranging themselves, leading to a revision of the modern canon. Such revision has already begun. One effect will be to resituate Lawrence and Joyce in relation to one another. Where family and gender relations are viewed as characteristic textual concerns, Lawrence and Joyce will not appear opposite one another in the modern canon but instead will be located adjacently along a continuum, both writers engaged in reimagining family and gender.

Modernism in the past was defined by a writer's interests in experimental form and language, in issuing manifestoes and testing theories. Using these measurements, Lawrence and Joyce seem poles apart. In *The Gender of Modernism* Bonnie Kime Scott points out that a major rethinking of these characteristics is already under way, as heretofore neglected women writers of the twentieth century are recovered. In addition to adding women to the traditional all-male modernist canon, feminist scholarship broadens definitions of the canon's distinguishing features to include a different set of interests. Along with issues of marginality in relation to the dominant culture and colonial oppression, gender and family have been undervalued as characteristic interests of modern writers. However, feminists have not invented these issues.

This study has shown that "gender" and "family" are recurring concerns in the texts of Lawrence and Joyce. Is this feature of their texts a sign of their modernity? After all, their interests in family and gender have often been written off as residual "leftovers" from the nineteenth-century novel of social relations. In *Marxism and Literature*, Raymond Williams argues that cultural change is "a specific and complex hegemonic process" "full of contradictions and unresolved conflicts" (118). Williams argues that in addition to the dominant culture, a work of art may incorporate emergent and residual alternatives. Thus, while gender and family concerns appear in modernist texts, it is likely they will be inscribed differently in the work of men and women.

Lawrence and Joyce are not feminists, but I believe their texts show an emergent rethinking of gender and family relations, even though both writers sometimes appear to, and do, carry over residual nineteenth century attitudes also. I conclude that they were implicitly questioning family and gender relations before we, their readers, were fully attuned to the cultural revisioning implicit in these issues.

Another revisionary effect of this study is to question the demarcation line between modernism and postmodernism. That is, I would argue that interest in reimagining family and gender relations is both modern *and* postmodern. The postmodern traits of fragmentation and multiplicity not only apply to formal features of a text but also are especially relevant to issues of gender and family. I have argued from a feminist's view that the questioning of gender roles and stereotypes, the fragmentation of personality, and the championing of polymorphous sexuality should not be considered regressive (as the ethics and narrative of psychoanalysis would judge) but as politically progressive. Questioning, destabilizing, or deconstructing the binary sex/gender system is a political act. Thus, in the broadest sense, this book argues for a redefinition of the political dimensions of modernism/postmodernism.

HOW DO LAWRENCE AND JOYCE
RETHINK FAMILY AND GENDER?

Both Lawrence and Joyce reject the Christian model of the family and turn to Egyptian family material because they dislike the Christian repression of sexuality. Both are alienated from the Western traditions they inherited from the nineteenth century, but their criticisms differ. Lawrence preserves his ambivalence toward the structures of culture he inherits. He welds Egyptian myth onto Western traditions. *The Man Who Died* preserves traditional cultural and symbolic patterns of psychic development and gender division. Analysis of its psychic structure reveals Lawrence's acceptance of, yet desire to change, the sex/gender roles of patriarchy in the romantic quest for the ideal mate—a doubled female figure and therefore a phallic woman. Even though he retains patriarchal structure, Lawrence minimizes the function of the father and all inherited structures of authority outside the individual (while patriarchy and authority are retained through their displacement onto the male hero).

In his earlier work, Lawrence delays reproduction of the family. Even in his later romances, family reproduction is implied but never really developed. These trends make Lawrence interesting to contemporary female readers who no longer achieve identity solely in the reproduction of the family, but who still inherit the dominant cultural formation of femaleness under patriarchy, finding their identity in affiliation and relationship with others. Further, Lawrence interests women readers because he explores the problems of separating from, and joining with, another that arise from dyadic relationships. Even when Lawrence retreats to stereotyped gender roles, as in his work of the mid-1920s, his interest in boundary states, in cross-cultural relations, and in experiencing the world of the Other through the Other mitigates somewhat his distasteful phallic idolatry. Freud's essays on female sexuality and later the work of feminists such as Nancy Chodorow remind us that even Lawrence's notorious problem with the mother figure makes him interesting to women readers, since they may also have experienced a "mother problem."

Focusing on the relation of two and on exchange with another leads outward toward boundary experiences. Lawrence's best writing warns against complacency, especially against ethnocentrism and perhaps gendercentrism (as in *Women in Love* and *The Fox*). Lawrence's romance quests have a psychostructural form that expresses ambivalence: accepting patriarchy and gender division but nostalgically desiring to return or revisit the earliest unity before gender division. The mother does not stand for that lost original unity because she is often the agent of castration. However, with the lover who may be a mother substitute, characters reexperience original unity in sexual union. Lawrence also posits an original notion of the unconscious, different from the Freudian unconscious. The Lawrentian unconscious represents an original unity in existence before thought and culture divide and alienate the individual. From a psychoanalytic point of view, of course, both the quest for a "genuine" Other and the desire to reexperience an "original unity" are romantic illusions.

I suggested in chapter 2 that Lawrence's attitude toward capitalism reflects a similar ambivalence. He bewails the lost communal ties of an imagined precapitalist era, while he also welcomes the creative conflict that the breaking up of the old and the proximity of the new provide. Juliet Mitchell argues that the economic mode of capitalism and the ideological mode of patriarchy are interlinked, but not the same thing. Both contain their own contradictions, Mitchell states, but "it is women who stand at the heart of the contradiction of patriarchy under capitalism" (412). Under patriarchy, women are cultural exchange objects; they remain defined by kinship patterns of organization even when that pattern of organization is no longer functional. Like Mrs. Morel, they have no way to enter into the structures of production and exchange except through personal relationship. When Lawrence attacks the personal in relationships, wishing instead to return to impersonal connections, he may appear to desire a return to a purely biological or "natural" primitivism in gender relations. Yet, combined with his delaying or canceling of family reproduction, his emphasis on impersonality can also be seen as rescuing the woman from the definition of femininity under patriarchy (which is personal affiliation).

I have characterized Lawrence's texts by their interest in exchange relationships and Joyce's in terms of serial relations. According to Freud, both kinds of relations express the connection to the mother. Both kinds of relations also reflect forces in capitalist ideology and modes of production. The nostalgia for a genuine exchange relationship haunts conservative, old-fashioned beliefs of value, for example, belief in the ideal meeting in the marketplace of "true" need (supply and demand) with "fair" price. Serial relations, on the other hand, resemble the fast-paced constant transformation of international, advanced capitalism, which rewards circulation and scoffs at such old-fashioned beliefs.

I have argued that Lawrence's best novels incorporate the contradictory psychology of two forces, the social relations under capitalism and the sexual relations of patriarchy, revealing an outdated ideology of masculinity and femininity and the need for new social structures. Though Lawrence provides no answers, his great novels imply that the new social structure will come out of conflict and destruction and will necessitate entirely new kinds of family relations based on individual independence-in-relation with another.

Even more than Lawrence, Joyce has been accused of abandoning the physical world, politics and history, for an ideal mental realm devoid of all concerns but linguistic experiment. Characters progressively disappear into textual flow itself and into sounds, sigla, and even single letter fragments. I have argued that Joyce so completely destabilizes point of view that the one characteristic of his texts is progressive, serial displacement at faster and faster rates. This characteristic overpowers any other tendency in his work, such as romanticizing the female or reproducing traditional family relations. We might say that notions of traditional gender division and family relations under patriarchy are subsumed, in Joyce's work, under the radical transformations of textual instability itself. So family stereotypes are there, though they are not particularly endorsed but are in the company of their opposites, while both are constantly being transformed into something else. Above all, however, Joyce cuts loose from Judeo-Christian (and Freudian) morality and judgment, offering in their place sexuality, creativity, and mutability.

Joyce's commitment to this last—to change itself—makes his work potentially revolutionary, I believe. The first and second wave of women scholars attacked Joyce's texts for female characters who were shallow and silly or who were unrealistic, all-loving earth mothers. However, I think those criticisms overlook the changes in Joyce's attitude to women and simplify the complex, psychological universe he portrays. I have argued that Joyce's representation of women changes. *A Portrait* presents a unified, male point of view, with its shadow repression, in a Family Romance. *Ulysses* begins with what appears to be a similar stance, but even in the first episode Buck Mulligan and Stephen split into two contending voices of young male views. Very quickly, thereafter, *Ulysses* gives way to plural points of view, and textual instability increases. *Ulysses* is not a Family Romance but an antiromantic comedy that refuses to authorize "better" family relations.

Finnegans Wake pushes the trends of *Ulysses* further. *Ulysses* portrays the break up of the too solid world into a stream of perception; the *Wake* portrays the piecemeal self of the unconscious. Whereas *Ulysses* gave us the womanly man and manly woman, the *Wake* draws a composite genital portrait of a bisexual, multiply perverse collective human. Joyce may, in fact, go easier on women than men, but I do not believe he idealizes women. A.L.P. is equally as perverse in her sexual practices as H.C.E., the twins as narcissistic as their sister, Issy as self-divided as the brothers. I believe the text insists on a common sexual human base, anarchic desires, and evolutionary change. *Finnegans Wake* is not a feminist tract, but I believe its characteristics implicitly support feminism—not by declaring women morally better than men nor by forcing women to adopt dominant "male" values but by suggesting the common sexual base of both men and women and their ability to create new forms.

FROM MODERN TO POSTMODERN

Although *Sons and Lovers* can be considered the literary text that began the practice of psychoanalytic literary criticism, it is surely *Finnegans Wake* that extends the limits of recent psycholiterary theory. Joyce's last and most experimental production has had a profound influence on post-structuralists, especially on French theorists such as Jacques Lacan, Hélène Cixous, Julia Kristeva, and Jacques Derrida. "Every time I write and even in the most academic pieces of work, Joyce's ghost is always coming on board," confesses Derrida in "Two Words for Joyce" (149). "The whole of *La Pharmacie de Platon* was only 'a reading of *Finnegans Wake*,'" he continues, and "*La Carte postale* is haunted by Joyce" (150).

The complex puns in *Finnegans Wake* enable a kind of thinking that defies the dominant Western logic based on a stable identity and the laws of noncontradiction. Hence skeptical philosophical textualists such as Derrida find the *Wake* an intriguing model. Criticism of Derrida, in fact, tends to be similar to criticism of Joyce: that despite their claim to an "unoriginal" writing their difficult styles display arrogant egotism; that they overemphasize language, making the world into texts; and that their subsuming of history to writing is politically reactionary and ultimately conservative.

Such an assessment underrates, I believe, the *Wake*'s capacity to criticize ideology. The *Wake*'s multidimensional puns and radically destabilized points of view mimic advanced capitalism's constant circulation but also reveal the contradiction between its ideology and practice. The ideology of capitalism insists that there is some aggregate good that comes from the so-called "spontaneous" marketplace distribution of supply and demand, capital and labor. Hence we often hear the term "market solution" for some social problem, as though the circulation of capital had a stable point of view capable of volition and purpose. But capital merely moves to where it finds the most profitable return. Joyce's style and message show that the desire to circulate itself cancels stable point of view, will, motive, plan. Circulation only serves the randomness of evolution (as opposed to any social good or progress) and open-ended creativity.

One of the most remarkable aspects of *Finnegans Wake* is that Joyce anticipates our hypermedia-ized world. The words, *"afterthoughtfully colliberated"* (FW 342.35), in the title of this chapter come from the TV skit by comics Butt and Taff in II.3. "Afterthoughtfully" suggests the retrospective nature of analysis and meaning in the postmodern world of continual movement. Meaning does not inhere "in" a moment, a word, a thing, but is a construction, one of many possible out of a network of relations with what has come before. "Colliberated" contains the collisions in a random universe and brings to mind guilt and accusation (berating oneself and being berated), the difficulty of calibrating precisely, the necessity of collaborating, which is partly always a co-optation of one's project (as in collaborating with the enemy) but also a communal activity that is co-liberating. Any reader of the *Wake* has to depend upon others who have come before, and writing about the text requires accepting dependence on other commentators, giving in to the anxiety of error, and acknowledging the profound debt that cannot ever be adequately repaid to all who have written about the book.

In retrospect, however, I see that *Finnegans Wake* may also be about the *dream* of resisting commodification by continual movement, one that may imply a warning about the debris that accompanies freedom. An article of trade that can be turned to commercial advantage, a commodity in literary terms could be a book that stands for X, or means Y, or that can be used for Z's cause, for example, as a book can become a hot property for a movie or as a rationale for someone's political agenda. The *Wake* expresses the dream of liberation, the utopian impulse of anarchy, as it eludes being turned into a commodity by virtue of its difficult, radical style of continual transformation, meaning in the making, and its resistent opacity.

Perhaps more than most texts, the book has managed to escape commodification (although "Joyce, the author," certainly has become a commodity). Free circulation, advanced capitalism, postmodern play—all have the liberating promise of openness in continual transformation and change. Yet, most often instead of transformation, the postmodern world just recirculates the same in a new package, like the box of soap that is constantly redefined, repackaged, and sold over and over again. If the *Wake* anticipates the postmodern, it also points to the threat in postmodernism. Despite the Utopian dream of endlessly remaking the world, we may awake to the nightmare of repetition compulsion. If the *Wake* dreams of litter being turned to letters, it also describes our contemporary condition of all letters being turned to litter, debris, bits and pieces to be reassembled and remarketed next week as a new miniseries, ad campaign, billboard sign, slogan.

On the other hand, the positive side of postmodernism is the constantly evolving, nonhierarchical network of multiple relations, for example, in the way computers can produce hypertextual writing spaces. Derrida has even compared Joyce's language experiment in the *Wake* to a kind of computer, and *Finnegans Wake* has been put on a "Hypertext" program. Yet, however compatible, the postmodern technology of the computer world also differs from Joyce's night world. Textual proliferation in the *Wake* is grounded in the human body. All the lexical transformations are sexually overdetermined, always coming back to the physical materialism of the human body from which arise perverse human desires. I have argued that the book does not enshrine the word ("ledn us alones of your lungorge, parsonifier propounde of our edelweissed idol worts!" [378.23–24]). Indeed, just as feminists do, the book connects "idol worts" to phallic dominance and the belief in a single God: "In the buginning is the woid" (378.29). The pun on buggery may suggest that belief in God derives from a homosexual longing of the male for his own image (similar to the critique of patriarchy made by Irigaray). Might it also suggest that the act of creation is like the phallic appropriation of the Other? The pun on void/word also suggests that in the beginning there is nothing, no God, and that the Word is empty, not the solid foundation of the universe as in the Book of John, but a mishmash (a sound associated with sexual intercourse in the *Wake*), human creation from gossip, rumor, murmuring in sleep, and memory.

Finnegans Wake speaks to feminist issues, I believe, because it is grounded in the material, human body and because it refuses the sentiment on which the patriarchal ego is founded. By only giving us fragments—which we must connect, interpret, and argue for—the book inscribes representation as eternally mediated. There is no direct relation between any figure, body part, or organ and meaning, but numerous, overdetermined pieces from which a reader must construct reading(s). If the text is a usurper in any way, it usurps our attempts at stabilizing meaning and asserting our own correct reading by constantly making us question our construction with its multiple punning possibilities and vast network of references. In "The Problem of Speaking for Others," feminist Linda Alcoff describes the "crisis of representation" that grows out of a postmodern awareness of multiplicity. From postmodern theory we understand that representation is "in every case mediated and the product of interpretation (which is connected to the claim that a speaker's location has epistemic salience)" (9). Faced with multiplicity and realizing all representation is mediated and therefore ideological, we may want to, but should not, Alcoff warns, withdraw from the arena of debate. She points out that there is no authentic location or truer self from which to speak but the one we inhabit. Although we always must confront the desire for mastery, she argues, we cannot flee from political effectivity by a desire to be transparent, bodiless, or located outside of a subject position. We must, she concludes, be responsible for an "analysis of effects" (28). The reception history of *Finnegans Wake* attests to a response similar to the one Alcoff warns us against. First, the audience for *Finnegans Wake,* it was thought, would withdraw in the face of such a complex text; no one would read the book. Then, critics denied its political effectivity; a book so obscure cannot be political, it was said. Now, however, when even "seemingly" realistic and political texts are deconstructed from postmodern points of view, *Finnegans Wake* seems less, rather than more, secretive. It does not conceal (as a realist text does), but flaunts, the processes and responsibilities of making meaning in discourse.

I also said *Finnegans Wake* speaks to feminism because it parodies the sentiment on which the patriarchal ego is founded. The patriarchal ego Freud describes is one constructed on loss, a point both Madelon Sprengnether (228) and Judith Butler (50) make in critiquing Freud's theory. Gender is produced within the "orbit of melancholy" (50), according to Butler, by internalizing and preserving loss within as the inner, homosexual counterpart of the normative "heterosexual frame" (57). While there is no escape from the patriarchal ego in a patriarchal culture, the *Wake* parodies both in the long passage about the "Willingdone Museyroom," satirizing the building of houses (the house-that-Jack-built parody), museums housing relics of the past, the construction of gender and sexuality, warfare, sexual antics, and heroes (8.9–10.22). The *Wake* does not memorialize loss, nor ignore it, but dismantles nostalgia, by breaking up the solid past into shards and thereby opening up a space for creativity from the pieces.

Although the book deconstructs phallic ideology, capitalist ideology, gender division, and the formation and control of the ego by repression, it does not stand in judgment nor propose a "better version" of these. The book itself does not make the mistake of Shem and Shaun, exchanging one tyrannical view for another. *Finnegans Wake* is not a romance but a comedy. The book gives us the bourgeois nuclear family and parodies it with perverse humor. To the end refusing any stable point of view necessary for criticism, refusing any utilitarian goal, the book affirms only the open-endedness of perverse sexual coupling and evolutionary change: "Of I be leib in the immoralities? O, you mean the strangle for love and the sowiveall of the prettiest? Yep, we open hap coseries in the home" (145.26–28).

**Notes
Works Cited
Index**

Notes

1. WRITING AND READING THE SCENE OF THE FAMILY

1. Jacques Derrida explores this "irreducible," yet "secondary," characteristic in his essay "Freud and the Scene of Writing." "Since the transition to consciousness is not a derivative or repetitive writing, a transcription duplicating an unconscious writing," Derrida states, "it occurs in an original manner and, in its very secondariness, is originary and irreducible" (*Writing and Difference* 212). In analyzing Freud's metaphor of the Mystic Writing Pad, Derrida credits Freud with moving from the old "preoccupation with *content*" to "concern for relations, locations, processes, and differences" (209). Derrida stresses the machinelike character of writing (consciousness does not write, but is written) and writing's relation to repression and death ("representation is death" [227]). In Derrida's characterization of writing as the absence of continual deferral, writing must always reinscribe itself: thus writing is like the repetition compulsion that Freud connected in *Beyond the Pleasure Principle* to the death drive. In the last chapter of this book I argue that in *Finnegans Wake* Joyce opens up repetition compulsion to the possibility of change. Looking backward from the point of view of loss, "there is no purity of the living present" (Derrida 212), but looking forward from the point of view of creativity, the gap of absence provides the opening space for the creative supplement fashioned out of the material remainder (the trace) of the past.

2. *Standard Edition of the Complete Psychological Works of Sigmund Freud*, 24 vols., 19: 178. All references to Freud are from this edition, except where otherwise indicated. Volume and page number appear in parentheses with the abbreviation *SE*.

3. For a recent study of the cultural construction of gender evidenced in intersex case management of hermaphroditism, see Suzanne J. Kessler, "The Medical Construction of Gender: Case Management of Intersexed Infants."

4. In fairness, though, I should add that Freud avoids using the idea of the norm prescriptively. He uses "the normal" more as an organizational device, as Fredric Jameson points out in "Imaginary and Symbolic in Lacan: Marxism, Psychoanalytic Criticism, and the Problem of the Subject" 372.

5. James Joyce, *Stephen Hero*, edited from the Manuscript in the Harvard College Library by Theodore Spencer, Incorporating Additional Manuscript Pages, ed. Slocum and Cahoon (New York: New Directions, 1963) 212. All references will be to this edition, page numbers given in parentheses.

6. D. H. Lawrence, *Studies in Classic American Literature*(Thomas Seltzer, 1923; rpt. New York: Doubleday Anchor, n.d.) 12. All references will be to this edition, page numbers given in parentheses.

7. James Joyce, *A Portrait of the Artist as a Young Man*, The definitive text, corrected from the Dublin holograph by Chester G. Anderson and edited by Richard Ellmann (New York: Viking, 1964) 215. All references will be to this edition, page numbers given in parentheses with the abbreviation *P*.

8. D. H. Lawrence, *Women in Love* (New York: Viking, 1920; rpt. The New Scholarly Text), ed. David Farmer, Lindeth Vasey, and John Worthen (Cambridge: Cambridge UP, 1987) 318. All references will be to this edition, page numbers given in parentheses.

9. See Lydia Blanchard's "*Women in Love*: Mourning Becomes Narcissism" for the parallels between Lawrence's diagnosis of his "sick" society and Freud's insights into depression and narcissism in "Mourning and Melancholia." Blanchard argues, "*Women in Love* is centrally concerned with narcissism and narcissistic rage. It provides not only one of our most profound statements of the relationship between the death of the past and both cultural and personal narcissism, but also, as a formal experiment, Lawrence's attempt to counteract what he saw as an increased narcissism in the shape of modern fiction" (106).

10. Despite the fact that such a reading of discourse has been influenced by Lacanianism, such a simple binary opposition between "male" logical discourse and "female" subversive nonspeech also seems to fall into the kind of dual thinking that in Lacan marks the register of the Imaginary.

11. My thinking on Freud has been influenced by Paul Ricoeur's *Freud and Philosophy*, Juliet Mitchell's *Psychoanalysis and Feminism*, and Peter Gay's biography, *Freud: A Life for Our Time*. In addition to Freud's *Standard Edition*, I have drawn on the *Introductory Lectures on Psychoanalysis*. Pointing out the significance of the *Introductory Lectures*, editor James Strachey says, they "may justly be regarded as a stock-taking of Freud's

views and the position of psycho-analysis at the time of the first World War" (7).

12. The fear of castration is a fantasy of the child's in response to a threat. Castration fear is variously explained as a real threat conveyed to the child by the mother or caretaker during the course of normal discipline ("Anatomical Distinction" 188–89) or as the reverse force of the child's own desire to kill the father (the Oedipus complex). Castration anxiety depends upon the child's psychic interpretation that a female has had her penis cut off. Of course, "penectomy" is not properly castration at all, but Freud always uses the term in this way.

13. In "Three Essays on the Theory of Sexuality" (*SE* 7: 125). Freud added material to this essay in 1915.

14. See *SE* 14 for "A Metapsychological Supplement to the Theory of Dreams" and "The Unconscious" as well as the closely related essay "The Instincts and Their Vicissitudes."

15. In his 1914 essay "On Narcissism: An Introduction," Freud wrote, "the formation of an ideal heightens the demands of the ego and is the most powerful factor favoring repression" (*SE* 14: 95).

16. James Joyce, *Finnegans Wake*, Embodying all author's corrections (New York: Viking, 1939; rpt. 1973). All references will be to this edition. The abbreviation *FW* and page and line numbers will be given in parentheses.

17. See Carol Dix, *D. H. Lawrence and Women*, and Bonnie Kime Scott, *Joyce and Feminism* for historical assessments of Lawrence's and Joyce's attitudes toward women and their relation to feminists. Though both writers spoke against feminism, each was connected to feminists, Lawrence in his early years in England, Joyce in the 1920s and 1930s in Paris. The historical record is only part of the story of their attitude to sex/gender issues. The other part resides in their texts.

18. V. N. Vološinov has often been treated as a mere pseudonym for M. M. Bakhtin, but the translator of *Freudianism: A Critical Sketch* argues that Vološinov should be considered as a separate individual and the author in his own right ("the case for attribution does not rest at any point on established facts" [xvi]). Vološinov, along with L. S. Vygotsky, was a member of the Bakhtin Circle.

19. "Neither is it true that every motive in contradiction with the official ideology must degenerate into indistinct inner speech and then die out—it might well engage in a struggle with that official ideology. If such a motive *is founded on the economic being of the whole group*, if it is not merely the motive of a déclassé loner, then it has a chance for a future and perhaps even a victorious future. There is no reason why such a motive should become asocial and lose contact with communica-

tion. Only, at first a motive of this sort will develop within a small social milieu and will depart into the underground—not the psychological underground of repressed complexes, but the salutary political underground" (Vološinov 89–90; italics in original).

20. Kelsey's and Pearce's books appeared after this manuscript was substantially complete, so I do not specifically engage their studies in later chapters. However, Kelsey's conclusions about Lawrence's portrayal of sexuality seem similar to mine. Kelsey remarks on the "representation of polymorphous desire" in *Women in Love*, but notes that polymorphous desires remain "but brief moments" "in the overall reduction of the text to the structure of the metaphysic, a heterosexual reduction" (179). I agree with Pearce that Joyce's texts have the potential to raise the consciousness of readers, that they inscribe competing political views, and thus are potentially liberatory.

21. For a feminist theory of resistant reading, see Patrocinio Schweickart's "Reading Ourselves: Toward a Feminist Theory of Reading."

22. "Lévi-Strauss's formalization of the elementary structures of kinship and its use of Jakobson's binarism provided the basis for Lacan's conception of the symbolic," states Alan Sheridan, translator of Lacan's *Four Fundamental Concepts of Psycho-Analysis* ("Translator's Note" 279).

23. In some ways arguments between structuralists and poststructuralists reproduce the disagreements among evolutionists in the nineteenth century over mechanisms of change, for example catastrophism vs. developmentalism, arguments that still continue in theorizing evolution. In *Darwin's Century,* Loren Eiseley maintains that evolution as a concept means "indeterminism" (349–52), and that time is "noncyclic, unreturning, and creative" (331). Eiseley also makes an interesting point about catastrophic theories of culture, similar to Lévi-Strauss's "one fell swoop":

By contrast [A. I. Hallowell] postulates what he terms a proto-cultural stage which might well have been reached early, "even before the development of speech." There may have been some slight degree of tool using, some learned behavior, but not the whole range of activities, including speech, which we now tend to regard as so uniquely human. Because Darwin and his associates pushed living apes too close to living men, a reaction set in which led anthropologists, even while rendering lip service to morphological evolution, to imply that culture is a whole with a "relatively constant categorical content." (323)

24. Whether or not Lacanian theory actually includes a poststructuralist critique of systems is debated in Johnson's *Critical Difference.*

25. "This statement refers to a field that is much more accessible to us today than at the time of Freud," Lacan states, "by the field that is explored, structured, elaborated by Claude Lévi-Strauss" (*The Four Fundamental Concepts* 20).

26. Lacan is often contradictory and is not entirely consistent on this point. In early seminars he connects desire to rivalry (as Freud does) and says desire exists before language: "before language, desire exists solely in the single plane of the imaginary relation of the specular stage, projected, alienated in the other" ("The See-saw of Desire," *The Seminar, I*: 170).

27. Jacques-Alain Miller, editor of Lacan, points out that Lacan himself warns that relying on schemata risks falling prey to the trap of the imaginary; however, this begs the question. Lacan is very fond of drawings, figures, maps, and he often does seem to reduce the complex and intuitive into a geometric figure.

28. Lacan insists that the phallus is not the referential, biological penis but an arbitrary signifier: "Because the phallus is not a question of a form, or of an image, or of a phantasy, but rather of a signifier, the signifier of desire. In Greek antiquity the phallus is not represented by an organ but as an insignia; it is the ultimate significative object, which appears when all the veils are lifted" (Wilden 187; quoting Lacan's seminar of April–June 1958).

In *Finnegans Wake,* when Shaun views his sister Issy with her veils lifted, he sees castration, a hole that he hails, on the one hand suggesting he is caught in the Imaginary order and on the other by the language's duplicitous condensation, which evokes its opposite, suggesting a negation of the Imaginary. Readers of the *Wake* after Lacan often consider that the book implies the truth of the third order, that all is language. I argue against this position in chapter 4, claiming that Shaun also sees himself in Issy's hole/hail and that the negation of the Imaginary order and castration is not the Symbolic order where all truth is language but the unconscious order of bisexual human desire below language and repression.

29. Judith Butler points out that "the *totality* and *closure* of language is both presumed and contested within structuralism." "This quasi-Leibnizian view," she continues, "effectively suppresses the moment of difference between signifier and signified, relating and unifying that moment of arbitrariness within a totalizing field" (*Gender Trouble* 40; italics in original).

30. Lacan's approach is "originally dependent upon analogies," which is "the weak point for its detractors," says Wilden (298).

31. Derrida criticizes Lacan's theory for its "phallogocentricism," the play on words pointing to the implicit though hidden referent to a

real situation and real penis, which in turn reveal the logocentrism at the center of the theory (see Barbara Johnson's *Critical Difference* chap. 7). When Derrida accuses Lacan of "logocentrism," he is concerned about the literal reference—in Lacan's terms, an error of the Imaginary order, believing in correspondence.

32. For a comprehensive but brief overview of Lacan's impact on Joyce studies in recent years, see the introductory essay by Sheldon Brivic, guest editor of "Joyce Between Genders" 13–21.

33. For example, in this special issue of *JJQ*, articles by Catherine Millot, Ellie Ragland-Sullivan, and Beryl Schlossman use Lacanian theory as the master narrative to "diagnose" Joyce/Joyce texts, and articles by Tony Jackson, Patrick Hogan, Kimberly Devlin, and Sheldon Brivic draw in part on Lacanian concepts as well as other strategies of reading to elucidate specific features of Joyce's work.

34. Lacan writes in his 1976 preface to *The Four Fundamental Concepts of Psycho-Analysis*, "I shall speak of Joyce, who has preoccupied me much this year, only to say that he is the simplest consequence of a refusal—such a mental refusal!—of a psycho-analysis, which, as a result, his work illustrates. But I have done no more than touch on this, in view of my embarrassment where art—an element in which Freud did not bathe without mishap—is concerned" (ix).

35. Joyce owned Freud's essay "Leonardo da Vinci and a Memory of Childhood," and Daniel Ferrer has uncovered evidence that Joyce took notes on Freud's case studies for *Finnegans Wake*. See chapters 3 and 4.

36. In "Castration and its Discontents: A Lacanian Approach to *Ulysses*," Kimberly Devlin argues that "Joyce offers no explicit cure for castration anxiety but traces instead its proliferative aggressive effects, exposing in the process the underside of various oppressive and dominant 'isms' (sexism, imperialism, snobbism, racism): their foundation in a profound ontological insecurity and, most depressingly, a purely fictional, yet symbolically effective, missing signifier" (140). In chapter 4, I argue quite the opposite, that the process of learning to negotiate the language of *Finnegans Wake* is a process of succumbing to the anxiety of castration and then a working through and overcoming it. Joyce's "cure" for castration anxiety, I argue, is to force us to make the creative leap across the gap. From a psychoanalytic view, however, "an inadequate acceptance of symbolic castration" can take the form of "fetishism and 'doubling' (reduplication of an image)" and is "the greatest of all obstacles to a full therapeutic 'cure,'" according to Juliet Mitchell (*Psychoanalysis and Feminism* 84).

37. In *Gender Trouble*, Judith Butler notes that Lacan's theory ro-

manticizes tragic failure (56), which is "symptomatic of a slave morality" (57).

38. American object-relations psychology and Lacanian theory are not truly opposites but are on different ends of the same continuum. Both incorporate Freudian and object-relations psychology, but they develop toward different poles—the external and cultural on the American side and the internal and symbolic on the French side.

39. Mitchell and Rose's criticisms would presumably apply to Sprengnether's rethinking of the mother, since Sprengnether suggests the mother functions as a *model* of self-division and absent plenitude, and thus the child's psyche would presumably develop from modeling what already exists.

40. See Daniel Dervin, "Play, Creativity and Matricide: The Implications of Lawrence's 'Smashed Doll' Episode" for an application to *Sons and Lovers* of the theories of D. W. Winnicott. Dervin's analysis is rich and interesting and avoids gender bias. However, I disagree with his interpretation of the "smashed doll" scene, which I believe is indeed implicated in gender issues. See chapter 2. Also see David Holbrook, *Where D. H. Lawrence Was Wrong about Woman,* and Margaret Storch, *Sons and Adversaries: Women in William Blake and D. H. Lawrence.* Storch declares "it is Kleinian theory that leads us to the truest meaning" of *Sons and Lovers* (98). For reasons I explain in the text below I disagree with this assertion.

41. I encountered Butler's *Gender Trouble* after this manuscript was substantially complete, so I do not specifically address the many interesting issues Butler raises. Butler employs a Foucaultian critique to argue that the incest taboo and earlier taboo against homosexuality exert a juridical force that both produces and represses desire for the mother/father (77). Thus she contends that bisexuality and homosexuality as well as the dominant heterosexuality are necessarily produced by the prohibition. Butler calls for "new possibilities for gender that contest the rigid codes of hierarchical binarism" (145). Butler argues against a primary bisexuality as psychic foundation, claiming that Freud actually begins with a "heterosexual matrix" (opposites attract) that must be there in order for him to read bisexual "dispositions" in the first place (60–63). While I agree that Freud conceptualizes pre-Oedipal relations in terms of "active" and "passive," I do not think this can be termed a "heterosexual matrix." First, one could argue, as Irigaray does, that active/passive is a single, homosexual economy, where "homosexual" refers to the single reflection of the male returned to him in "heterosexual" relations (not to alternative gay and lesbian filiations of desire). Second, Freud stipulates that desires are multiple, perverse, and unat-

tached *until* they pass through the regulating of the Oedipus complex and emerge gendered. Gendering under patriarchy regulates desire into active/passive, male/female.

42. See Joan Tempelton, "The *Doll House* Backlash: Criticism, Feminism, and Ibsen."

2. D. H. LAWRENCE: THE SEXUAL STRUGGLE
DISPLACES THE CLASS STRUGGLE

1. See Daniel A. Weiss's *Oedipus in Nottingham: D. H. Lawrence* and David Cavitch's *D. H. Lawrence and the New World* for examples of Freudian studies. For an example of a study drawing on the theories of Jacques Lacan, see David J. Gordon's article on the "sexualization of style," "Sex and Language in D. H. Lawrence."

2. In *D. H. Lawrence and Women,* Carol Dix also begins with this perplexing question and concludes that women readers respond to Lawrence's work because "Lawrence treats women with a respect hardly ever accorded them by male writers, let alone female writers. . . . it is women who explore, progress, advance, think and feel. The real heroes . . . are the women" (12). Two recent books also explore this seeming contradiction, Nigel Kelsey's *D. H. Lawrence: Sexual Crisis* and Carol Siegel's *Lawrence Among the Women: Wavering Boundaries in Women's Literary Traditions.*

3. According to Tristram, Lawrence was first introduced to Freud's ideas in 1912 and became acquainted with professional Freudians in 1914 (138). Burwell notes in a "Catalogue Addenda" of Lawrence's reading that he sent a copy of *Psychoanalytic Review* to Dr. Barbara Low, a friend and Freudian analyst, in 1916. Ruderman notes that he read Jung in the autumn of 1918 (254).

4. D. H. Lawrence, *Sons and Lovers* (Thomas Seltzer, 1913; rpt. The New Scholarly Text, Cambridge: Cambridge UP, 1992) 9. This is the first line of the novel. All references will be to this edition, page numbers given in parentheses.

5. See, for example, Donald E. Mortland, "The Conclusion of *Sons and Lovers:* A Reconsideration"; and Daniel R. Schwarz, "Speaking of Paul Morel: Voice, Unity, and Meaning in *Sons and Lovers.*"

6. For an analysis of the shortchanging of feminism in traditional Marxist theory, see Simone de Beauvoir's essay in *New French Feminisms* and the collectively written "Variations on Common Themes," whose authors point out the "inherent gaps" and "inconsistencies" in the way Marxism situates oppression in capitalism alone and ignores the structures that oppress women: "these structures are part of a specific

system different from the capitalist system, and we call this system 'patriarchy'" (217). See also Sandra Harding, "The Instability of the Analytical Categories of Feminist Theory," for a critique of how Marxist epistemology excludes the labor of women, slaves, and colonized peoples from the proletariat's relations to production, which, according to Marxism, confer revolutionary knowledge.

7. Schwarz 269, but he regards this "intercourse with flowers" as proof of the sexual frustration of Lawrence's characters.

8. "Vulgar economic thought," states Adorno in "Reification of Logic," "attributes value to goods in themselves and does not determine it through social relations" (*Against Epistemology* 65), just as, Adorno argues, the reification of logic abstracts logic "from all facticity" (60). For a secondary discussion of Adorno's concept of reification, see Gillian Rose's *Melancholy Science: An Introduction to the Thought of Theodor W. Adorno*, chap. 3, "The Lament Over Reification."

9. See Freud, "Some Psychical Consequences of the Anatomical Distinction between the Sexes," and "Female Sexuality," in *SE*, vols. 19 and 21.

10. In "The Father of All Things: The Oral and the Oedipal in *Sons and Lovers*," T. H. Adamowski argues that Paul and all Lawrentian male characters show that Lawrence got stuck at the negative Oedipal phase, that he is like a woman (this is bad), he fears for his safety in intercourse (83) and that "anal penetration haunted Lawrence and tempted him, and that in some way it allowed him to deal with a woman as though she were a man" (86). I would like to describe in more specific ways how Lawrence's central characters are "like" women, in ways that are not pejorative to women, and in ways that do not depend on the dominance of male experience as normal. (What is wrong, by the way, with treating a woman like a man? Or a man like a woman? What is such treatment anyhow? And why would it supposedly be abnormal for a man to fear for his safety in intercourse, but not for a woman?)

11. "A Checklist of Lawrence's Reading" shows that in 1908 he read Ernst Haeckel's *Riddle of the Universe* (Sagar 70). In this work Haeckel applied the doctrine of evolution to philosophy and argued that organic and inorganic life were essentially unified, the highest animal forms having evolved from simpler forms and inorganic matter. Psychology, he argued, derived from physical properties, and he believed even cell life had psychic properties. These ideas seem very similar to Lawrence's, and it is tempting to consider that Haeckel may be a source for them.

12. In Freudian terms, Mrs. Morel suffers from a transference neurosis. She substitutes the love of her sons for the love of her husband, because in loving her sons she has authority and can carry out her will

and gain satisfaction, whereas her husband is dominant, intractable and unpredictable. Freud says that neurotic symptoms substitute for sexual satisfaction (see "The Dynamics of Transference" and "Types of Onset of Neurosis" *SE:* 12). Taken literally, her neurosis can be seen as her dissatisfaction with her sexual identity—the limitations and contradictions of being female.

13. In *Lawrence among the Women,* Carol Siegel traces the metaphor of flow in Lawrence and cautions against a simple binary male, female reading. His works "defy categorizaton" (170), she concludes. Siegel sees Lawrence's contradictions as the result of the "discrepancy between male and female world views" (9), credits him for inscribing oppositional female voices in his texts (10), and argues that he presents women as "wholesome," portraying a "feminized cosmos" (10) that replaces the father "with the Mother as the primary source of life and art" (13). Siegel connects Lawrence to "liberal humanism" (18) in his emphasis on choice for women, and she argues he parts from liberalism "at precisely the same point that feminism does"—at the point where gender identity causes problems (18). Siegel situates Lawrence with women writers in a "common tradition" (18). I argue that binary gender difference is a product of patriarchy, as is "liberal humanism," which I think explains why both Lawrence and liberal humanism can accommodate misogyny as well as female freedom.

14. Freud states that "the concept of repression involves no relation to sexuality. . . . It indicates a purely psychological process, which we can characterize still better if we call it a 'topographical' one" (*Introductory Lectures* 342). But Freud uses a metaphor drawn from class division to describe that supposedly neutral location (topography). He compares the unconscious to a large, common entrance hall where individual impulses crudely jostle one another. Adjoining this large room is a narrower one, whose threshold is guarded by a "watchman, the censor" who allows only certain impulses to cross over into the next room, where consciousness resides (*Introductory Lectures* 295). According to Freud's own, quite didactic list, rooms, houses, and especially doorways and thresholds are symbols of women, so there is reasonable evidence from Freud's writings that the unconscious is associated with the female and is implicated in class issues in the metaphor above, even though Freud consciously denies the connection.

15. D. H. Lawrence, *The Rainbow* (New York: Viking, 1915; rpt. The New Scholarly Text, Cambridge: Cambridge UP, 1989). All references will be to this edition, page numbers given in parentheses.

16. For example, Scott Sanders says Lawrence's "Freudian paradigm of politics as the interaction of an authoritarian father-figure who craves affection with subservient children who crave authority, outlined

here in the relation between Gerald and his workers, is projected again on a fuller screen in *Kangaroo* and *The Plumed Serpent*" (*The World of the Five Major Novels* 112–13).

17. "She had thought there was no source deeper than the phallic source. And now, behold, from the smitten rock of the man's body, from the strange marvellous flanks and thighs, deeper, further in mystery than the phallic source, came the floods of ineffable darkness and ineffable riches" (*Women in Love* 314).

18. See Pierre Vitoux, "The Chapter 'Excurse' in *Women in Love:* Its Genesis and the Critical Problem." I am deeply indebted to this fine study of the composition process of this chapter of the novel and to Vitoux's explanation of how it relates to Lawrence's conception of the unconscious and gender roles. "We can safely dismiss all speculations about 'what really happened' sexually," during Ursula and Birkin's sexual exchange in "Excurse" concludes Vitoux. Nothing happens, Vitoux argues, but Ursula becomes tapped in to a deeper source of connection than the merely phallic "what in another deleted part of the TS [p. 498], he had called 'a mating beyond love and passion'" (831). Vitoux also argues that Birkin rejects "Platonic Man and Woman" (829) for a new kind of relational, equal sexuality, an idea I agree with.

19. In "Apropos of *Lady Chatterley's Lover*" (1930), Lawrence commented, "Never was an age more sentimental, more devoid of real feeling, more exaggerated in false feeling, than our own. Sentimentality and counterfeit feeling have become a sort of game, everybody trying to outdo his neighbour. The radio and the film are mere counterfeit emotion all the time, the current press and literature the same. People wallow in emotion: counterfeit emotion. They lap it up: they live in it and on it. They ooze with it" (*Phoenix II:* 493).

20. "When works of art are exchanged as commodities, they become detached from the context of social use and ritual and thus become 'autonomous'" (Rose 116). This passage explains one element in Adorno's critique of modernism. Adorno rejects the nostalgic view of lost cultural unity. Instead he argues that culture always arises from the contradictions in society, but only in capitalism do cultural forms achieve autonomy. He then goes on to argue that their autonomy destroys the illusion of wholeness and unity of culture, thereby revealing its contradictions. And so Adorno champions avant-garde art. Lawrence's attitude to the modern world that emerges from his best novels seems quite similar to Adorno's. On the other hand, Lawrence has a tendency to lament lost cultural unity in some of his writing such as *The Plumed Serpent.*

21. Pierre Vitoux agrees that the problem of male dominance "remains, and it is central to the novel: the theoretical equality between

two independent stars is, in fact, as Ursula was quick to detect before her conversion, very close to the relation of a planet to its satellite. . . . What is in theory a purely qualitative difference between the male and the female principles becomes the support of male domination. . . . the problem is dramatized (not hypocritically passed over), but it is not solved" (832–33). Lawrence's 1923 novella, *The Fox*, also explores the desire to dominate in homosexual and heterosexual relations and ends ironically, I believe, with a heterosexual rescue that threatens to become male domination: "And he! He did not want her to watch any more, to see any more, to understand any more. He wanted to veil her woman's spirit, as Orientals veil the woman's face. He wanted her to commit herself to him, and to put her independent spirit to sleep. He wanted to take away from her all her effort, all that seemed her very *raison d'etre*. He wanted to make her submit, yield, blindly pass away out of all her strenuous consciousness. He wanted to take away her consciousness, and make her just his woman. . . . He wanted her at peace, asleep in him" (*The Fox* 103–4).

22. In "Lawrence's *Götterdämmerung:* The Tragic Vision of *Women in Love*," Joyce Carol Oates notes that Lawrence values the feminine and opposes its qualities to those of "the patriarchal cosmos": "Where in more traditional tragedy—Shakespeare's *King Lear* comes immediately to mind—it is the feminine, irrational 'dark and vicious' elements that must be resisted, since they disturb the status quo, the patriarchal cosmos, in Lawrence it is precisely the darkness, the passion, the mind-obliterating, terrible, and even vicious experience of erotic love that is necessary for salvation" (571–72).

3. JAMES JOYCE: OVERDETERMINATION
REPLACES CAUSE AND EFFECT

1. In "Silence in Dubliners," Jean-Michel Rabate states, "to stress the link between *Dubliners* and *Finnegans Wake*, a link attested by the note-books, I would be tempted to say that the Father hesitates between the paralysis of heresy and sexual sin—this would be best figured out by the GPI, or syphilitic 'general paralysis of the insane' affecting Father Flynn, and the paralysis of mute orthodoxy, the GPO, or General Post Office, the pure ballast of an empty symbolic structure, defining the void centre of the capital 'to the wustworts of Finntown's generous poet's office' [*FW* 265]" (71). The link between *Dubliners* and *Finnegans Wake* is a backward one, it should be noted. I shall address the question of the GPO, or empty symbolic structure, below.

2. James Joyce, *"Ulysses": The Corrected Text*, ed. Hans Walter Gabler

(New York: Random House, 1986). All references will be to this text. The abbreviation *U*, with episode and line numbers, will be given in parentheses.

3. There is a connection, however, between the historicist ideas of Dilthey, a Gestaltist, and Croce, who wrote a book about Vico in 1924, and whose earlier work Joyce probably was aware of in the early years in Trieste. See Manganiello, *Joyce's Politics*. Vico's "statement, '*verum et factum convertuntur*', that truth and fact are convertible, lies at the root of his view, which was to be echoed by Marx and Dilthey, that man can understand history because he made it himself" explains Bleicher in *Contemporary Hermeneutics* (16).

4. Gestaltists were arguing against notions of undifferentiated, raw sense perceptions like those of William James. That stream of "discontinuity" is to be distinguished from what I describe below as Stephen's final claim of achieving a constant position of discontinuity by always moving through and beyond controlling structures. For discussion of the differences between Gestaltists and William James, see Allan Strauss, *A Critical Study of Freud's Concept of Unconscious Mental Processes: With Special Reference to Gestalt Psychology*, 68.

5. In *Beyond Egotism: The Fiction of James Joyce, Virginia Woolf, and D. H. Lawrence*, Robert Kiely compares the struggles of the two heroes in *A Portrait* and *Sons and Lovers*, concluding that for each character the struggle to maturity is "defined largely in terms of his efforts to attain sexual and emotional maturity in his relations with women" (62). I agree that this is the case with Paul Morel, but I argue that Stephen defends himself against the sexual by refuge in the mental. Even in *Ulysses*, where Stephen more openly articulates a desire for a relationship with a woman, his relations are presented indirectly, obliquely, through hypotheses, displacements, and substitutions.

6. Stephen Heath in "Ambiviolences" calls this negative, dialectical movement "the strategy of hesitation": "This is the context of the necessity of the strategies of hesitation of Joyce's texts. Gripped in a general paralysis, Joyce's writing is obliged to effect a constant activity of refusal of available meanings, explications, discursive forms, all the very texture of the paralysis. It is precisely the evasion and baffling of the available, the given, its hesitation, to which the writing of Joyce's early texts is devoted and which defines their negativity" (34).

7. Earlier I argued that Stephen's mother stands for the materiality of the body, flesh, and the senses. There are few other women represented in the novel. Emma Clery, for instance, who had a substantial reality in *Stephen Hero* speaks only two sentences and becomes an oblique, unnamed diary entry in *A Portrait*. Some might point to Stephen's vision of the bird girl in objecting to my conclusion that women are seen as

materiality. I would argue that the bird girl is merely one of Stephen's images created from the patriarchal structures that shape him. In the same way that he uses Mariology to think of Eileen Vance, he fashions a phantasm of a female muse, whose associations with purity and spirituality are entirely conventional (see *P* 171–72).

8. See Henke and Unkeless, eds., *Women in Joyce*. Many contributors to this volume do just that, directly correlating a character or cultural type with Joyce's attitude. The editors conclude that Joyce "could imagine woman as both goddess and muse, but not as an intellectual equal" (xxi).

9. In *Finnegans Wake* Joyce seems to parody the simplistic phallic dominance of *Lady Chatterley's Lover* in a long passage on p. 92 that contains fragments of Lawrentian theme words such as polar opposites and lunar and that refers to "stincking thyacinths through his curls" (92.16–17) from the famous lovemaking scene in *LCL*. Joyce reverses everything, though. The woman is on top, "heruponhim" (92.28). Rather than phallic victory, the feminine aspects of sexual climax are suggested: "the shaym of his hisu shifting into the shimmering of her hers, (youthsy, beautsy, hee's her chap and shey'll tell memmas when she gays whom) till the wild wishwish of her sheeshea melted most musically mid the dark deepdeep of his shayshaun" (92.28–32). (Hyacinths and lisping sexuality are also probably associated with Oscar Wilde. See chap. 4, n. 31.)

10. M. J. C. Hodgart in his essay "Aeolus" notes that little was manufactured in Dublin in 1904 "except porter and biscuits" (116), and he makes the point that it was a "city of consumers" (116) rather than producers. My argument that in the book we do not see the family relations of advanced consumer capitalism does not, I think, contradict Hodgart's economic portrait. The Dublin of *Ulysses* is neither a farm nor an industrial society but a *simple* consumer society with widespread poverty and unemployment.

11. For a Lacanian reading of "eyes," see Kimberly J. Devlin, "'See ourselves as others see us'": Joyce's Look at the Eye of the Other."

12. The "Aeolus" chapter went through three stages of revision, representative of, and almost simultaneous with, the three stages of revision of the whole work. Joyce began the chapter in the summer of 1919, revised it briefly between 1920 and mid-1921, and made more numerous revisions right up to publication in February 1922. "'Aeolus' serves as a microcosm of Joyce's work on *Ulysses*," says Michael Groden in *Ulysses in Progress* (64).

13. The close connection between the "Aeolus" episode and the "Cyclops" episode is embodied in the figure (including the figurative sense of) Admiral Nelson. About the time of the second stage of revision

of "Aeolus," in September 1920, Joyce prepared the Linati schemata, listing "Sense (Meaning)—The Mockery of Victory" (Groden 100).

14. Adaline Glasheen, for example, states that Bloom and Molly's "sin" is "against human fecundity. They have not replaced their dead son, Rudy" (56). Glasheen indicts Bloom for not coming home to the vagina in "domestic duty" (60). Molly's crime is that "she is pushy about sex, too enthusiastically yes-saying" (56). The values by which such kinds of judgments are made are not fixed but culturally and historically produced. Any reader should ask whether these are not the very mores Joyce is satirizing in *Ulysses*. At the very least, we require the norms Glasheen draws on to be textually based. Why should a reader accept "fecundity" as an unquestioned virtue when *Ulysses* parodies the doctrine of "copulation without population" in Theodore Purefoy's pompous Victorian tirade in "Oxen of the Sun"? "Copulation without population! No, says I! Herod's slaughter of the innocents were the truer name. Vegetables, forsooth, and sterile cohabitation! Give her beefsteaks, red, raw, bleeding!" (*U* 14.1422–24).

15. See Elaine Unkeless, "Leopold Bloom as Womanly Man."

16. Sadism and masochism are essential concepts in Freudianism. From little Hans ("Analysis of a Phobia in a Five-Year-Old Boy" [1909]), Freud developed the Sadistic Theory. That is, that a pre-Oedipal understanding of where babies come from develops through three phases: the omnipresent penis, the cloacal, the sadistic (Mitchell 24–25). Men and women both pass through the sadistic stage. Moreover, masochism (pleasure in pain) is "inherent in both sexes" (Mitchell 114), although "it is 'feminine' in whichever sex it occurs" (Mitchell 115) because it expresses a passive relation. In "The Freudful Couchmare of ∧d: Joyce's Notes on Freud and the Composition of Chapter XVI of *Finnegans Wake*," Daniel Ferrer argues that Joyce read this Freud case.

17. This is also the name of a work by the German mystic and heretic Jakob Boehme (1575–1624), who believed that the human mind could directly perceive the contrasting discordancies (such as hardness and softness, love and hate, heaven and hell) as a root structure of the world, and who believed in a divine principle of immanence out of which all things are generated. He argued against creation from nothing and that divine energy operates through the natural principles of contraction and diffusion. He rejected orthodox notions of sin and evil, believing that the divine spirit manifested itself as love, expression, and variety; in place of good and evil, he saw good and good fallen (Christ and Lucifer). Stephen muses on Boehme's philosophy, attracted to him no doubt as he is to the ideas of other heretics, because of his attitude of proud rebellion and his desire to penetrate the mysteries of the universe. Some notions of Boehme's philosophy resemble the character-

istics of *Ulysses* I gather under the terms overdetermination and anarchy. Inflation and deflation of the textual tone resemble the principles of contraction and diffusion; textual repetition, parody, and exfoliation resemble the principle of variety. Boehme's emphasis on love, and his rejection of notions of evil, and his belief in a multitudinous, evolving universe resemble the overdetermined psychological world of *Ulysses*, where secrets and repression replace sin, and where desire and love generate a creative, anarchic order (something like a balanced flow of opposite forces such as contraction and diffusion or entropy and disentropy in modern scientific terms). According to Ellmann and Gillespie, Joyce owned Boehme's *Signature* and left it behind in Trieste in 1920 when he moved to Paris (102). Does his leaving it behind suggest he had appropriated as much of Boehme as he needed?

18. Max Jammer, "Indeterminacy in Physics," 589. Jammer further explains, "If we know exactly the present, we can predict the future," according to the "strong formulation" of causality. But because "the present can never be known exactly," in view of the relations of position, momentum and energy as understood in modern physics, then "the causality principle as formulated, though logically *[sic]* and not refuted, must necessarily remain an 'empty' statement; for it is not the conclusion, but rather the premiss which is false" (589).

4. "RETOURNEYS POSTEXILIC": OVERTHROWING THE CHRISTIAN HOLY FAMILY AND RETURNING TO EGYPT

1. This novel was published in Paris by the Black Sun Press in 1929 as *The Escaped Cock*. In 1931 it was published in London by Martin Secker and in New York by Alfred A. Knopf as *The Man Who Died*. I will refer to it by this last title. All references will be from the reprint in *The Later D. H. Lawrence*, selected and with Introductions by William York Tindall (New York: Knopf, 1952), page numbers given in parentheses.

2. See Mark L. Troy, *Mummeries of Resurrection*, for a concise study of Joyce's Egyptian source material and John Bishop, *Joyce's Book of the Dark*, for an extended analysis of how *Finnegans Wake* is a book of the dead.

3. See "A Checklist of Lawrence's Reading," by Rose Marie Burwell, in *A D. H. Lawrence Handbook*, chap. 2. Burwell notes that Lawrence read Jung in 1918 (89); may have read his friend Barbara Low's *Psychoanalysis: A Brief Outline of the Freudian Theory* when it came out in 1920 (91); probably read Poul Carl Bjerre's *History and Practice of Psychoanalysis* sometime in 1920 (93); and comments that he read A. A. Brill's transla-

tions of *The Interpretation of Dreams, Three Contributions to the Theory of Sex,* and *Totem and Taboo* by 1922 (94).

4. See Jean Kimball, "Freud, Leonardo, and Joyce: The Dimensions of a Childhood Memory." Kimball connects Freud's Leonardo piece to *A Portrait* and *Ulysses,* arguing that Leopold Bloom is like Leonardo. Kimball does not really discuss the essay's significance to *Finnegans Wake,* which I take up in this chapter. I agree with Kimball's assessment that this Freud essay is important to Joyce, but I think Freud's influence took a longer time to find its way into Joyce's work than Kimball does.

5. I argue below that Joyce may have incorporated references to Lawrence into existing structures of *Finnegans Wake* in the mid to late 1930s. I hedge with "perhaps" because proving that he did is a complex matter. Since the text of the *Wake* is overdetermined, each "word" has multiple references. Making a persuasive case would require constructing a genealogy of all additions to every passage and making a case for each one in the context of all the other allusions in that passage. Although we have Joyce's notebooks, it is not clear how to interpret their contents. For example, do they record only what Joyce could not otherwise remember, suggesting that the most important material may not be written in them? I intuitively sense that a lot of what enters the *Wake* may have had its source in daily ephemera, from newspapers and "talk." But tracking down such sources is a difficult task. As I argue below, there are a few additions Joyce made in the mid-to-late 1930s that might be evidence that he is adding Lawrence allusions. Then again, maybe not.

6. Freud would not return to considerations of the mother's importance until very late in life in his two late essays on female sexuality. Actually, these earlier essays do not focus on the female directly at all but on the son's coming to terms with parental sexuality. Both essays, however, are concerned with the relationship of the mother and child, the relationship Freud has been many times accused of neglecting or covering over himself. See, for example, Peter Gay, *Freud: A Life for Our Time,* 335ff.; Juliet Mitchell, *Psychoanalysis and Feminism,* 55ff.; and Madelon Sprengnether's *Spectral Mother: Freud, Feminism, and Psychoanalysis.*

7. James C. Cowan in "Allusions and Symbols in D. H. Lawrence's *The Escaped Cock,*" sees the novella as "a hymn to the resurrection of the body, not the glorified body of Christianity but the instinctual body of physical being" (187). Cowan defends the story against the charge of heresy, concluding it is addressed to contemporary civilization and contains a message about "the rebirth of the whole man through tenderness in the sexual relationship" (187). While I agree the novella is more Christian than Egyptian (what Cowan refers to as "pagan vitalism"

[185]), my conclusion rests on my argument that the story is built on the gender relations of patriarchy (which also includes the gender roles of Christianity, a patriarchal religion). Cowan does not critique the implications of gender in the story. Rather than being reborn through "tenderness," I argue the hero is reborn through the patriarchal male fantasy of the submissive woman.

8. For a discussion of totemism in Lawrence, see Judith Ruderman, *D. H. Lawrence and the Devouring Mother*, 52ff. Ruderman cites John Vickery's 1959 "Myth and Ritual in the Shorter Fiction of D. H. Lawrence" in which he argues that the fox is a phallic animal, Grenfel's totem, and that Grenfel rescues March with his phallic power. This reading affirms the male version of the Family Romance, involving rescue, which I shall discuss later in this chapter. Ruderman contends that "Grenfel as the fox exerts a power over March that she both desires and fears" (52), that the totem animal is a sign of primitivism pointing to the pre-Oedipal mother-child relationship, and that Grenfel is actually a "devouring mother" (53). Ruderman's reading is more complex and satisfying than Vickery's, but she does not submit the "devouring mother" concept to any critical analysis for gender bias. I conclude below that Lawrence's interest in dyadic relationships reproduces—with an important post-Oedipal difference—pre-Oedipal interests. The wish to create balanced, polar relationships can be seen as an attempt to rewrite the mother-child relationship in better, more mature, adult terms, and thus can be seen as a form of Family Romance, incorporating the themes of rescue and revenge.

9. Perhaps the clearest statement about how to read the *Wake* comes in I.5 in a long aside on how to interpret the envelope of the hen's letter:

Yet to concentrate solely on the literal sense or even the psychological content of any document to the sore neglect of the enveloping facts themselves circumstantiating it is just as hurtful to sound sense (and let it be added to the truest taste) as were some fellow in the act of perhaps getting an intro from another fellow turning out to be a friend in need of his, say, to a lady of the latter's acquaintance . . . (109.12–18)

The speaker here, sounding very Swiftian, veers off into sexual speculation about that lady's clothes, what's under her clothes

for better survey by the deft hand of an expert, don't you know? Who in his heart doubts either that the facts of feminine clothiering are there all the time or that the feminine fiction, stranger than the facts, is there also at the same time, only a little to the rere? Or that one may be separated from the other? Or that both may then be contemplated simultaneously? Or that each may be taken up and considered in turn apart from the other? (109.29–36)

I take these directions to mean that all ways of reading are authorized, but that the sexual at bottom is the foundation of all others.

10. See chap. 7, "Tea," in Margaret Solomon, *Eternal Geomater*, 77–80.

11. Solomon declares that "history—time—is the female force" (109), because she connects history to "flow," the female's most distinct attribute in the *Wake*. Although I am very indebted to Solomon's analysis, I disagree with this particular point. I believe the *Wake* more often depicts history growing from male conflict (developed in the rivalry of the brother figures in *FW*), and the homosexual slant of the "back side" reinforces the male-to-male action history represents to Joyce. Insofar as the rivals are analogous to the *rivae*, banks of the female river, and all figures condense into the unity of "the genital family" (Solomon 49), as I agree they do, then the female flow flows into male history, as Anna flows into the father sea at her death. In the sense that the woman reproduces the family she also participates in historical time, but her action is circular, *re*producing, which is different from the male productions of linear time. I believe it is more accurate to say that time past (history, judgment, law) is male. Time present (nurturing, living) is female, and time future is the androgynous fetus of the next generation. As the text itself declares, "the gist of the pantomime, from cannibal king to the property horse, being, slumply and slopely, to remind us how, in this drury world of ours, Father Times and Mother Spacies boil their kettle with their crutch" (599.36–600.1–3).

12. Daniel Ferrer believes Joyce knew of Freud's writing on Schreber. In "The Freudful Couchmare of ∧d: Joyce's Notes on Freud and the Composition of Chapter XVI of *Finnegans Wake*," Ferrer states there is "indirect but conclusive evidence that 'Dora,' 'The Rat Man,' and 'President Schreber' ('Fragments of an Analysis of a Case of Hysteria,' 'Notes upon a Case of Obsessional Neurosis' and 'Psycho-Analytic Notes upon an Autobiographical Account of a Case of Paranoia [Dementia Paranoides]') passed through [Joyce's] hands, although we do not yet know whether he actually read them" (367). Freud repeated the equation of feces, money, gift, baby, penis in other essays, so the idea was widely disseminated, and Joyce may have read the connection elsewhere in Freud. Interestingly, a recent Freud biographer, Peter Gay, notes the close connection between Freud's Schreber study and his paper on Leonardo: "Emotionally, chronologically, and in other ways, Freud's paper on Schreber is a pendant to his 'Leonardo'" (277).

13. Other *Wake* analogues to the missing phallus may be the Chris-

tian myth of the Fall, Finnegan's fall, the father's crime, H.C.E.'s inter-rupted intercourse, the missing phallus that the Shem and Shaun sigla have, since they are not yet men who have replaced the father.

14. Actually, I claim below that the female figure acquires a phallus symbolically through the doubling process.

15. I quote the Ms. A version of "The Ship of Death" from D. H. Lawrence, *Last Poems*, ed. Richard Aldington and Giuseppe Orioli (New York: Viking, 1933) 56–61. See Aldington's introduction for a descrip-tion of the versions of this poem.

16. This point needs qualifying, though, since there is the very slight presence of the castrating female in the brief mention of the raped slave girl who resentfully strips the pigeons. As I noted earlier in this text, the pigeons fall into the symbolic male set, and her (re)action results from male violence done to her.

17. A criticism of Mitchell and also of Fredric Jameson, whose position is similar to Mitchell's, might be that when she says the uncon-scious is "the domain of the reproduction of culture or ideology" (413), she seems to turn the irrational unconscious into some kind of repository of laws, thereby canceling any true Freudian concept of the unconscious as irrational. It is important to correct this possible criticism, however, by pointing out that Mitchell and Jameson, as Marxians, believe that ideology is *irrational* by definition. (For them, "ideology" is not synony-mous with "belief"). The contradictions of ideology are repressed, how-ever. They might say that analysis brings the repressed contradictions into conscious awareness, where we come to understand, by working through, how the irrational and contradictory have shaped our present practices. Then, we overthrow the old and institute new practices. If we merely exchange one ideology for another, we then in turn repress the contradictions of the new ideology in our unconscious. As psychoan-alytic Marxians, Mitchell and Jameson would claim that their method is exempt from the deconstructive chain because it is not "ideology" (with its own repressed contradictions) but a process of analysis.

18. I believe *The Fox* develops by a similar negative structure as *Women in Love*, and I think the novella can be seen as an exploration of female bisexuality, just as *Women in Love* explores male bisexuality. In both, the bisexual partner is killed, and the remaining couple are left in uneasy alliance.

19. See Kimberly Devlin, "Castration and its Discontents: A Lacan-ian Approach to *Ulysses*." Devlin reads issues of gender in *Ulysses* with subtlety, and I agree with her that the book presents gender as culturally constructed (131). She concludes that "Joyce offers no cure for castration anxiety but traces instead its proliferative aggressive effects" (140). I propose that *Finnegans Wake* may actually offer a model for living with

castration anxiety. That is, Joyce recasts castration anxiety onto the experience of reading itself, making the reader first experience anxiety and castration and then experience a partial working through it as he or she begins to construct a reading and work *toward* meaning.

20. As I understand the book, *Finnegans Wake* is an overdetermined construction and hence can be read in a multitude of different ways.

21. These definitions and etymologies and all that follow are taken from *The American Heritage Dictionary of the English Language,* ed. William Morris (Boston: Houghton Mifflin, 1969).

22. Margaret Solomon notes the two-three patterns in the book and attributes these to genital symbols: female (two), male (three). I also read a core genital symbolism in the book, but I perceive a three-three genital pattern. I would not like to make a sexual theme out of the two-three pattern, because I believe the book presents an androgynous universe, and because I believe the two-three pattern derives from the conventions of language: two from irony, three from dialectics.

23. Juan in the barrel is the dying sun god Osiris, a growing fetus in amniotic fluid who is using up his space, and a barrel of beer, too. He is "maybe nine score or so barrelhours distance off" (429.20–21). "[G]racious helpings, at this rate of growing our cotted child of yestereve will soon fill space and burst in systems, so speeds the instant!" (429.23–25). "Yes, faith, I am as mew let freer, beneath me corthage, bound. I'm as bored now bawling beersgrace at sorepaws there as Andrew Clays was sharing sawdust with Daniel's old collie. This shack's not big enough for me now" (468.31–34).

24. This signature also suggests the castrated female, and so is another example of the reversibility/identity of opposites, the male letter of the law inscribes the female castration under the law.

25. There may be other references to Lawrence and his work throughout the text. Other possible references may occur at 5.2–3: "with a burning bush abob off its baubletop and with larrons o'toolers clittering up" (Lawrence title, *The Boy in the Bush?*); 92.6–32: long sexual passage perhaps parodying *Lady Chatterley's Lover* "stincking thyacinths through his curls (O feen! O deur!)"; 112.3–8: "You is feeling like you was lost in the bush, boy?" (possible references to *The Lost Girl* and *The Boy in the Bush?*); 179.11–12: "and the whole mesa redonda of Lorencao Otulass in convocacaon" (Portuguese words listed in 1938 workbook slightly changed as it makes its way into 1939 edition, so may also be a reference to Lawrence in New Mexico, echoing Mabel Dodge Luhan's *Lorenzo at Taos* [1933]?); 211.25–26: "a change of naves and joys of ills for Armoricus Tristram Amoor Saint Lawrence" (a condensation of Laurence Sterne, *Tristram Shandy,* St. Lawrence O'Toole, Lawrence of Arabia—T. E. Lawrence, and D. H. Lawrence in list of gifts to literati?);

228.16–34: a long passage on the exiled writer, includes "ban's for's book," "From the safe side of distance! Libera, nostalgia! Beate Laurentie O'Tuli, Euro pra nobis!"; and long passages on 419.24–36; 587.30–588.1–14; and 613.14–23.

26. My speculation rests on the assumptions spelled out by Danis Rose about the *Wake*'s composition and governing principles: that is, that the book developed by a process of accretion, layering, and retrospective cross-referencing, resulting in a broadening out and overdetermination of referents. David Hayman in *The Wake in Transit* argues for the importance of changes made to the *Wake* in the 1930s (14). After a series of depressing personal problems with his eyes, Lucia's increasing illness, and his own possible writer's block, according to Hayman, Joyce underwent a "creative epiphany," making "important changes" (55) in the book and consolidating the whole by drawing more and more contemporary parallels to the early mythic foundations.

27. Joyce's reluctance to meet Lawrence might be explained by the fact that while Lawrence was alive, the two writers were rivals. Their lives did have thematic links and connecting moments, though; both suffered from censorship and perceived persecution. Joyce may well have come more to identify with the dead than the living Lawrence.

28. The *Wake* has many passages that repeat the core theme. One of these incorporates the tree and stone, and this passage suggests that the movement from stone to tree is not just revivifying the phallic father but marks the evolution from brute, dumb nature (stone), like Mutt and Jute, to living consciousness:

Postreintroducing Jeremy, the chastenot coulter, the flowing taal that brooks no brooking runs on to say how, as it was mutualiter foretold of him by a timekiller to his spacemaker, velos ambos and arubyat knychts, with their tales within wheels and stucks between spokes, on the hike from Elmstree to Stene and back, how, running awage with the use of reason (sics) and ramming amok at the brake of his voice (secs), his lasterhalft was set for getting the besterwhole of his yougendtougend, for control number thrice was operating the subliminal of his invaded personality. (246.36–247.1–9)

Translating as best I can, I take the passage as a description of the evolution of humans to the present. Running away with the use of reason (sick), they create a wage culture (capitalism) from the fear or threat caused when the Viconian thunder voice interrupted their sexual coupling in the cave (running amuck at the sound of his voice [sex]). But this underlying cause of the present has been repressed, and is known only in the spaces of the tales we tell ("tales within wheels and stucks between spokes").

29. Joyce owned a copy of Lawrence's *Rainbow* (see Ellmann, *Consciousness* 116; Gillespie 95).

30. In *The Decentered Universe of Finnegans Wake*, Margot Norris points out the mirror aspects of Shem, Shaun, and Issy (47–54). Norris argues that the three play out triangular desire, with Issy as the mediating object. Issy is narcissistic, rather than alienated from herself as the male twins are, Norris claims, showing that Joyce treats female desire as "primitive" (53) and lacking in the "precondition for human knowledge" (53). In their alienation from the mirror image, the twins act out the Hegelian master, slave dialectic, Norris states. While I agree with her statements about male and female aspects of the mirror state, I also argue that the male and female aspects fold into one another, so that Shem/Shaun share Issy's narcissism, and Issy their alienation.

31. For example, in his review of the revised edition of McHugh's *Annotations*, R. J. Schork notes that the passage on 587.36ff., "my own sweet boosy love, which he puts his feeler to me behind," refers to Oscar Wilde's lover, Sir Alfred Douglas, also known as "Bosie." Because of condensation and multiple referents, I see no contradiction in suggesting this passage may also slyly refer to Lawrence and Joyce (as boozer). See R. J. Schork, Review of *Annotations to "Finnegans Wake."*

32. "It is of note that one method of 'killing' the Father, as evidenced in the Captain and tailor and the Russian general stories (as well as in the park episode), is homosexual union—man replacing God by uniting with Him pervertedly" (Solomon 87).

33. See *This Sex Which Is Not One* 25. In *Speculum of the Other Woman* Irigaray meditates on the "heliotropic" characteristic of Western patriarchy. "The sun," she says, is "the keystone supporting the whole—phallic—edifice of representation that it dominates" (267).

34. Her torn "witwee's mite" recalls Molly's disclosure in "Penelope" that when they were courting, Bloom had requested a piece of her underdrawers as a keepsake.

35. In *This Sex Which Is Not One*, Luce Irigaray discusses the perceptual aspect of sexual difference under patriarchy, pointing out that "female sexuality has always been conceptualized on the basis of masculine parameters" (23) in which desire is male, external, and visual, and woman "a 'hole' in its scoptophilic lens" (26).

36. This may be another condensation/reference to Osiris's substitute phallus.

37. Issy writes in reverse mirror language in her footnote: "O Evol, kool in the salg and ees how Dozi pits what a drows er" (262.F2).

38. This last is probably the best-known passage of *Finnegans Wake*, so I will quote only a part of it:

> he shall produce nichthemerically from his unheavenly body a no uncertain quantity of obscene matter not protected by copriright in the United Stars of Ourania or bedeed and bedood and bedang and bedung to him, with this double dye, brought to blood heat, gallic acid on iron ore, through the bowels of his misery, flashly, faithly, nastily, appropriately, this Esuan Menschavik and the first till last alshemist wrote over every square inch of the only foolscap available, his own body (185.28–36).

39. Incidentally, while Tristan and Iseult make love on their ship, they are watched by the voyeuristic four old men. Their watching is similar to the mother's in *The Man Who Died,* but in the *Wake* the voyeurism is clearly satiric.

40. I am indebted to Margaret Solomon's analysis of genital signs in *Eternal Geomater,* but I differ somewhat in my conclusions. Solomon believes that five is the important number to describe the sexual and genital shenanigans, a male three and a female two (chap. 10). She argues in chap. 11 that the "coach with the sex insides" (*FW* 359.24) is the cube of man, which opened up, reveals the six kinds of sexual relations: romantic idealism (Tristan and Iseult story), brother-to-brother rivalry and male impotence, complete heterosexuality, fornication, sodomy, and narcissism (Issy's mirror love). I agree that all these kinds of relations are present in the book, but I stress more than she does that the *Wake* presents an androgynous universe. I see the six genital regions as symmetrical and balanced. However, I grant that certain episodes present male threes and female twos, such as in The Tale of Kersse the Tailor and the Norwegian captain: "the threelegged man and the tulippied dewydress" (331.8–9). However, hidden in this is "two-lip" and "peed" (little p), the female sign of three.

41. The twins and Issy together are also three peas in a pod or "tripods" ("On the name of the tizzer and off the tongs and off the mythametical tripods" [286.22–24]), forming a sort of holy trinity, with the sister as tizzer (teaser, clitoris, small penis) and the twins as tongs (testicles, labia).

42. The Prankquean, since she combines p's and q's (she knows what's what), is an analogue of the adult A.L.P. The children only partially participate in her knowledge, since they have not really figured out the answer to the riddle of life.

43. "And they bare falls witless against thee how slight becomes a hidden wound?" (247.22–23) seems to mean that Chuff denies the wound as he sees it: "He knows for he's seen it in black and white

through his eyetrompit trained upon jenny's and all that sort of thing which is dandymount to a clearobscure" (247.32–34). In contrast, in the nightlessons Shem's left-columned comment is *"Thsight near left me eyes when I seen her put thounce otay ithpot"* (262. L2), suggesting he is almost blinded by the sight of the female genitals. In the Chuff/Glugg episode, Shem/Glugg hears, Chuff/Shaun sees (but sees "clearobscure").

44. Another transformation of the mirror-refracting rainbow occurs in book IV where the "archdruid of islish chinchinjoss in the his heptachromatic sevenhued septicoloured roranyellgreenlindigan mantle finish" (611.5–7) seems to debate with "Same Patholic" [Saint Patrick] about the "true inwardness of reality, the Ding hvad in idself id est, all objects (of panepiwor) allside showed themselves in trues coloribus resplendent with sextuple gloria of light actually retained, untisintus, inside them (obs of epiwo)" (611.21–24). Just as when Shaun looks at Issy, he sees and does not see, and finds his own reflection, this passage seems to suggest that what is seen is determined by the psychological needs of the observer (the id), *and* it also seems to say that all objects possess their own inner light (their whatness, as Stephen Dedalus would say).

45. The key in Issy's kiss refers to the play *Arrah-na-Pogue* by Dion Boucicault, where Arrah saves her brother by passing plans for escape to him through her kiss. See Norris 71–72 for a discussion of other references to this play.

46. In III.4, the Earwickers or Porters in bed have their lovemaking interrupted by their child crying out in the night, and they apparently never "wet the tea!" (585.31).

47. In the Prankquean story, Jarl is called "the arkway of trihump" (22.28). Analogue of H.C.E., van Hoother is three-humped, like the sigla for and the initials of H.C.E, and all are like Old Testament father figures. Natal and naval connects the sea with all the origination myths of the book, from Noah and the Flood, to Egyptian myths of laying eggs on the water (connected with the eggs in amniotic fluid), to evolution.

48. It is well known, for example, that Joyce knew there were errors, transpositions, and accidental additions to his text, but left them there. He felt these added to the book's potential meaning.

49. See Freud, "The Premisses and Technique of Interpretation," *Introductory Lectures on Psychoanalysis*, lecture vi. Freud explains that the dream *process* is determined (not its content); therefore the analysand begins to free associate (106), and the analyst arbitrarily chooses a stimulus word to focus interpretation on (110). Any order—as well as every order—is significant.

50. "Pigott's forged Parnell letter begins 'Dear E! . . . let there be an end of this hesitency'" (McHugh 29).

51. "And it is as though where Agni araflammed and Mithra moni-shed and Shiva slew as mayamutras the obluvial waters of our noarchic memory withdrew, windingly goharksome, to some hastyswasty timber-man torchpriest, flamenfan, the ward of the wind that lightened the fire that lay in the wood that Jove bolt, at his rude word" (*FW* 80.23–28). In place of every culture's myth of origin is an unremembered watery beginning.

Works Cited

Adamowski, T. H. "The Father of All Things: The Oral and the Oedipal in *Sons and Lovers*." *Mosaic* 14 (1981): 69–88.

Adorno, Theodor W. *Against Epistemology: A Metacritique*. Trans. Willis Domingo. Cambridge: MIT UP, 1983.

———. *Negative Dialectics*. Trans. E. B. Ashton. New York: Seabury, 1973.

Alarcón, Norma. "The Theoretical Subject(s) of This Bridge Called My Back and Anglo-American Feminism." *Making Face, Making Soul— Haciendo Caras: Creative and Critical Perspectives by Feminists of Color*. Ed. Gloria Anzaldúa. San Francisco: Spinsters Aunt Lute, 1990. 356–69.

Alcoff, Linda. "The Problem of Speaking for Others." *Cultural Critique* 20 (Winter 1991–92): 5–32.

Aldington, Richard. Introduction. *Last Poems* by D. H. Lawrence. Ed. Richard Aldington and Giuseppe Orioli. New York: Viking, 1933.

Anderson, Chester G. "Leopold Bloom as Dr. Sigmund Freud." *Mosaic* 6 (1973): 23–43.

Beauvoir, Simone de. From interviews with Alice Schwarzer. Trans. Helen Eustis and Elaine Marks. *New French Feminisms: An Anthology*. Ed. Elaine Marks and Isabelle de Courtivron. New York: Schocken, 1981. 142–53.

Begnal, Michael H. *Dreamscheme: Narrative and Voice in "Finnegans Wake."* Syracuse: Syracuse UP, 1988.

Benstock, Bernard. *Joyce-Again's Wake: An Analysis of "Finnegans Wake."* Seattle: U of Washington P, 1965.

Bishop, John. *Joyce's Book of the Dark: "Finnegans Wake."* Madison: U of Wisconsin P, 1986.

Blanchard, Lydia. "*Women in Love*: Mourning Becomes Narcissism." *Mosaic* 15 (1982): 105–18.

Bleicher, Josef. *Contemporary Hermeneutics*. London: Routledge, 1980.

Brivic, Sheldon. "Joyce Between Genders: Lacanian Views." *James Joyce Quarterly* 29.1 (Fall 1991): 13–21.

Budge, Sir E. A. Wallis. *The Gods of the Egyptians: or Studies in Egyptian Mythology*. Vol. 2. London: Methuen, 1904.

Burke, Kenneth. "'Stages' in 'The Dead.'" *Dubliners: Text, Criticism, and Notes.* Ed. Robert Scholes and A. Walton Litz. Penguin, 1976. 410–16.

Burwell, Rose Marie. "A Checklist of Lawrence's Reading." *A D. H. Lawrence Handbook.* Ed. Keith Sagar. New York: Barnes, 1982. Chap. 2.

Butler, Judith. *Gender Trouble: Feminism and the Subversion of Identity.* New York: Routledge, 1990.

Cavitch, David. *D. H. Lawrence and the New World.* New York: Oxford UP, 1969.

The Challenge of D. H. Lawrence. Ed. Michael Squires and Keith Cushman. Madison: U of Wisconsin P, 1990.

Chodorow, Nancy. "Gender, Relation, and Difference in Psychoanalytic Perspective." *The Future of Difference.* Ed. Hester Eisenstein and Alice Jardine. New Brunswick: Rutgers UP, 1985. 3–19.

———. *The Reproduction of Mothering: Psychoanalysis and the Sociology of Gender.* Berkeley: U of California P, 1978.

Cixous, Hélène. "Joyce: The (r)use of writing." Trans. Judith Still. *Post-structuralist Joyce.* Ed. Derek Attridge and Daniel Ferrer. Cambridge: Cambridge UP, 1984. 15–30.

Cixous, Hélène, and Cathérine Clément. *The Newly Born Woman.* Trans. Betsy Wing. Minneapolis: U of Minnesota P, 1986.

Cowan, James C. "Allusions and Symbols in D. H. Lawrence's *The Escaped Cock.*" *Critical Essays on D. H. Lawrence.* Ed. Dennis Jackson and Fleda Brown Jackson. Boston: Hall, 1988. 174–88.

Crosby, Harry. *Shadows of the Sun: The Diaries of Harry Crosby.* Ed. Edward Germain. Santa Barbara: Black Sparrow, 1977.

Derrida, Jacques. "Two Words for Joyce." Trans. Geoff Bennington. *Post-structuralist Joyce: Essays from the French.* Ed. Derek Attridge and Daniel Ferrer. Cambridge: Cambridge UP, 1984. 145–59.

———. *Writing and Difference.* Trans. Alan Bass. Chicago: U of Chicago P, 1978.

Dervin, Daniel. "Play, Creativity and Matricide: The Implications of Lawrence's 'Smashed Doll' Episode." *Mosaic* 14 (1981): 81–94.

Devlin, Kimberly. "Castration and its Discontents: A Lacanian Approach to *Ulysses.*" *James Joyce Quarterly* 29.1 (Fall 1991): 117–44.

———. "'See ourselves as others see us': Joyce's Look at the Eye of the Other." *PMLA* 104.5 (Oct. 1989): 882–93.

Dix, Carol. *D. H. Lawrence and Women.* Totowa, NJ: Rowman, 1980.

Eagleton, Terry. *Criticism and Ideology: A Study in Marxist Literary Theory.* London: Verso, 1978.

———. *Exiles and Emigrés.* New York: Schocken, 1970.

Eiseley, Loren. *Darwin's Century.* New York: Anchor, 1961.

Ellmann, Richard. *The Consciousness of Joyce.* New York: Oxford UP, 1977.

———. *James Joyce.* New and Revised Edition. New York: Oxford UP, 1983.

Felman, Shoshana. "Turning the Screw of Interpretation." *Literature and Psychoanalysis: The Question of Reading Otherwise.* Baltimore: Johns Hopkins UP, 1982. 94–207.

Feminism and Materialism. Ed. Annette Kuhn and AnnMarie Wolpe. London: Routledge, 1978.

Ferrer, Daniel. "The Freudful Couchmare of ∧d: Joyce's Notes on Freud and the Composition of Chapter XVI of *Finnegans Wake.*" *James Joyce Quarterly* 22 (1985): 367–82.

"For the Etruscans: Sexual Difference and Artistic Production—The Debate Over a Female Aesthetic." By Rachel Blau DuPlessis and Members of Workshop 9. *The Future of Difference.* Ed. Hester Eisenstein and Alice Jardine. New Brunswick: Rutgers UP, 1985. 128–56.

Freud, Sigmund. *Introductory Lectures on Psychoanalysis.* Trans. and ed. James Strachey. New York: Norton, 1977.

———. *Standard Edition of the Complete Psychological Works of Sigmund Freud.* Trans. under the general editorship of James Strachey in collaboration with Anna Freud, assisted by Alix Strachey and Alan Tyson. 24 vols. London: Hogarth, 1953–1974.

The Future of Difference. Ed. Hester Eisenstein and Alice Jardine. New Brunswick: Rutgers UP, 1985.

Gallop, Jane. *The Daughter's Seduction: Feminism and Psychoanalysis.* Ithaca: Cornell UP, 1982.

Gay, Peter. *Freud: A Life for Our Time.* New York: Norton, 1988.

Gender and Reading: Essays in Readers, Texts, and Contexts. Ed. Elizabeth Flynn and Patrocinio Schweickart. Baltimore: Johns Hopkins UP, 1986.

Gillespie, Mark Patrick. *Inverted Volumes Improperly Arranged: James Joyce and His Trieste Library.* Ann Arbor: UMI Research P, 1983.

Glasheen, Adaline. "Calypso." *James Joyce's "Ulysses": Critical Essays.* Ed. Clive Hart and David Hayman. Berkeley: U of California P, 1974. Rpt. 1977. 51–70.

———. *A Second Census of "Finnegans Wake."* Evanston: Northwestern UP, 1963.

Gordon, David J. "Sex and Language in D. H. Lawrence." *Twentieth Century Literature* 27 (1981): 362–75.

Groden, Michael. *Ulysses in Progress.* Princeton: Princeton UP, 1977.

Hamilton, Edith. *Mythology.* New York: New American Library, 1942.

Harding, Sandra. "The Instability of the Analytical Categories of Feminist Theory." *Signs: Journal of Women in Culture and Society* 11.4 (Summer 1986): 645–64.

Hart, Clive. *A Concordance to "Finnegans Wake."* Minneapolis: U of Minnesota P, 1963.

Hayman, David. *A First-Draft Version of "Finnegans Wake."* Austin: U of Texas P, 1963.

———. *The "Wake" in Transit.* Ithaca: Cornell UP, 1990.

Heath, Stephen. "Ambiviolences: Notes for reading Joyce." *Post-structuralist Joyce: Essays from the French.* Ed. Derek Attridge and Daniel Ferrer. Cambridge: Cambridge UP, 1984. 31–68.

———. "Joyce in Language." *James Joyce: New Perspectives.* Ed. Colin MacCabe. Bloomington: Indiana UP, 1982. 129–48.

Hinz, Evelyn J. "The Beginning and the End: D. H. Lawrence's *Psychoanalysis* and *Fantasia.*" *Dalhousie Review* 52 (1972): 251–65.

Hodgart, M. J. C. "Aeolus." *James Joyce's "Ulysses": Critical Essays.* Ed. Clive Hart and David Hayman. Berkeley: U of California P, 1974. Rpt. 1977. 115–30.

Hoffmann, Frederick. *Freudianism and the Literary Mind.* Baton Rouge: Louisiana State UP, 1945.

Holbrook, David. *Where D. H. Lawrence Was Wrong about Women.* Lewisburg: Bucknell UP, 1992.

Holderness, Graham. *D. H. Lawrence: History, Ideology and Fiction.* Atlantic Highlands, NJ: Humanities P, 1982.

In Dora's Case: Freud—Hysteria—Feminism. Ed. Charles Bernheimer and Claire Kahane. New York: Columbia UP, 1985.

Irigaray, Luce. *Speculum of the Other Woman.* Trans. Gillian C. Gill. Ithaca: Cornell UP, 1985.

———. *This Sex Which Is Not One.* Trans. Catherine Porter with Carolyn Burke. Ithaca: Cornell UP, 1985.

Jackson, Tony E. "'Cyclops,' 'Nausicaa,' and Joyce's Imaginary Irish Couple." *James Joyce Quarterly* 29.1 (Fall 1991): 63–83.

The James Joyce Archive. Vols. 57–62. Gen. ed. Michael Groden. New York: Garland, 1978.

James Joyce: The Critical Heritage. 2 vols. Ed. Robert H. Deming. London: Routledge, 1970.

James Joyce: New Perspectives. Ed. Colin MacCabe. Bloomington: Indiana UP, 1982.

James Joyce's The Index Manuscript FW Holograph Workbook VI.B.46. Ed. Danis Rose. Colchester, Essex England: Wake Newslitter P, 1978.

James Joyce's "Ulysses": Critical Essays. Ed. Clive Hart and David Hayman. Berkeley: U of California P, 1974. Rpt. 1977.

Jameson, Fredric. "Imaginary and Symbolic in Lacan: Marxism, Psychoanalytic Criticism, and the Problem of the Subject." *Literature and Psychoanalysis: The Question of Reading Otherwise*. Ed. Shoshana Felman. Baltimore: Johns Hopkins UP, 1982. 338–95.

———. *The Political Unconscious: Narrative as a Socially Symbolic Act*. Ithaca: Cornell UP, 1981.

———. "Seriality in Modern Literature." *Bucknell Review* 18.1 (1970): 63–80.

Jammer, Max. "Indeterminacy in Physics." *Dictionary of the History of Ideas*. Vol 2. Ed. Philip Wiener. New York: Charles Scribner's Sons, 1973. 586–94.

Johnson, Barbara. *The Critical Difference: Essays in the Contemporary Rhetoric of Reading*. Baltimore: Johns Hopkins UP, 1981.

"Joyce Between Genders: Lacanian Views." Guest ed: Sheldon Brivic. *James Joyce Quarterly* 29.1 (Fall 1991).

Joyce, James. *Dubliners: Text, Criticism, and Notes*. Rpt. of the 1969 ed. The Viking Critical Edition. Ed. Robert Scholes and A. Walton Litz. Penguin, 1976.

———. *Finnegans Wake*. Embodying all author's corrections. New York: Viking, 1939. Rpt. Viking Compass, 1973.

———. *The Letters of James Joyce*. Vol. 2. Ed. Richard Ellmann. London: Faber, 1966.

———. *A Portrait of the Artist as a Young Man*. The definitive text, corrected from the Dublin holograph by Chester G. Anderson and edited by Richard Ellmann. New York: Viking, 1964. Rpt. Viking Compass, 1969.

———. *Stephen Hero*. Ed. from the Manuscript in the Harvard College Library by Theodore Spencer, Incorporating the Additional Manuscript Pages in the Yale University Library and the Cornell University Library edited by Slocum and Cahoon. New York: New Directions, 1963.

———. *"Ulysses": The Corrected Text*. Ed. Hans Walter Gabler. New York: Random House, 1986.

Kahane, Claire. Introduction: Part Two. *In Dora's Case: Freud—Hysteria—Feminism*. Ed. Charles Bernheimer and Claire Kahane. New York: Columbia UP, 1985. 19–32.

Kelsey, Nigel. *D. H. Lawrence: Sexual Crisis*. New York: St. Martin's, 1991.

Kessler, Suzanne J. "The Medical Construction of Gender: Case Management of Intersexed Infants." *Signs: Journal of Women in Culture and Society* 16.1 (Autumn 1990): 3–26.

Kiely, Robert. *Beyond Egotism: The Fiction of James Joyce, Virginia Woolf, and D. H. Lawrence*. Cambridge, MA: Harvard UP, 1980.

Kimball, Jean. "Family Romance and Hero Myth: A Psychoanalytic Context for the Paternity Theme in *Ulysses.*" *James Joyce Quarterly* 20 (1983): 161–73.

——. "Freud, Leonardo, and Joyce: The Dimensions of a Childhood Memory." *James Joyce Quarterly* 17 (1980): 165–82.

——. "James Joyce and Otto Rank." *James Joyce Quarterly* 13 (1976): 366–82.

Kristeva, Julia. *Desire in Language: A Semiotic Approach to Literature and Art.* Ed. Leon S. Roudiez. Trans. Thomas Gora, Alice Jardine, and Leon S. Roudiez. New York: Columbia UP, 1980.

Kuhn, Annette. "Structures of Patriarchy and Capital in the Family." *Feminism and Materialism.* Eds. Annette Kuhn and AnnMarie Wolpe. London: Routledge, 1978. 42–67.

Lacan, Jacques. *Écrits: A Selection.* Trans. Alan Sheridan. London: Tavistock, 1977.

——. *Feminine Sexuality.* Ed. Juliet Mitchell and Jacqueline Rose. Trans. Jacqueline Rose. New York: Norton, 1982.

——. *The Four Fundamental Concepts of Psycho-Analysis.* Ed. Jacques-Alain Miller. Trans. Alan Sheridan. London: Hogarth, 1977.

——. *The Language of Self: The Function of Language in Psychoanalysis.* Trans. with notes and commentary by Anthony Wilden. New York: Dell, 1975.

——. *The Seminar of Jacques Lacan: Book I, Freud's Papers on Technique 1953–1954.* Ed. Jacques-Alain Miller. Trans. John Forrester. New York: Norton, 1988.

——. *The Seminar of Jacques Lacan: Book II, The Ego in Freud's Theory and in the Technique of Psychoanalysis 1954–1955.* Ed. Jacques-Alain Miller. Trans. Sylvana Tomaselli. New York: Norton, 1988.

Lawrence, D. H. *The Fox.* New York: Viking, 1923. Rpt. Bantam, 1967.

——. *Last Poems.* Ed. Richard Aldington and Giuseppe Orioli. New York: Viking, 1933.

——. *The Letters of D. H. Lawrence.* Vol. 1. Ed. by James T. Boulton. New York: Cambridge UP, 1979.

——. *The Man Who Died.* New York: Knopf, 1931. Rpt. in *The Later D. H. Lawrence.* Ed. William York Tindall. New York: Knopf, 1952. 397–449.

——. *Phoenix: The Posthumous Papers of D. H. Lawrence.* Ed. and with an Introduction by Edward D. McDonald. London: Heinemann, 1936. Rpt. New York: Viking, 1968.

——. *Phoenix II: Uncollected, Unpublished and Other Prose Works by D. H. Lawrence.* Collected and edited with an Introduction and notes by Warren Roberts and Harry T. Moore. London: Heinemann, 1968.

———. *The Rainbow*. William Heinemann Ltd., 1915. Rpt. The New Scholarly Text. Ed. Mark Kinkead-Weekes. Cambridge: Cambridge UP, 1989.

———. *Sons and Lovers*. Selzter, 1913. Rpt. The New Scholarly Text. Ed. Helen Baron and Carl Baron. Cambridge: Cambridge UP, 1992.

———. *Studies in Classic American Literature*. Seltzer, 1923. Rpt. New York: Doubleday, n.d.

———. *Women in Love*. Seltzer, 1920. Rpt. The New Scholarly Text. Ed. David Farmer, Lindeth Vasey, and John Worthen. Cambridge: Cambridge UP, 1987.

Lawrence and Women. Ed. Anne Smith. New York: Barnes, 1978.

Lerner, Gerda. *The Creation of Patriarchy*. New York: Oxford UP, 1986.

Literature and Psychoanalysis: The Question of Reading Otherwise. Ed. Shoshana Felman. Baltimore: Johns Hopkins UP, 1982.

Lukács, Georg. *Realism in Our Time*. New York: Harper, 1964.

MacCabe, Colin. "An Introduction to *Finnegans Wake*." *James Joyce: New Perspectives*. Ed. Colin MacCabe. Bloomington: Indiana UP, 1982. 29–41.

———. *James Joyce and the Revolution of the Word*. London: Macmillan, 1979.

McGee, Patrick. *Paperspace: Style as Ideology in Joyce's "Ulysses."* Lincoln: U of Nebraska P, 1988.

McHugh, Roland. *Annotations to "Finnegans Wake."* Baltimore: Johns Hopkins UP, 1980.

Mackward, Christine. "To Be or Not to Be . . . A Feminist Speaker." Trans. Marlene Barsoum, Alice Jardine, and Hester Eisenstein. *The Future of Difference*. Ed. Hester Eisenstein and Alice Jardine. New Brunswick: Rutgers UP, 1985. 95–105.

Mahaffey, Vicki. *Reauthorizing Joyce*. Cambridge: Cambridge UP, 1988.

Making Face, Making Soul—Haciendo Caras: Creative and Critical Perspectives by Feminists of Color. Ed. Gloria Anzaldúa. San Francisco: Spinsters Aunt Lute, 1990.

Manganiello, Dominic. *Joyce's Politics*. London: Routledge, 1980.

Mensch, Barbara. *D. H. Lawrence and the Authoritarian Personality*. New York: St. Martin's, 1991.

Mitchell, Juliet. *Psychoanalysis and Feminism*. New York: Pantheon, 1974. Rpt. Random Vintage, 1975.

Mortland, Donald E. "The Conclusion of *Sons and Lovers:* A Reconsideration." *Studies in the Novel, North Texas State* 3 (1971): 305–15.

Nelson, Jane. "The Familial Isotopy in *The Fox*." *The Challenge of D. H. Lawrence*. Ed. Michael Squires and Keith Cushman. Madison: U of Wisconsin P, 1990. 129–42.

New French Feminisms: An Anthology. Edited and with Introductions by Elaine Marks and Isabelle de Courtivron. New York: Schocken, 1981.

Norris, Margot. *The Decentered Universe of Finnegans Wake: A Structuralist Analysis.* Baltimore: Johns Hopkins UP, 1974.

Oates, Joyce Carol. "Lawrence's *Götterdämmerung:* The Tragic Vision of *Women in Love.*" *Critical Inquiry* 4 (1978): 559–78.

Pearce, Richard. *The Politics of Narration: James Joyce, William Faulkner, and Virginia Woolf.* New Brunswick: Rutgers UP, 1991.

Post-structuralist Joyce: Essays from the French. Ed. Derek Attridge and Daniel Ferrer. Cambridge: Cambridge UP, 1984.

Rabate, Jean-Michel. "Silence in *Dubliners.*" *James Joyce: New Perspectives.* Ed. Colin MacCabe. Bloomington: Indiana UP, 1982. 45–72.

Ramas, Maria. "Freud's Dora, Dora's Hysteria." *In Dora's Case: Freud— Hysteria—Feminism.* Ed. Charles Bernheimer and Claire Kahane. New York: Columbia UP, 1985. 149–80.

Ricoeur, Paul. *Freud and Philosophy.* Trans. Denis Savage. New Haven: Yale UP, 1970.

Rose, Gillian. *The Melancholy Science: An Introduction to the Thought of Theodor W. Adorno.* New York: Columbia UP, 1978.

Ruderman, Judith. *D. H. Lawrence and the Devouring Mother: The Search for a Patriarchal Ideal of Leadership.* Durham: Duke UP, 1984.

Sabin, Margery. *The Dialect of the Tribe: Speech and Community in Modern Fiction.* New York: Oxford UP, 1987.

Sagar, Keith, ed. *A D. H. Lawrence Handbook.* New York: Barnes, 1982.

Said, Edward W. *Beginnings: Intention and Method.* Baltimore: Johns Hopkins UP, 1975.

Sanders, Scott. *D. H. Lawrence: The World of the Five Major Novels.* New York: Viking, 1973.

Schechner, Mark. *Ulysses in Nighttown: A Psychoanalytic Inquiry into "Ulysses."* Berkeley: U of California P, 1974.

Schork, R. J. Review of Roland McHugh's *Annotations to "Finnegans Wake,"* Revised Edition. *James Joyce Quarterly* 29.4 (Summer 1992): 849–53.

Schwarz, Daniel R. "Speaking of Paul Morel: Voice, Unity, and Meaning in *Sons and Lovers.*" *Studies in the Novel* 8 (1976): 255–77.

Schweickart, Patrocinio. "Reading Ourselves: Towards a Feminist Theory of Reading." *Gender and Reading: Essays on Readers, Texts, and Contexts.* Ed. Elizabeth Flynn and Patrocinio Schweickart. Baltimore: Johns Hopkins UP, 1986. 31–62.

Scott, Bonnie Kime. Introduction. *The Gender of Modernism.* Ed. Bonnie Kime Scott. Bloomington: Indiana UP, 1990. 1–18.

———. *Joyce and Feminism.* Bloomington: Indiana UP, 1984.

Siegel, Carol. *Lawrence among the Women*. Charlottesville: UP of Virginia, 1991.

Simpson, Hilary. *D. H. Lawrence and Feminism*. London: Croom Helm, 1982.

Smith, Anne. "A New Adam and a New Eve—Lawrence and Woman: A Biographical Overview." *Lawrence and Women*. New York: Barnes, 1978. 9–48.

Solomon, Margaret C. *Eternal Geomater: The Sexual Universe of "Finnegans Wake."* Carbondale: Southern Illinois UP, 1969.

"Sons and Lovers: A Freudian Appreciation." *Psychoanalytic Review* July 1916: 295–317.

Spivak, Gayatri Chakravorty. "The Letter as Cutting Edge." *Literature and Psychoanalysis: The Question of Reading Otherwise*. Ed. Shoshana Felman. Baltimore: Johns Hopkins UP, 1982. 208–26.

Sprengnether, Madelon. *The Spectral Mother: Freud, Feminism, and Psychoanalysis*. Ithaca: Cornell UP, 1990.

Storch, Margaret. *Sons and Adversaries: Women in William Blake and D. H. Lawrence*. Knoxville: U of Tenn. P, 1990.

Strauss, Allan. *A Critical Study of Freud's Concept of Unconscious Mental Processes: With Special Reference to Gestalt Psychology*. Smithtown, NY: Exposition, 1980.

Templeton, Joan. "The *Doll House* Backlash: Criticism, Feminism, and Ibsen." *PMLA* 104.1 (1989): 28–40.

Tindall, William York. Introduction. *The Man Who Died. The Later D. H. Lawrence*. Ed. William York Tindall. New York: Knopf, 1952. 397–98.

Tristram, Philippe. "Eros and Death (Lawrence, Freud and Women)." *Lawrence and Women*. New York: Barnes, 1978. 136–55.

Troy, Mark L. *Mummeries of Resurrection: The Cycle of Osiris in "Finnegans Wake."* Uppsala: Alqvist, 1976.

Unkeless, Elaine. "Leopold Bloom as Womanly Man." *Modernist Studies* 2 (1976): 35–44.

Van Boheemen, Christine. *The Novel as Family Romance: Language, Gender, and Authority from Fielding to Joyce*. Ithaca: Cornell UP, 1987.

Vitoux, Pierre. "The Chapter 'Excurse' in *Women in Love:* Its Genesis and the Critical Problem." *Texas Studies in Literature and Language* 17 (1976): 821–36.

Vološinov, V. N. *Freudianism: A Critical Sketch*. Trans. I. R. Titunik. Bloomington: Indiana UP, 1987.

Walzl, Florence. "*Dubliners:* Women in Irish Society." *Women in Joyce*. Ed. Suzette Henke and Elaine Unkeless. Urbana: U of Illinois P, 1982. 31–56.

———. "Gabriel and Michael: The Conclusion of 'The Dead.'" *Dublin-*

ers: Text, Criticism, and Notes. Ed. Robert Scholes and A. Walton Litz. Penguin, 1976. 423–43.

Watt, Ian. *The Rise of the Novel.* Berkeley: U of California P, 1957.

Weiss, Daniel. *Oedipus in Nottingham: D. H. Lawrence.* Seattle: U of Washington P, 1962.

Wilden, Anthony, ed. and trans. *The Language of the Self: The Function of Language in Psychoanalysis.* By Jacques Lacan. New York: Dell, 1975.

Williams, Raymond. *Marxism and Literature.* Oxford: Oxford UP, 1977.

Wolff, Geoffrey. *Black Sun: The Brief Transit and Violent Eclipse of Harry Crosby.* New York: Random House, 1976.

Women in Joyce. Ed. Suzette Henke and Elaine Unkeless. Urbana: U of Illinois P, 1982.

Index

293

Cynthia Lewiecki-Wilson received her Ph.D. degree in English from the University of New Mexico and is currently an assistant professor of English at Miami University, Middletown, where she teaches a variety of writing and literature courses, with a special interest in modernism and feminist theory. She has presented papers on Lawrence, Joyce, feminism, and writing at national and international conferences. Her current research interest is in the relation between theory and practice, more specifically, how teaching and writing might be reconceptualized after postmodernist and feminist critiques.